# BUILDING A BRIDGE:

## A Divorced Parent's Guide

## to

## Long-distance Loving

### by

### Pamela Payne

*Disclaimer*

The intent of the author of this book is only to offer information of a general nature to help you in your quest for a healthier and more loving family relationship with your long-distance children. It is also the intent to assist you toward improved associations with the other parents and involved third parties. In the event you use any of the information in this book for yourself, which is your constitutional right, the author and the publisher assume no responsibility for your actions or the outcomes. The information in this book is in no way meant to take the place of professional counseling for personal or parenting matters, professional legal advice or spiritual guidance.

ISBN 1-58747-C26-8
Copyright, 2001
by Pale Horse Publishing, Inc.

All rights reserved. No part of this work may be reproduced, stored in a retrieval system, or transmitted in any form or by any means, electronic, mechanical, photocopying, recording, or otherwise, or adapted to any other medium without the prior written permission of the publisher. Brief quotations in articles or reviews are permitted and publisher requests a copy of the article or review.

The publisher may be contacted at:
Pale Horse Publishing
T (936) 327-1104 F (936) 967-8962
E-Mail: divorce@livingston.net
WWW: http://www.custodywar.com
P.O. Box 1447 Livingston, Texas 77351-11351 U.S.A.
Printed in Canada

Cover design by Joy Goodgame and Frank L. Mitchell

Praise for Building A Bridge ...

Once in a while I get to edit something that makes me feel good to be a human being. This book is one of those things. It is full of great ideas and resources and should be useful to both professionals and ordinary folks who become long-distance parents. You have taken a situation that might have made you bitter, addressed your creativity and warmth to it, and produced a book that will prove a blessing to many. I am proud to have a small part in your effort. God Bless!

Carol Dennis, Editor

Being geographically separated from a child does not mean a parent must be out of that child's life. Pamela Payne shows parents how to actually strengthen the parent-child relationship while being physically apart. This book is an invaluable guide for all parents who find themselves away from their children for whatever reason. *Building a Bridge* will help build better relationships.

Michael L. Oddenino, General Counsel, Children's Rights Council, Washington, DC

The many great teachings and religions present to us a common thread that today's youth seem to incorporate in their genetic code as we grown-ups struggle to get it right in our behavior. Pamela gets all this. She teaches us, together with Louise Hay, Bryon Katie, Caroline Myss and Deepak Chopra, how to remember that we are all yet another version of each other and of God. She has so much love in her – it illuminates this work. Whether parenting our children or friendly-ing our co-workers, we all have bridges to build. This is an instruction book on how to do that. We begin at home with our spouses (ex or current), our children, our families, our friends, our co-workers, our bosses, our employees. Bravo, Pamela! Thank you for touching our lives with material that brings richness to us that we can pass along to our children. Thank you for the gift of your book. Finally an instruction book, sweet and kind and gentle and clear, to teach me how to BE and make a joyful noise with my children as well as with all others in my life.

Regina Swimmer Brown, M.D., Ouray, Colorado

To

Sarah and Jason,

Thank you for choosing me

to be your Mother.

You have been, and continue to be,

the greatest teachers in my life.

I love you.

For

every long-distance parent

who wants to transcend the miles.

LAUGH, LEARN, LIVE, LOVE

## *Letter to My Loves*

July 26, 1999

Dearest Sarah and Jason,

      For the past three years I have been working on how to be a long-distance parent to you. The real issue has been to figure out how to demonstrate to you my love with the miles between us. Being a hands-on mom offered one set of challenges, but being a long-distance mom has offered me an entirely new set of challenges. I hope that if you have read this book, or heard about it, you will have an appreciation for how seriously I have taken my responsibilities as your mother.

      Even though I have been apart from you for three years, I have never been separated from you. You are in my every thought. Each time my heart beats, my soul sends my love for you through the universe. Each time I breathe, my spirit calls out your names. An invisible line of communication dances through space between Houston and Chicago, and I am ever present for you.

      Words cannot express my deep and sacred love for you. That is why I have lived so passionately. I believe the only voice that could even possibly speak to the caliber of my love for you is my daily life. It remains my sincerest desire to **be** an example of the fullness of life that I want for you.

      I thank you for all the love notes you have written, the pictures you have drawn, the moments we have shared. I surround myself with photographs of our joyous unions and the trinkets you have bestowed to me. I celebrate you in every blink of an eye.

      I want you to know that Daddy Fred and I accepted this position in Houston because we believed that it would offer our family powerful opportunities for personal growth. It was never our intention to distance you from your father or the family you have with him.

*Building a Bridge*

I no longer believe that we could have a better life here – I know that we do. We have this better life because we have focused on becoming better people. Each morning we place our feet firmly on the floor and welcome the new day with thanksgiving. We open our arms and bless whatever experiences come our way. We know that whatever happens in the next twenty-four hours will be for our highest good. I pray that you will choose to live this way. I pray that you will always embrace change as an opportunity to explore yourself and your world. I pray that you will look at life as a gift to savor and cherish.

While I have missed you greatly, I must acknowledge that as a result of our separation a powerful work has been accomplished. If you would have moved to Houston with us, I would not have sought the way for long-distance parents to connect with their children. Has a Divine Mission been fulfilled by our separation? My work was for our benefit, but now as I share what I have learned, many will embrace the meaningful relationship we enjoy. Your acceptance of this situation and your faith in my love for you made this possible. We have made a beautiful contribution to this world. I thank you for your participation in this endeavor.

Sarah and Jason, I plan to live a very long life. I hope to grow older and wiser and more beautiful. But should God have other plans for me, I want you to know that I will always be with you. Oh, I do not hold any insightful keys about what happens after I leave this Earth. I do, however, know that within you are memories of our shared life. Those precious moments are safely and securely nestled in your hearts and souls ... protected forever. In any thirsty instant you can be with me and draw from my well of love.

You never need doubt how deeply I love you.

Your mother,

*Pamela* ♥

*Building a Bridge*

## *Acknowledgements*

The acknowledgements that you are about read may seem long. You might think, "She acknowledged everyone but the tax collector!" The reason for this is important. Working through a long-distance parenting situation is a big job. While you, the parent, must personally do the work, you cannot do it alone. You must have a support network. I have included those in my support network in the acknowledgements. As you read through my list, I hope you will think of those individuals in your life who offer you encouragement and support. Make the effort to applaud them for their contribution to your life ... no matter how the long the list.

♥

I thank You, God that even when I walked through the darkest and loneliest portion of my path, You were there for me. I am sure you wondered on many occasions why I did not listen for Your voice or act on Your guidance. In retrospect, I wonder too. You were faithful and loving and patient. Whatever I am today, I owe to Your love. I know You have created me for a sacred mission. I am just beginning to get a glimpse of myself and my potential.

Fred deserves and receives my deepest gratitude. He has been understanding and patient with me as I have worked through my hurts and hang-ups. He is always loving; not only to me, but to our children as well.

I have thanked Sarah and Jason already, but certainly their contribution in my life is worthy of another statement of appreciation. Hugs and kisses!

I want to thank my parents for the love and energy they give to the children. They have demonstrated that by ignoring labels, all children can be celebrated and enjoyed. I appreciate the life and instruction they have given me and hope that my life is a source of delight for them.

*Building a Bridge*

The children's father and his wife are due my appreciation for the valuable contribution they make on a daily basis to the children's lives. I am also grateful for the role they have played in my life. For a long while I despised them. As a result, my dealings with them were contemptible. I have made huge strides in my spiritual growth and now understand the vital contribution they have made to me and the children. I release them in love to experience their own journeys. I sincerely hope that their individual and mutual journeys are lined with peace and prosperity.

Carol Dennis, my editor, has been an enormous asset to this book and therefore, to the healing process of many families. I am grateful for the instruction she has given, as it has not only made a positive difference in this work, but will also contribute to all my future writings.

Charlotte Hardwick, my publisher, is answered prayer. Her expertise on the subject of custody and her knowledge of the publishing business, have provided me wisdom and guidance. I respect her as a business associate and admire her as a person. I am a better servant to my readers because of her input in my life and this book.

Mary Kragel has coached me through this book when I wondered if a book was my ego or the Spirit. I thank her for sharing with me those things she learned from the books she read. I also appreciate her openness with me – she tells me like it is – and I know it is for my own good. Everyone needs a "kick-my-fanny" friend! Above all, I observe Mary with awe as I watch her guide her children. She is a marvelous mother. She has my deepest respect and admiration.

Diane Mason has been a source of strength. We met at the onset of my long-distance parenting; a time when I was not feeling my inner best (and I know it showed externally.) Her compassion toward me and her confidence in me have been cherished assets during many tough times. She has applauded me when I haven't been in the frame of mind to even think I had any reason for applause.

*Building a Bridge*

Carla Medlenka is my angel prayer partner. I appreciate that she has prayed with me – for my soul growth – so I would have something valuable to write. She has also been a fabulous springboard for ideas and observations. Her experiences with long-distance parenting and blending a family have also provided great food for thought. I also thank her for her editing skills.

Jennifer Myles has consistently reminded me that while I say I have something important to do, I have actually been doing it. She and I share a beautiful friendship and she has also been a true companion to Sarah and Jason. I am grateful for her college studies in child psychology and counseling which have guided me through many of my personal trials. Jennifer and her family have also given me the opportunity to transcend traditional family lines and "adopt" them.

Lisa Sealine has been a dear friend along my path of life for over thirteen years. She and I have been through many potholes together and have always found the beauty and laughter in those times. Lisa and I have shared a sisterhood since we met and have deliciously blended our families – which have always been long distance from each other. When I made the decision to stop the legal proceedings and rewrite the parenting agreement, Lisa was tremendously supportive. Ironically, as I wrote this book, she was involved in her own custody case. I have been able to be supportive of her and she has opened my mind to consider additional issues. She, too, tells me like it is and keeps my thinking straight. I am grateful that she helps me to see the humor in situations and from tickling my funny bone I am able to see myself more accurately. Lisa is a "magic mommy" as she has a unique talent for making every moment memorable.

Paula Vargas did the wonderful graphics in this book. Since we met, Paula has called me "Pamelina." It always makes me feel like an angel. I thank her for her support of this book and I am always grateful for the friendship we share. She is an angel herself.

Naomi Warren has been a tremendous inspiration to me. When I think about all the hardships she has triumphed over in her life, I am in awe of her courage. She has used her experiences to shape herself into a beautiful soul. As a result, she is a very successful and admired woman. I look to her for guidance and wisdom. I am always nourished by her presence in my life.

*Building a Bridge*

Dr. Jack Williams, a mentor and friend, encouraged me to write. Jack has been my bridge builder, and for his contribution to my life, I am forever in his debt. Perhaps the greatest honor I can bestow on him, my teacher, is working toward fulfillment of my potential.

The staff and volunteers of Big Brothers/Big Sisters have reminded me that I am great with kids and have given me lots of opportunities to participate with children. I am thankful that I have been able to be a part of this wonderful organization that truly makes a difference in the lives of young people.

The faculty and staff at Edgewood Elementary School in Woodridge, Illinois, are due a huge round of applause as they gave me complete freedom to try new ideas for staying active in Sarah and Jason's education. They went above-and-beyond in communicating with me and as a result, the children benefited from the relationship we shared.

The employees of International Trading Company, our friends, and neighbors are owed my genuine appreciation for not laughing out loud as I worked to find myself over these past few years. I also delight that many of you have called me a writer because I write and not judged me based on my not being published up to this point.

Finally, a word of thanks to those who kept their negative thoughts to themselves. You obviously know who you are better than I, but I know you are out there. You are the ones who thought, "This chick is dreaming if she thinks she can write a book!"

My reply to you is...**DREAMS DO COME TRUE!**

*Building a Bridge*

## *Introduction*

On October 24, 1996, I walked out of the family law courtroom into a corridor that led me to a new life. Ten months prior I had married a wonderful man, Fred, who subsequent to our marriage accepted a career opportunity in another state. From a previous marriage I had two children, a daughter, Sarah, who was at that time eight years old and a son, Jason, who was six. They knew of our pending move, and in their minds they would be moving, too. That is certainly what Fred and I had hoped for also. But that is not what happened.

I had a joint parenting agreement with the children's father, and we shared a split-week arrangement. When the children were small, it worked fairly well. When they grew a bit older and more involved with friends and school activities, it became more of a challenge. I recognized that they were moving into a phase in their lives when they would probably want to make a choice to live in one home more fulltime and the other more part-time. Our relocation certainly put the need for this change on the front line.

Fred conditionally accepted the new position. Our stipulation was that we could take all the time we needed to work through the custodial arrangements for the children. Then we notified the other parent and his wife of our situation and offered them a possible alternative arrangement with the children moving with us.

I could not fathom that their father would honestly consider the children living with him. His new wife had a daughter of her own, and they had birthed a child together. In my opinion she had her hands full. In living with me the children would have my complete attention because I was able to remain at home and focus on the family. We offered their father a very generous proposal – which he did not even consider.

*Building a Bridge*

Unfortunately, a custody battle ensued. After ten months and twenty-five thousand dollars, we found ourselves facing a brick wall. The county we lived in had a law on the books that stated that the moving parent would bear the burden of the loss if the non-moving parent refused the children the right to relocate. Because he said the children could not go, they could not go. He had the law to support him.

No one looked at the parenting of the two households. We did meet with a conciliator on a few occasions, but my questions regarding the stepmother's ability and willingness to parent the children were disregarded. I was told that how the father conducted his household was none of my business so long as the children were not abused or neglected.

I desperately prayed that a miracle would occur – either the father would see the light or the judge would intervene. Neither happened. The attorneys kept the turmoil stirring and the invoices coming. By this time Fred and I were living in separate cities and supporting separate households. The children were emotionally drained. The stress was mounting, and showing, on all of us.

After much soul searching and many tears, I made the decision to stop the proceedings. Fred and I rewrote our original agreement stating the children could remain in the father's household, but only if the other elements of our proposal were agreed upon. When their father gave us a verbal confirmation of acceptance, we each gave a copy of the agreement to our attorneys for submission to the judge and official filing.

Peace washed over me. I knew God was holding my hand and would see me through this darkness. So when I walked out of the courtroom that day, I felt that I must take a deep, purposeful breath and strengthen myself for the journey I had before me. I did not see myself as a victim, but I was certainly in an undesirable situation. Bemoaning the position would have helped no one – not me, not my marriage, not the children. What I did have clarity about was that changes needed to occur **in** me.

*Building a Bridge*

Therefore, for nearly three years I have been working to create a sense of communication and cooperation with the children's father and new wife, maintain a healthy and meaningful relationship with my children, and develop a life for myself. In an effort to seriously accomplish these goals I have read countless books, listened to numerous counselors, followed my heart and thumped my head.

This book has been written by a long-distance mom. I am not a psychologist, lawyer, teacher or religious instructor. I am a mother who deeply loves her children and wants to be a part of their lives.

I feel that what I have learned is of value and needs to be shared. I offer this book to you with the greatest respect for the mission you have before you. Being physically distanced from our children is a traumatic event, but it need not be tragic. I pray that you will find in these pages honesty, understanding, encouragement and inspiration.

*Building a Bridge*

*14*

*Building a Bridge*

## Table of Contents

| | |
|---|---|
| **CHAPTER 1: WHO ARE LONG-DISTANCE PARENTS?** | 19 |
| **CHAPTER 2: FIVE STEPS FOR BUILDING A RELATIONSHIP WITH OUR CHILDREN** | 21 |
| **CHAPTER 3: STEP ONE: EVALUATING YOUR FEARS STEP TWO: RELEASING YOUR FEARS STEP THREE: EMBRACING YOUR LOVE** | 25 |
| **Don't Be Afraid To Fail** | 36 |
|    Alienation | 42 |
| **Separation is Impossible** | 49 |
|    Prayer | 50 |
| **Visualization** | 55 |
| **Anger** | 64 |
|    Release the Anger | 68 |
|    Sense of Humor | 70 |
|    Arrogance | 76 |
|    Blame | 83 |
|    Act Responsibly | 84 |
|    Despair | 87 |
|    Focus on Contributing | 87 |
|    Envy | 93 |
|    Do Not Compete | 93 |
|    Greed | 99 |
| **Child's Bill of Rights** | 111 |
| **Parent's Bill of Rights** | 112 |
|    Grief | 113 |
|    Draw on Creative Ability | 114 |
|    Acceptance | 116 |
|    Guilt | 118 |
|    Release the Past | 119 |
|    Hatefulness | 122 |
|    Inferiority | 126 |
|    Focus on Your Value and Your Child's Value | 130 |

*Building a Bridge*

| | |
|---|---|
| Laziness | 133 |
| Focus on Today – Get to Work! | 134 |
| Loneliness | 137 |
| Reach Out to Others – Celebrate Your Connectedness | 137 |
| Listening Skills | 139 |
| Problem Solving | 144 |
| Holidays | 145 |
| Regret | 149 |
| Forgiveness | 150 |
| Resentment | 156 |
| Practice Letting Go | 157 |
| Legal System | 159 |
| Money | 162 |
| Self-pity | 169 |
| Stop Being a Victim | 169 |
| Spite | 170 |
| Superiority | 173 |
| Building a Bridge for Your Children | 176 |

## CHAPTER 4: WORST CASE SCENARIOS — 181

## CHAPTER 5: STEP FOUR: OUR GREATEST MISSION: TO BE A LIVING EXAMPLE — 185
- Let There Be Peace On Earth — 188
- The Steps to Personal Fulfillment — 189

**Plan of Pursuit** — 194
- We Make Our Own World — 197
- Volunteer Work — 197
- Teachers — 198

**Journaling** — 202
- Making Peace with Imperfection — 203
- In Search of Balance — 204

## CHAPTER 6: OUR RELATIONSHIPS WITH THE THIRD PARTIES — 205

**The Residential Parent** — 205

**Your Spouse or Partner** — 208

**Stepparents** — 216

| | |
|---|---|
| Stepsiblings | 219 |
| New Family | 222 |
| Grandparents | 223 |
| School Personnel/Teachers | 226 |
| Medical/Dental Professionals | 232 |
| Attorneys | 233 |
| Support Groups | 237 |
|    Support Network | 239 |
| **CHAPTER 7: OUR CHILDREN AT HOME** | 243 |
| Creating Schedules | 243 |
| Home: From the Inside | 245 |
|    Creating a Room for Your Children | 247 |
|    Pets and Plants | 249 |
|    Routines | 249 |
|    Chores | 252 |
|    Policies/Procedures | 252 |
|    Making Life Fun | 256 |
| Home: From the Outside | 258 |
|    Friends | 258 |
|    Church | 259 |
|    Family Business | 260 |
|    Community | 261 |
|    Good-byes | 261 |
|    Post Together Follow-ups | 262 |
| **CHAPTER 8: STEP FIVE: IDEAS FOR STAYING IN TOUCH** | 263 |
|    Resources | 263 |
|    Responsibility for Co-Communicating | 264 |
|    Address Books | 265 |
|    Answering Machines | 266 |
|    Books | 266 |
|    Business Cards | 268 |
|    Business Connections | 268 |
|    Calendars | 269 |

| | |
|---|---|
| Cameras | 270 |
| Cassettes | 271 |
| Computer | 272 |
| Cookie Kits | 274 |
| Suggestions for Shipping | 275 |
| Fan clubs | 276 |
| Fax Machines | 276 |
| Gifts | 277 |
| Letters | 278 |
| Lunchtime Love Notes | 280 |
| **Meet In The Middle** | **282** |
| Monthly Information | 282 |
| Pagers | 301 |
| Postal and Parcel Services | 302 |
| Same Time "Stuff" | 304 |
| **Scrapbooks** | **304** |
| Special Notes of Love and Support | 306 |
| Summer | 307 |
| Evaluate Your Needs | 307 |
| Evaluate Your Child's Needs: | 308 |
| Consider Your Finances | 310 |
| Consider the Other Parent's Needs | 310 |
| Talents and Hobbies | 310 |
| Telephone | 312 |
| Travel | 314 |
| The Backpack | 316 |
| Traveling by Airplane | 317 |
| Traveling by Bus | 320 |
| Traveling by Car | 321 |
| Make a Treat Bag | 322 |
| Trading Places | 322 |
| Hotel Accommodations | 323 |
| Traveling by Train | 323 |
| Treat Bags | 325 |
| Video Recorders | 325 |
| **CHAPTER 9: AVAILABLE SUPPORT** | **328** |
| **CHAPTER 10: FINAL THOUGHTS** | **332** |
| **BIBLIOGRAPHY** | **334** |

*Building a Bridge*

## Chapter 1: Who Are Long-distance Parents?

Who are long-distance parents? Geoffrey L. Grief, author of *Out of Touch*, gathered from his research that "the Census Bureau report states that 7.6 million women were raising children without the father in the household … and 1.3 million fathers were raising children without the mother in the household." He further documents:

> Estimates of the number of fathers who have stopped visiting their children at least annually after a breakup run from as high as two-thirds to slightly under 10 percent, with the Census Bureau placing the figure at 47 percent … much less data exist on mothers' rates on non-visitation, though it is estimated by the Census Bureau to be 30 percent.

Let's do some math

Forty-seven percent of fathers who engage in no visitation with their children would be approximately 3,572,000.

*Building a Bridge*

Non-visitation fathers and thirty percent of mothers who engage in no visitation with their children would be approximately 390,000 non-visitation mothers. That adds up to be 3,962,000 non-visitation parents. This figure does not account for long-distance parents who do exercise visitation.

Long-distance parents are not a small group. If you get nothing else from this book, get this: you are not alone.

We are a part of every walk of life. Our professions touch every scope of industry. Our incomes cover the very top to the very bottom of salary ranges. We vary in age and ethnic background. We live in every community. We worship in every church. We are men. We are women. Some of us believe the children living with the other parent or grandparent is for the best. Some of us do not. Some of us manage to cooperate with the other parent. Some of us do not. Some of us are honest about our situations. Some of us are not. Some of us have accepted it. Some of us have not.

Why do so few parents stay in contact and maintain relationships with their children? Mr. Grief further learned that "the visiting parent starts to drift away, either because of emotional problems, anger at the breakup, problems with visitation, miscommunication, or the desire/need to avoid financial obligation."

I certainly don't have to tell you that this is an emotionally devastating and potentially overwhelming experience. The unresolved issues that reside within us about the relationship with the other parent, the failure of that relationship, the divorce proceedings and the custody outcomes gnaw at us. Is it any surprise that there are long-distance parents that break down or lose touch? There is a feeling of hopelessness. But hope does exist. Sometimes hope is all we have. Sometimes it is all we need.

*Building a Bridge*

## Chapter 2: Five Steps for Building a Relationship with Our Children

I am writing to you because I believe that it is not what we get in this life that matters, but what we do with what we get that counts. Having said that, I believe that regardless of the current condition of our relationship with the other parent, our children or other persons involved, we can heal those old wounds and create genuine, meaningful relationships with our kids.

While I know this can be done, I also know that it takes a strong intention, honesty, patience and perseverance. The results of our efforts may not be seen for years, but we must remain committed regardless.

From my experience, I see this work as being a five-part process:

1. Face our fears, which are fearful thoughts manifested into actions. Fear can be demonstrated in many ways. These include, but are not limited to:

    alienation                    inferiority                    anger

*Building a Bridge*

| | | |
|---|---|---|
| laziness | arrogance | loneliness |
| blame | regret | despair |
| resentment | grief | self-pity |
| guilt | hatefulness | spite |
| superiority | | |

2. Release the fear by changing our thinking and thereby release the fear-based behaviors.

3. Embrace loving thoughts and thereby act accordingly. Love can be demonstrated in many ways. These include, but are not limited to:

| | | |
|---|---|---|
| acceptance | kindness | listening |
| acting responsibly | compassion | respect |
| courtesy | self-worth | creativity |
| honesty | forgiveness | surrender |
| spiritual development | friendliness | wisdom |

4. Focus our energies on becoming a quality person – becoming an example for our children to follow.

5. Participate in activities that connect us to our children.

    I applaud you for stepping up to the plate and wanting to reestablish a relationship with your children. I know that you want to have a relationship with your children because you have this book in your hand. This effort takes courage; you are respected for this choice.

    Now that I have explained what you need to do, you may be asking yourself why. Why is this really important?

*Building a Bridge*

Why do I need to do this work? Why not leave the past behind? Maybe someone else is parenting your child, so why rock the boat?

There are five reasons why I think you need to continue reading this book and start or continue to work on your relationship with your child.

1. Your children need you. They need contact with you.

2. You need your children. You need contact with them.

3. Your family and friends need to see that you will do whatever it takes to keep your family intact.

4. The courts need to see that you maintain contact in the event that something happens to the custodial parent. Otherwise, custody could remain with a non-blood-related person, such as the stepparent.

5. Society needs responsible parents. When we take responsibility and care for our children, we contribute to society becoming stronger and healthier.

These are five of my ideas, but the only reason that matters is the one you hold in your heart.

*Building a Bridge*

*24*

*Building a Bridge*

# Chapter 3: Step One: Evaluating Your Fears Step Two: Releasing Your Fears Step Three: Embracing Your Love

Healthy and meaningful relationships require whole people. Whole people are not perfect people, because "perfect" does not exist. Whole people are people in process. In order to be a whole person, we must begin a healing process that starts with facing our fears. These fears have created soul wounds that lie deep within us and will not simply go away by themselves. If left buried, they eat away at us and become cancer, diabetes, heart trouble, mental illness, or a combination of these. They must be exposed and dealt with – a job that only you can do.

We are all fear filled and hurting. I have said to myself and aloud, "I am afraid and I hurt." It is OK to say this. Give yourself permission to say what you feel. When you identify what you are feeling, you can begin to evaluate what is causing the pain and what you can do to heal the hurt. Our pain is here to help us – to guide us to wholeness.

*Building a Bridge*

## 26

### "Those things that hurt, instruct."

### Benjamin Franklin

The first step in the process of exposing these fears and hurts, requires you to:

- be honest with yourself
- accept responsibility for yourself and your fears
- be willing to release the fear once it is acknowledged
- open yourself to new thoughts – and the resulting behaviors
- be prepared to accept this new behavior without skepticism or sarcasm

F.E.A.R., **F**alse **E**vidence **A**ppearing **R**eal, is what fear is. Fear is an illusion; it is fake. What we need to do is look at reality. The foundation of reality lies in our thinking. Everything starts with the thinking process. We behave based on our thinking. All of our life experiences are a result of our thinking. The real work for us to do is to clear up our thinking. The fear areas where we need to concentrate our efforts for change exist in how we think about alienation, anger, arrogance, blame, despair, grief, guilt, hatefulness, inferiority, laziness, loneliness, regret, resentment, self-pity, spite and superiority.

### "Those who cannot change their minds cannot change anything."

### George Bernard Shaw

*Building a Bridge*

Does changing your thought patterns sound pretty simple? It is simple. It is not easy. Your thoughts play in your mind like a cassette tape that has run continuously for the length of your life. Many of the thoughts we think are rooted deeply into our brains from childhood – as a result of our experiences, observations or the lessons that our parents taught us.

Unfortunately, many of those experiences, observations or lessons were unloving and have produced fearful, negative thoughts. When we attempt to change those thought processes, we challenge the very core of who we are. That is a time when our ego is put on alert and works diligently to justify the old, familiar and fear-based thoughts and resulting behaviors. The ego is exceptionally convincing. Often we fall back into old routines.

**"The biggest problem any of us ever face is our own negative thinking."**

**Dr. Robert H. Schuller**

Because we have spent our entire lives engrossed in negative thinking, we don't notice we are doing it. So how can we stop doing something we are not aware we are doing? By listening to ourselves. Dr. Shad Helmstetter writes in his book, *What to Say When You Talk to Yourself*, "During the first eighteen years of our lives, if we grew up in fairly average, reasonably positive homes, we were told "No!," or what we could not do, more than 148,000 times!"

Let's do more math.

18 years x 365 days per year = 6, 570 days.

148,000 times ÷ 6,570 days = 22.53 times a day!

*Building a Bridge*

You think we don't negative self-talk? We have been conditioned to do so. Dr. Helmstetter continues by reporting that "Leading behavioral researchers have told us that as much as seventy-seven percent of everything we think is negative, counterproductive, and works against us."

Some examples of negative self-talk might me:

- "I am so stupid."

- "I dream but know my dreams will never come true."

- "I will never have any money – no one in my family ever has."

- "College is too hard for me."

- "Why would my kid want to have a relationship with a loser like me?"

Make a list of the negative messages you send to yourself. Go through the list and write a positive message (or two) for each negative one. Using a message board, like the one that follows, can help you refocus your negative messages into positive ones.

*Building a Bridge*

| MESSAGE BOARD ||
|---|---|
| **Negative Message** | **Positive Message** |
| I am a loser. | I have the right to experience love and joy in my life. I claim this right – right now! <br><br> I have talents and abilities and use them for my good and the good of others. |
| I do not understand math. | I keep my checkbook up-to-date and in order. <br><br> Anything I do not understand, I can study and learn. |

The remedy for our negative message affliction is to feed ourselves massive amounts of positive thinking. Through the various ways listed below we can generate positive input into our lives:

| | |
|---|---|
| Affirmations | Motivational cassette tapes |
| Books | Seminars |
| Workshops | Visualization exercises |
| Symbolic exercises | Journaling positive talk |
| Messages in music/movies | Creating a support network |

What in the world are symbolic exercises? Symbolic exercises are those activities we can use symbolically to communicate messages. Here are a few examples:

*Building a Bridge*

- If you feel that you do not have enough love in your life, buy or make heart-shaped confetti. Sprinkle it at the entrances to your home and on the floor of your car. By doing this you can remind yourself that you are stepping into love and carrying that love with you everywhere you go. You can also take a marker and draw hearts on the inside of your shoe for the same message.

- Do you want to get connected with people? Take an extension cord (which represents energy) and plug it into itself to make a circle. Make some tags with the names of the people you want to connect with and fasten them to the cord. The cord represents you and your life. By adding the names to the cord, you are symbolizing your connection with them. You can also add situations you want to connect with, such as a new career or companion or support network.

- If you need to weed out problems in your life, try gardening. The actual exercise of pulling weeds is a powerful metaphor for clearing out the weeds in life – clearing space for the beautiful and healthy parts of your life to flourish.

- If you find yourself getting into heated discussions with others, write your name on a piece of paper and place the paper in your refrigerator. This will give you a "cooling off" opportunity.

- Cleaning house is also a symbolic exercise for cleaning up our lives. As you dust, you will be ridding your life of old dusty thoughts. As you remove clutter from closets and drawers, you will be releasing old thoughts and habits that no longer serve you.

- If you want to be more open-minded about life, try to see things from different viewpoints. For example, lie on the ground to look at a tree and its sprawling branches or lay on the bed with your head hanging over the edge to see the room upside-down or visit a high-rise observation floor to broaden your views.

- Have you caught yourself driving fast or getting speeding tickets? This is a symbolic message telling you that you are living fast. Try to slow down a little. If you are getting tickets, life is definitely telling you to slow down.

*Building a Bridge*

Speaking of a support network, do you have one? A support network is the collection of family members and friends who encourage you in your efforts to fulfill your goals, offer input and inspiration when you need advice or a boost to your morale. Each person in a support network has a special gift to offer you. You might turn to one wise friend for advice, while a family member might be your personal cheerleading squad.

Appreciate each person for the gift they bring to you. A word of caution – do not abuse your support network by wallowing in your problems. Everyone has tough days, but you will quickly find yourself without a support team if you linger too long in self-pity.

A support network or team is different from a support group. A support network is developed from your inner circle of family and friends. They are individuals who offer you positive energy and insight in dealing with life. A support group is a group of individuals who may not know each other outside of the group. While the group can, and often does, offer a positive contribution to your life, everyone in a support group is dealing with the same situation. Having both a support group and support network can be helpful. The support group will know the issue first-hand so you may feel more understood in that group, however, you need the support network to remind you that there is more going on in life than those issues you are personally managing. (More information on support groups can be found in Chapter 6.)

If you find it difficult to ask for help, take a lesson from professional athletes. I am not an avid sports viewer, but on those occasions when I do watch a game, I notice that when one player gets knocked down, another always lends a hand to help that player up. Don't be afraid to accept a helping hand – and don't be slow to offer one.

We need, we must, practice positive thinking on a daily thought-by-thought basis and there is no time like the present! James Allen, author of *As A Man Thinketh*, supports positive thinking. He said, "Good thoughts bear good fruit, bad thoughts bear bad fruit – and man is his own gardener."

*Building a Bridge*

## "As a man thinketh, so is he."

### King Solomon, Proverbs 23:7

We need to give careful consideration to the childhood experiences that formed our thinking. Our minds are cluttered with hurtful experiences that have been buried or allowed to fester. They have haunted us and grown into ghosts that echo when we attempt to step out and face a challenge or ourselves. These voices have tricked us into thinking that we are not worthy. Try this exercise:

- Recall a childhood experience that haunts you.

- Think on that experience and relive the scene in your mind.

- Observe how the adults around you were treating you.

- Allow yourself to feel the emotions you were expressing in those moments.

- Evaluate your real role in the scene – Were you a little child trying to learn? Did you make a simple childlike mistake and find yourself in a huge ordeal over it? Were the adults involved verbally or physically abusive?

- Forgive the people in your scene for the role they played in your experience.

- Look at the little child you were in the scene and love him. Kneel down and look into his eyes and tell him that it is OK to learn, to figure life out. Express your compassion and understanding.

- Think about what you said to your child-self and use that as your affirmation. (For example, "It is OK to learn and attempt new things. I am worthy and deserving of those opportunities although the outcome is not perfect.")

- Now allow yourself, the adult you, to embrace those same words of encouragement and support.

- Let go of the experience, but keep the lesson and love.

*Building a Bridge*

By doing this exercise, you can release the ugly memories of the past and free yourself of the negative thoughts that linger as a result.

If this exercise of visualization does not work for you, try some of these ideas:

- Write the experience down – every detail. Work through your story using the same steps as the visualization.

- Talk through the experience using a cassette recorder. Set up the recorder in a living room setting so you can be comfortable. Pretend you are sharing this story with someone. As you talk, you will become aware of things about the situation or people that you had not previously noticed. After you have gone through the entire story, listen to the cassette recording as if someone else is telling you the story. Be the friend of this person and help him by offering insight.

- If the cassette recorder doesn't feel comfortable, find a caring soul or therapist to listen to you as you work through the story.

If God is a part of your life, ask God for a miracle. Miracles happen all the time – everyday. Many of the things that occur in our lives are miracles, but if we are in an unappreciative frame of mind, we don't acknowledge them as such. Miracles happen when we are grateful, so try opening your heart to a miracle and see what happens.

Please do not shut down at the mention of God. When God comes up in conversation or text, many people want to disconnect. Maybe you feel that you, too, want to close this book and say, "Oh boy, I am not interested in any religious ideas about how to connect with my kid." Before you toss the book aside and throw your hands to the air, consider what author and minister J. Douglas Bottorff has to offer from his book, *The Practical Guide to Meditation and Prayer*:

> "In your consciousness, your body, and your affairs, you are seeking to express more of God. You may not have called your desire for healing, prosperity, and harmony a desire for God, but that is exactly what it is. Perhaps by

*Building a Bridge*

exchanging the word God for the word good, as someone has suggested, you can see it clearly."

Moving closer to God frightens some of us. We resist more of God because we have been taught that God despises our behavior. We consider our behavior to be who we really are. If our behavior is unlovable, then we must be unlovable. If I think this of me, God must too.

We think our thinking is God's thinking. If all we see is ugliness, how can God see anything different? We reject any effort to get to know God because, after all, why should we solicit more pain? It is a vicious cycle – and a lie.

We have bought a lie. God loves us and wants us to love ourselves. In Mark 12:31 we received this instruction: "Thou shall love thy neighbor as thyself." God has requested this of us, because we cannot genuinely love others unless we genuinely love ourselves. Often we confuse loving ourselves with being self-centered and egotistical. Genuine love of ourselves produces a healthy soul that takes us out of our ego. Working through these fears, releasing them and embracing what heals our lives moves us closer to God – closer to the loving relationship between God and ourselves. From this place we experience healing and wholeness.

Another word that makes us nervous is love. When I speak of love and love-based behavior, I am not talking about the popular easy-come-easy-go type of love. I am talking about agape love – the love of God. God's love is strong, bold and honest. It is love that transcends our understanding, brings peace and heals our soul wounds.

The apostle Paul wrote of God's love in I Corinthians 13:4-7:

"Love is patient and kind. Love is not jealous or boastful or proud or rude. Love does not demand its own way. Love is not irritable, and it keeps no record of when it has been wronged. It is never glad about injustice but rejoices whenever the truth wins out. Love never gives up, never loses faith, is always hopeful, and endures through every circumstance."

*Building a Bridge*

When I have spoken to my family and friends during the development of this book, I have shared what I believe with every fiber of my being: we must learn to love one another. When loving each other happens, healing will be accomplished. The response I get is "What? You are being a Pollyanna. You need to look at reality." I ask, "Why is my positive outlook any less real than your negative outlook?"

Here is the real kicker. We cannot avoid this work. We cannot begin to create an authentic relationship with our children unless we clear out the fear that stands between us and pave the way with love. The question is not "Will you do the work?" The question is "When?"

You may be thinking that you are too angry or weak or "far gone" for healing. Bah! When we work on ourselves, we turn our weakness into our strength. History is paved with such testimonies.

Consider, for example, Albert Einstein. In Laurence Santrey's biography of Albert Einstein, he writes of Albert's struggled through his entire school years. His Greek teacher told him "You will never amount to anything." On another occasion Albert's father asked the school's headmaster "What profession should Albert consider?" The headmaster replied, "It doesn't matter, Mr. Einstein. He will never make a success of himself at anything." But Albert's years of study and dedication to his ideas – by honoring himself – proved that he was something. The December 31, 1999 issue of Time Magazine named Albert Einstein the Person of the Century. A nothing? Or a someone very awesome?

Wilma Rudolf is another powerful example. She was born the twentieth child in a family with twenty-two children. When she was six years old, her legs were so weak from childhood illnesses that she had to wear leg braces. At age twenty Wilma became an Olympic star during the games in Rome. Do you think Wilma Rudolf had naysayers nipping at her heals? Do you think she had obstacles to overcome? Of course, she did!

Years ago the Wall Street Journal published an article entitled "Don't Be Afraid To Fail." It made such a powerful impact on me that I cut it from the paper and have kept it for over thirteen years.

*Building a Bridge*

## 36
### *Don't Be Afraid to Fail*

You've failed many times, although you may not remember. You fell down the first time you tried to walk. You almost drowned the first time to tried to swim, didn't you? Did you hit the ball the first time you swung a bat? Heavy hitters, the ones who hit the most home runs, also strike out a lot. R. H. Macy failed seven times before his store in New York caught on. English novelist John Creasey got 753 rejection slips before he published 564 books. Babe Ruth struck out 1,330 times, but he also hit 714 home runs. Don't worry about failure. Worry about the chances you miss when you don't even try.

People do not always see our potential because our seeds of greatness lie deep within us. We must believe in ourselves, follow our hearts, and stay committed to our purpose.

How does this transformation happen?

Focused energy.

The key is to set an intention and concentrate on the desired outcome. Gary Zukav, author of *The Seat of the Soul* states, "An intention is not only a desire. It is a use of will." When we set our intentions and use our will power, we will see results. These results do not come from our manipulation of events, but as a result of the law of the universe. Whatever energy we send out, we get back. When we emit fear, we receive fear in return. As an example, if we demonstrate anger (a fear-based behavior) to someone, we will receive hostility (another fear-based behavior) in return. This law of the universe is true also for love. When we demonstrate love, we experience love in return. Have you ever extended a kindness to someone and found the rest of your day to be more pleasant?

Have you read the children's book, *Because Brian Hugged His Mother* by David L. Rice? Young Brian awakens one morning and embraces his Mother with an awesome hug. She feels so good, as a result, that she extends a kindness, then that person does the same and so on. Throughout the day love is shared from person to person and by evening the kindness is returned to Brian. This is a fabulous

*Building a Bridge*

story for children of all ages. I highly recommend it be added to your library.

This little poem from the book *Apples of Gold* also demonstrates this law:

I did a favor yesterday, A kindly little deed …
And then I called to all the world to stop and look and heed.
They stopped and looked and flattered me in words I could not trust,
And when the world had gone away my good deed had turned to dust.

A very tiny courtesy I found to do today;
'twas quickly done, with none to see, and then I ran away …
But Someone must have witnessed it, for – truly I declare –
As I sped back the stony path roses were blooming there!

The following section of this chapter is a list of fears – and the manifestations of those fears – that I have personally encountered.

I have faced my thinking about these fears, released the old, and work to embrace the love. I say work because we are never done. We do not "arrive" at "finish" and sit back on our laurels. The work we have to do is work we will do our whole lives. Our mission is a day-to-day process, but one that will lead us to peace.

Our mission is to build a bridge for our children to safely travel between ourselves and the other parent. Our separation has left a gap in the foundation of our children's lives. This bridge is necessary in order for our children to grow up safely and securely. The work involves removing the fears – similar to excavating the land before the actual building begins. As we clear away the fears, we can begin the construction phase of building a bridge – the work of demonstrating love. Parents must constantly work to keep the foundation of the bridge solid. As you work through each section of this book, I encourage you to make notes regarding your feelings and thoughts. These notes will help you to build your own bridge.

*Building a Bridge*

Being separated from my children offered me the opportunity to build this bridge in my own life. Knowing how challenging this endeavor is, I want to help you build your bridge using the information and wisdom I gained along the way. As your bridge becomes solid and stable, you too will reach out to help other parents. The poem, "The Bridge Builder," beautifully expresses how we can take our lessons and use them to help others that follow.

*Building a Bridge*

## The Bridge Builder

An old man, going a lone highway,
Came at the evening, cold and gray,
To a chasm, vast and deep and wide
Through which was flowing a sullen tide.

The old man crossed in the twilight dim;
The sullen stream had no fears for him;
But he turned when safe on the other side
And built a bridge to span the tide.
"Old Man," said a fellow pilgrim near,
"You are wasting strength with building here;
Your journey will end with the ending day;
You never again must pass this way;
You have crossed the chasm, deep and wide –
Why build you the bridge at the eventide?"

The builder lifted his old gray head;
"Good friend, in the path I have come," he said,
"There followeth after me today
A youth whose feet must pass this way,
This chasm that has been naught to me
To that fair-haired youth may a pitfall be.
He, too, must cross in the twilight dim;
Good friend, I am building the bridge for him!"

Will Allen Dromgoole

*****

Personal Reflections

Have you given yourself permission to feel? Write down what you are feeling – list both your negative and positive feelings. (For example: sad, ashamed, angry, stupid, victimized, lost, lonely, scared, weak or valuable, hopeful, creative, loved.)

Do you know the source (or experience) of these feelings? If so, write them down. If not, take some time to trace the history of your feelings. (For example, The first time I remember feeling this way was ….")

*Building a Bridge*

Decide if you are ready and willing to take the steps necessary for exposing your fears and hurts? If you are ready, write yourself a contract.

> I, _____, am ready and willing to take the necessary steps for exposing my fears and hurts.

Listen to yourself. What do you say to you? List the negative messages. Rewrite those into positive messages.

**Negative Messages**     *Positive Messages*

Check off the method(s) you want you try for putting more positives into your life.

| | |
|---|---|
| Affirmations | Workshops |
| Motivational cassette tapes | Books |
| Seminars | Create a support network |
| Visualization exercises | Symbolic exercises |
| Journaling | Positive talk |
| Messages in music/movies | |

Draw a picture of yourself as a child. Write a list of loving things you want to say to your child-self. (For example, "You have a beautiful smile," or "You have a terrific laugh" or "I love your bright eyes.")

Write a letter to the adults in your childhood situation(s) telling them how you felt about the experience(s). In the letter release your hurts and fears. Once written, destroy the letter. Get rid of the letter and the hurts.

> Dear Dad,
>
> When I was ten you smacked my face for getting into your tool chest. You yelled at me for touching your belongings. I was so hurt. I loved you and wanted to be just like you. After you hit me, I hated you and never again wanted to be

*Building a Bridge*

like you. I'm grown up now, but don't know how to use tools because whenever I get around tools I remember that ugly day. To help me forget, I never touch tools. Now I feel useless around my own home and am afraid to tell anyone the truth so I pretend I don't care about fixing things.

John

How do you feel about involving God in your effort to reconnect with your child(ren)? Your thoughts/feelings are:

Do you have anyone you admire that you can look to for inspiration? (For example, Albert Einstein, Michael Jordan, or Oprah Winfrey.) If so, get a biography of this person's life and make notes about how they handled their difficult experiences. Also note the wisdom that is offered in the book – what they have learned from life.

Have you set your intention – your will power – on reconnecting with your children? How will you reconnect with them? (For example, write, call or plan a trip.)

What we give out, we get back. Each day look for an opportunity to do something nice for someone else – even if the person doesn't acknowledge your kindness. You might even do something they are not aware of, such as, putting a shopping cart in the designated area so it does not ram into their vehicle. For the next week, make a list of these acts and say "Thank you" for each good thing you were able to do.

Sunday:

Monday:

Tuesday:

Wednesday:

Thursday:

Friday:

Saturday:

After a week of demonstrating kindness, write down how it felt when you were doing these acts of kindness? (For example, happy, excited, uncomfortable, worried about what others will think?) Do you see how you can incorporate kindness into your life on a daily basis?

Did this exercise affect your sense of appreciation? Make a list of things you appreciate. (For example, "I am thankful for: my children, my life, food, clothing, a home, my car …")

### *Alienation*

**Alienation is "a conveyance of property to another; a withdrawing or separation of a person or his affections from an object or position of former attachment; isolation; exile."**

We are attached to nothing else like we are attached to our children. We regard our children with an element of ownership. Each parent experiences attachment, the "this child belongs to me" thinking. During marriage, parents view themselves as equal partners in rearing the children, even when the responsibilities of parenting are not equally divided. When the divorce occurs and the custody matters are established, one parent generally finds himself in a secondary, or supportive, parenting role. Having formerly considered himself on equal footing with the other parent, some divorced parents feel demoted. Since parents feel a prior sense of real attachment to the child, the change in the parenting role can create a sense of detachment; a court mandated form of exile for the parent who loses the day-to-day contact. In an effort to defend oneself, an "all or nothing" attitude is developed. We take the approach that "if I can't have the children when I want them or on my terms, then forget it." In our pain, we isolate ourselves from the time we are allotted to be with our children and therefore, alienate, or separate, ourselves from them.

If you have been separated from your child for a long time, you may think that your relationship is beyond hope or repair. Do not throw in the towel. It is never too late. Building a meaningful relationship does not happen overnight. With consistent and committed effort, you can experience the joy of reuniting.

Mark Bryan, author of *The Prodigal Father* and founder of The Father Project, was separated from his son for fourteen years. His effort to find himself and reconnect with his child is powerful and inspirational. I encourage you to study Mr. Bryan's work.

If you want to reconnect with your child, you will need to start by introducing (or reintroducing) yourself to your child. I suggest you write a letter. A letter is invitational and non-confrontational. It is also tangible. If you have been apart for a while, a letter can provide your child with something solid from you. Keep your letter short and keep it honest. Here is a sample letter:

Dear Son/Daughter,

You are probably surprised to hear from me.

I know I have not done a good job of staying in touch with you or being a parent to you. This has been on my mind. I just read a book about long-distance parenting. I now know and respect how important it is to stay in touch.

I miss you and would like to work things out between us. If this is something you want also, please write me a note. I have enclosed a pre-addressed, pre-stamped envelope for you.

I hope to hear from you, but if you are not ready, that is OK. Please know that I do love you.

Your father/mother, (name)


If you have more than one child, you need to address a separate letter to each child and respect each child's right to answer according to his own heart. One child might be ready to connect with you when another is not.

As parents we often attempt to keep the dealings with our children on an equal plane. Dr. T. Berry Brazelton offers this insight, "Parents who have more than one child often wonder how to treat each child equally. The answer is simple. You can't – and you shouldn't try to. Each child is a different personality and needs a different approach." If you have more than one child, take some time to consider the individualism of each child – his or her specific needs – and then proceed appropriately.

*Building a Bridge*

At the same time, you also should write a letter or note to the other parent. An example is as follows:

Dear (custodial parent),

You may be wondering why I have sent you and the children letters. I know it has been a long time since I talked to you or the kids, but I really want to reconnect with them. I do not want you to be afraid of my desire to establish a relationship with them, nor do I have any secret agendas in doing so. I simply miss my children.

I know that you have been a very responsible parent to the children for a number of months (years). I appreciate everything you have done for them. I apologize that I have not been around to help you with them or support you in raising them.

I know you and I have a lot of old baggage, but I hope you will not use the past against me.

name


I have written this book because I want to encourage long-distance parents to reconnect with their child(ren). I also encourage you to finish this book and understand fully that to have a relationship with our children means we must:

- live with respect for ourselves

- create a cooperative association with the other parent

- be committed to our children and demonstrate that commitment through our actions

To think that we can reach out to our children without these elements means that we are fooling ourselves and, in that case, no real relationship can exist.

The choices made by the residential parent can further alienate us from our children. In their anger over the divorce or the settlement, residential parents often make decisions that distance the children from the other parent. Sometimes these decisions are not consciously made, but the effects nonetheless carry hurtful consequences. Tragically, many times the residential parent does purposely attempt to alienate the children from the long-distance parent.

When this happens, a long-distance parent that is working to create or maintain a relationship with his children may feel that all doors are closed – even locked.

If your former spouse has – or is attempting to – create a barrier between you and the children, you need to determine why this has happened.

- Do you possess any behaviors or habits that could genuinely harm or inappropriately influence the child?

- Do you abuse alcohol?

- Do you participate in drug use?

- Do you use physical or emotional intimidation in order to have your demands met or wishes carried out?

- Does your spouse have a valid reason for keeping the children from you?

Only you can answer these questions.

If any of these, or other issues, are present in your life:

- You need to seek professional counseling. Get help. Wonderful support systems are available to assist with all types of addictions and behavior problems.

    Alcoholic's Anonymous has local chapters throughout the world. Consult your local Yellow Pages or refer to the web site at http://www.recovery.org/aa.

    National Clearing House for Alcohol and Drug Information, 800-729-6686 or at http://alcoholhelpline.com.

*Building a Bridge*

1470 support resources for a wide range of problems are available through Dr. John Grohol's Mental Health Page at www.grohol.com. He addresses issues such as online/internet addictions, sexual abuses, eating disorders, anxiety/panic disorders, mental health issues, obsessive-compulsive disorders, and post-traumatic stress disorder.

The book, *Help & Where To Find It* compiled by Charlotte Hardwick, offers countless valuable resources for assistance. The book is updated annually, so you can be confident the information is accurate. You can order the book online at http://www.custodywar.com or by calling 936 327-1104 or 800 646-5590.

United Way offices can also offer referrals to assist you with a variety of issues. United Way is not only familiar with the programs offered through their own services, but also those offered in the community.

- Contact a minister. She/he will also know of programs or support groups that can assist you.

- Have your progress documented by someone who is helping you and journal the progress yourself. If you sincerely want to create or maintain a relationship with your child, several parties will want confirmation that you have acknowledged the problem and dealt with it in a positive, constructive manner. Those parties will include, but might not be limited to: the other parent, the children, and perhaps the courts.

- Although you have worked through your issue, your life will need to be the strongest evidence of the change. Simply saying that you attend a support program or see a counselor will not be enough to create trust in you. You must be a living example of the decisions you have made for lifestyle improvement.

If this is not the case, if the former spouse is simply blowing smoke in an effort to appear (or in her mind be) the superior parent, let go of the nonsense. Remain committed to your contribution to the children. Rise above the trash talk and live so those observing you – especially your children – know better about you. The trash the other parent may sling at you can only stick if it is true. Otherwise, it becomes like a boomerang and will end up right back in her face. Stay focused on your character and your reputation will take care of itself.

*Building a Bridge*

You might experience times when your children say negative things about you. Maybe they have overheard conversations from adults or maybe they are simply testing you to get your reaction to their comments. While we generally expect and prepare ourselves for some disturbing dialog about us from the other parent, we are rarely ready for hurtful comments from our children. Some examples of those painful words are:

- "Dad says you're a lousy housekeeper."
- "Mom says you only care about your work."
- "You don't always send the child support."

If our kids engage in this talk towards us, we need to:

- Take an honest look at ourselves. How much truth exists in what we are hearing?

    If there is truth to the comments:

- You must respond to your child with an honest answer. To do anything else will make you a fraud and jeopardize any chance you may have of a genuine relationship. While it is difficult to admit to our weaknesses, not admitting to them is a price too high to pay.

    If there is no truth to the comments:

- Take a moment to consider the possible origin of the remarks. Is this simply a matter of their repeating what they have overheard or is this their pain screaming out?

- We need to respond to their comments in a thoughtful and respectful mannor. You might say, "I am very sorry to hear you say these things about me. I would like to tell you about _____ so you know my point of view. Would you be willing to listen to my comments?" or "What in my behavior indicates to you that I am _____?"

- When we speak to our children in deliberate and gentle tones, they listen. By presenting ourselves in this manner, it indicates to them that we are not threatened and they will hear honest information. When we blurt out reactionary remarks in defensive

*Building a Bridge*

protection of ourselves, listeners shut down and all we become is noise.

- Live so your children will **see** who you are. Your living testimony will stand so solid that it will not be shaken by cutting comments or negative jabs.

- 

> "As I grow older, I pay less attention to what men say.
> I just watch what they do."
>
> **Andrew Carnegie**

Sometimes children isolate themselves from the long-distance parent. They may be confused about who you are or whom to trust. They may be holding a grudge over an old hurt – a missed birthday, infrequency of phone calls, or a lack of consistent contact. If our children feel we have rejected them, they will protect themselves by isolation. Sometimes blocking out what they perceive as rejection seems the best course of action.

Have you ever excused yourself from a business meeting or family discussion because it was getting ridiculous? Have you ever walked away from an argument because it was loud voices instead of productive communication?

I wonder if our children are doing this to us? I wonder if they eventually get a belly full of parental bickering and fighting and feel that the only positive thing they can do is escape?

Abandonment is a major concern for children of divorce. We once said that we loved the parent, but later divorced that person. Then we say we love our children and they wait in fear, wondering if or when we will divorce them. They feel vulnerable and unsure of the future. We must be careful to not feed this fear, but work to establish a sense of security in them. Our children need to know that we are here for them. They need solid evidence of our love. We show them our love and secure them emotionally by:

- Calling on a regular basis

- Writing regularly and sending them tangible evidences of our affection

- Physically being together

- Making positive memories

- Paying our child support according to our agreements and accounting for our spending of those funds

- Behaving in a respectful manner toward the other parent

- Having consideration for the other parent's and the children's views

- Being polite

- Attempting to understand the other parties' situation

- Being on time when picking up or returning the children

- Keeping promises made to the other parent and children

- Being considerate of the problems the other parent faces

- Expecting the children to show respect for the other parent

- Not telling the children negative things about your relationship with the other parent

- Emphasizing the love both you and the other parent feel for the children

- Being non-judgmental about the other parent's actions when speaking to the children

### Separation is Impossible

From a spiritual standpoint, the idea of separation is impossible. We are all connected to each other and to everything in the universe. Metaphysical scientists know that at the subatomic level everything is equal. Everything is energy. When we attempt to alienate ourselves from others or when others attempt to alienate us, the flow of energy is blocked, but is not completely inaccessible. Consider that old saying, "When a door closes, God opens a window."

*Building a Bridge*

The day-to-day role we play in our children's lives may have changed, but this does not mean that we cannot make a profound contribution to their lives. While your child may be alienated from you at this time, if you consistently send love out, it will eventually be received. It may not be in the time frame we would choose, but we must remain focused on our effort. This is our opportunity to express unconditional love.

As I refer to sending your child love, you may be wondering how to do that. When discussing alienation, you may not feel that the traditional ways of connecting through calling, letter writing, and visiting are available to you. Consider sending your child love in a manner that cannot be blocked – through prayer, meditation or visualization.

### *Prayer*

We generally think of prayer as asking God for something – usually an offer of bargain or barter. Is it any wonder we doubt if God is listening? "… the purpose of prayer", Bottorff writes, "is to integrate the attributes of God into your consciousness which, in turn, will manifest as corresponding conditions....Our problems are solved from the inside out, not from the outside in." Therefore, when we pray, it should be for understanding and guidance on how we need to think differently – asking to think as God thinks. Once we have this awareness, we can respond to the situations of our life with confidence that our actions will not only be for our own good, but the good of others as well.

> **"I do not pray so God will change circumstances.**
> **I pray so God will change me."**
>
> **C. S. Lewis**

If you are not familiar with prayer and long for words, Iyanla Vanzant, author of *One Day My Soul Just Opened Up and In The Meantime* and other wonderful books, offers these beautiful prayers:

*Building a Bridge*

## *A Prayer For A Child*

(to be spoken to a sleeping child)

My beloved child, _____, I call forth your holiness.

I now see you as God created you – whole, complete and perfectly capable of making choices that will take you to your highest good.

I see the good in you and I see you attracting more good into your life.

I see your mind filled with divine light.

I see our life filled with divine good, which is your inheritance from God.

I now surrender all fears I have about you or for you.

I now surrender all judgments and criticisms about you.

I now ask your forgiveness for anything I have done consciously or unconsciously to deny the Spirit in you.

I now affirm for you, and the Divine Spirit in you, perfect peace, total well-being, joy and abundance.

I direct you toward your perfect place, your divine purpose and your true identity as a child of God.

I surround you in love.

I surround you in light.

I see you as you were meant to be – a blessed child of God.

And I call forth your holiness.

*Building a Bridge*

## A Prayer For Parents

Remind me to teach my children to call on You in times of challenge and difficulty and to thank you afterwards.

Remind me to teach by example to always begin and end each day with prayer.

Teach me how to understand my children's needs, to listen patiently to what they have to say, and to answer their questions with kindness and wisdom.

Help me to be as courteous, compassionate and cooperative with them as I want them to be with me.

Heal me of all thoughts, habits and actions that lead me to shame and ridicule them when they make mistakes. May I never punish them out of spite, anger, or to show my power.

Help me to demonstrate by all that I do and say that honesty, honor, and humility will produce joy.

Eliminate any meanness in me, when I am out of sorts, and help me to hold my tongue.

May I be ever mindful that my children are Your children, who are complete and perfect just as they are.

Let me not rob them of any opportunity to do things for themselves or to make their own decisions.

Help me to grant them all reasonable requests and give me the courage to deny them privileges that may be harmful.

Help me to be fair, just and kind so that I may earn their love and respect.

Most of all remind me that what I can't do for them, You can and will do.

*Building a Bridge*

As you pray, you will find your own words. Remember that in prayer you are talking to God. God loves you. God knows the heart and hears the heart even when we can't or don't verbalize, but saying the words aloud reminds us that we are sharing a conversation with God.

Here are more ideas regarding prayer:

- Sing prayers. When I go on a walk, work in the garden or kitchen, I often sing out my concerns, hurts, hopes and dreams. Sound crazy? So what? If you like to sing, give it a try.

- Write a letter to God and mail it.

- Get a God Can. God Cans are available through Tiger Mountain Press at 800-893-1000. The idea is to write your concern on a slip of paper and place that concern in the can. You have now given your concern to God. When you can't handle a situation, God can! The can also comes with an inspirational cassette tape. (I have also seen these cans for sale at local Christian bookstores and shops that handle spiritual materials.)

- Give your name and concern to a prayer group. If you are not ready to pray for yourself, allow others the opportunity to help you. Nearly every church has a prayer group. Send an index card with your name and your children's names written on it. Simply say "Please pray for us."

- You can also contact Guideposts Prayer Ministries, The Prayer Line at 800-204-3772 or online at prayerconfid@guideposts.org.

- Unity School of Christianity, publisher of the Daily Word, offers a prayer service as well. You can write them at Silent Unity, 1901 NW Blue Parkway, Unity Village, MO 64065-0001, call at 816-969-2000, email at www.unityworldhq.org or call them at 800-669-7729. They request that you use the 800 number only if have no means of paying for the call.

- America On Line (AOL) offers prayer circle options for a variety of faiths at http://aol.beliefnet.com.

*Building a Bridge*

## Meditation

Rev. Bottorff writes:

"… is a general term that can be and is used to describe a variety of mental and spiritual exercises." at a higher level it is a method for creating an environment where "The continual chatter of the thinking mind is silenced, giving way to the rejuvenating spring of pure, unadulterated life."

For myself, I consider my meditation time as allowing myself to experience pure silence. I focus my energies towards the center of my being and concentrate on this very moment – the now. In our daily routines we are caught up in the past or the future.

Learning to be in the moment, where our real power exists, is the lesson meditation teaches. In this "now" state I often discover the keys that unlock the mysteries in my life. Sometimes I simply stay in the quiet moment and absorb the beauty of silence. Regardless of what occurs during my meditation time, I always find it healing and peaceful.

There is no "right way" to meditate, but if you are unfamiliar with meditation, you can begin by following these suggestions. Once you practice meditation, you will begin to develop your own methods. These are offered to you simply as an encouragement for getting started.

- Get comfortable whether seated or lying flat.

- Close your eyes and take a few slow, deep breaths.

- You may want to repeat a phrase, such as "release and relax" or you can simply sit silently.

- Release the tension in your body. Begin at the top of your head and work down through each part of your body concentrating on releasing and relaxing.

- Now gently shift your thinking to your mind. Clear your mind of the daily thoughts. The "to do" list can be thought about later. I think about a limitless clear blue sky. You might choose to focus on golden light, a vast ocean, or the immensity of outer space.

- Once you have quieted your mind, thoughts will flow in and out of your awareness. These are the thoughts that will unlock the mysteries in your life. Sometimes when I meditate, I experience a powerful epiphany about myself or a situation. Other times I sit quietly and benefit from getting off of life's fast track.

- There is no amount of time for you to meditate. One day you might meditate for twenty minutes, another day forty. Time is not the important factor – the goal is to get yourself centered and relaxed. Try to set time aside each day for meditation. While you initially may think it is a waste of time, you will soon appreciate the beauty of meditation.

### *Visualization*

We have all engaged in visualization through daydreams. This is a great place to start! Get into the habit of thinking about your child through daydreams. In the morning, visualize your child waking from a good sleep and welcoming a new day. Then see him getting ready for school or running to the bus or on the playground with school friends or at basketball or football or band practice. In the afternoon you can picture her returning from school with exciting stories, information about upcoming events or returned homework. In the evening develop pictures of your child sharing dinner with you, reading or watching a favorite program before preparing for bed. Bedtime is a precious time to mentally tuck your child in and send blessings for a good rest and sweet dreams.

Perhaps you and your child have had a dispute. Make this the focus of your visualization. Work through the problem. Approach the situation as you would if you were observing another parent/child in conflict. As you watch the behavior of the observed parent/child, notice how you feel, what you might say to them if you could interject. Or can you put yourself in your child's shoes by recalling when you were his age? Do you have a similar experience that you can draw from? What kind of support is your child longing for? Stay in a loving

*Building a Bridge*

and compassionate mode. Communicate your concerns and fears to your child. Be still so your child can communicate his thoughts and feelings. Listen. Be willing in mind and heart to receive answers and guidance. Allow the constructive information to come to you and be confident that these insights are your Higher-Self counseling you. You will be amazed at how the solution to the situation will come to you.

- Find a comfortable place to relax by lying down or sitting.

- Play a cassette tape of instrumental or meditation music, if you like.

- Close your eyes and be still.

- Clear your mind of the thoughts that race through the day.

- Concentrate on your breathing.

- With each breath, silently say the name of your child.

- Get a happy, loving picture of your child clearly in your mind. If your relationship with your child is or has been under stress for sometime, go back as far as you need to get a happy, loving image – even that means going back to your child's birth.

- Hold that picture steady and admire the smile, the bright eyes, the laugh, the enthusiasm, the energy your child projects.

- Now invite your child to join you. Extend a tender greeting and a warm embrace to your child. Tell your child that you have missed him. Be patient with the reunion – don't rush into any form of activity. Just **be** together for a few moments.

- Then picture yourselves enjoying time together: playing together at the park or riding bikes or enjoying a meal or a sporting event or sharing a sensitive and compassionate conversation.

- Be patient and allow your visualization to flow and develop. Cherish being in the moment.

*Building a Bridge*

- When you have finished with your activity, again embrace your child. Express your appreciation for being together. Remind your child that you are always available. Allow the departure to be freeing – don't allow separation anxiety to enter into the space. Confirm that you are individuals and you each have a path to follow while simultaneously keeping the connection flowing between you.

- When your child has moved away from your visualization, give yourself time to savor the experience of being together. Do not rush yourself.

- Slowly bring yourself back by concentrating on your breathing.

When you have completed your visualization, you will feel the warmth and energy of your child surrounding you. These moments will be powerful and real. As you continue this practice on a regular basis, you will manifest your visualizations into your physical times together. Keep your visualizations focused on healing and loving each other. Do not underestimate the power of visualization.

If you feel that you are not ready to try visualization, write down a story of how you would like to spend time with your child. Use the cassette recorder or share your hopes with a friend.

You can demonstrate prayer, meditation and visualization in your daily life by:

- Being quiet

- Allowing yourself to daydream

- Allowing yourself to night dream

If you are looking for more tangible was for connecting with your child during a "disconnect" time, consider some of the following ideas:

- Stay in touch with grandparents, friends and teachers. If they know the status of your life, they might find opportunities in conversation when they can update your child. If the other person

*Building a Bridge*

is comfortable in communicating a short message, they could express your love and concern for you. "I spoke to your dad last night. He misses you and sends his love." Or "Your mom asked me to say Hello to you." Do not ask anyone to relay difficult messages as that might jeopardize the relationship they have with your child.

- Purchase an "I love you" or "I am thinking of you" ad in your child's local paper. If your child does not personally see it, I bet someone from his circle of life will and tell him about it.

### Respect Your Child's Individual Path

From the day our children come into our lives, we cannot know what experiences we will encounter with them. We cannot know what "makes them tick." We cannot know what work they came to do on this planet. In 1923 Kahlil Gibran wrote *The Prophet* offering spiritual insight on a number of subjects, parenting included. His thoughtful prose offers a perspective that is still valid today.

### The Prophet

"And a woman who held a babe against her bosom said,
Speak to us of Children.
And he said:
Your children are not your children.
They are the sons and daughters of Life's longing for itself.
They come through you but not from you,
And though they are with you yet they belong not to you.

You may give them your love but not your thoughts,
For they have their own thoughts.
You may house their bodies but not their souls,
For their souls dwell in the house of tomorrow,
which you cannot visit, not even in your dreams.
You may strive to be like them, but seek not to make them like you.
For life goes not backward nor tarries with yesterday.

You are the bows from which your children
as living arrows are sent forth.
The archer sees the mark upon the path of the infinite,
and He bends you with His might that His arrows may go swift and far.

*Building a Bridge*

> Let your bending in the archer's hand be for gladness;
> For even as He loves the arrow that flies,
> so He loves also the bow that is stable.

I encourage you to spend some time in careful consideration of Gibran's words:

- Carefully evaluate your view of the parent/child relationship. Have you ever considered a birth certificate a certificate of ownership?

- Ask yourself how his writing can lead you into a higher level of parenting.

- Search your soul to understand how you are trying to make your child like you, when perhaps this is not in his best interest.

- Consider how you can let her go in gladness while always being a stable presence that she can turn to.

- Take time to know that you too are loved and appreciated, although that may not be verbally communicated to you.

> **"Allow children to be happy their own way;
> for what better way will they ever find?"**
>
> **Samuel Johnson**

In your efforts to love your child, how do you handle your child's request that he wants no contact with you? When a child attempts to alienate herself from a parent, it is an extremely painful and hurtful experience for all parties. Put into practice these following suggestions:

- Honor the request. Show that you respect what your child is asking for.

- Tell him you will still send communications, but he is not obligated to respond. Make sure the communication does not require a response.

*Building a Bridge*

If the request comes verbally, you may respond by saying that you will honor the wishes, but remind him that you are and will always be his parent and that you love him and will always be there for him when he is ready to receive that love.

If you only suspect your child is trying to distance herself from you because you are getting no communication from that child, you can write a note sharing these thoughts.

> Dear Son/Daughter,
>
> It has been quite a long while since you and I shared a telephone visit or letter. I have left messages and written to you, but since I have not had any responses, I must say that I am concerned.
>
> If this is a matter of your being busy at school, I understand how quickly days can go by. I hope you will take time to call or write a note.
>
> If something has happened between us that has caused you to be upset or feel uncertain, I invite you to share that situation with me. If I have done something to hurt or offend you, please let me know. I want us to be able to speak freely with each other.
>
> I love you and miss you. I have enclosed a phone card and a pre-addressed stamped envelope. I close this note hoping you will use them to connect with me.
>
> Dad/Mom

But once said, let the matter go. Give her the time and space she needs to think things out, to consider what she really wants, to see a bigger – and perhaps more truthful – picture.

*Building a Bridge*

During this period of separation it is difficult to know if it is appropriate to send a birthday card or holiday gift. When we are walking on eggshells our steps must be taken lightly. Use your best judgment. Do you have communication with your other children? If so, continue including your "separation child" in the birthday/holiday loop. If you are completely uncertain as how to proceed, simply send a card. In this manner you are acknowledging the day and your child. By not sending a gift there can be no accusations of a "buy off."

- Practice daily meditation, prayer and visualization.

If you think the other parent is actively working to keep you away from your child, consider the following actions:

- Proceed with caution. Your ego can really go to work in this situation. Before you know it, a drama is created. Ask yourself, "Will the steps I am considering help or hurt our chances for a real relationship?"

- Send "important" mail via registered mail, return receipt requested. You will at least know if it has been refused or accepted. Important mail would be a letter that communicates any change of information (address, telephone number, etc.) that the residential parent is entitled to under the custody decree.

- Stay focused on the quality of your person.

- Write a monthly update letter. Children (like everyone) are interested in themselves and how things directly relate to them. So in your letter, include things of direct interest to your child, such as happenings in the child's extended family and your life, of course. Even if these just get put into a folder for a while, your child may someday be interested in knowing what you have done and how you have grown.

- If you think the letters aren't getting to your child because of interference with their mail, send a copy to the child's name at your address. When they arrive, don't open them. Save them to give to your child when the opportunity arises.

*Building a Bridge*

- Keep a scrapbook of your life. (Need ideas? See Scrapbooks in Chapter 8.)

- Keep a scrapbook of your child's life.

- Practice daily meditation, prayer, visualization and/or journaling.

Please do not go off into a dramatic scenario and do crazy and foolish things. Foolish things? Who me? YES! Do not give into the urge to call the local news investigative reporter or Prime Time Live in hopes that you can sensationalize your story. Resist the temptation to call the other parent and declare war. Instead, stay focused on your thoughts and behaviors and allow God to work on your behalf. Of course, you will need to demonstrate some patience and that is generally where we lose hope. I caution you against soliciting legal aid in this matter as it will only lead to deeper heartache and take you on a more difficult path to your desire of a healthy relationship with your child.

*****

Personal Reflections

What do you think and feel about your present relationship with your child(ren)?

Thoughts: (For example, we are emotionally distant or we are communicating better.)

Feelings: (For example, "I feel lonesome for my children and worry about them" or "I enjoy them more now than ever before. I feel the love we have for each other.")

Do you have respect for yourself? How do you demonstrate that respect? (For example, set healthy boundaries, honor your responsibilities or other ways.)

Do you have respect for your parenting responsibilities? How do you demonstrate that respect? (For example, call regularly, friendly with other parent, try to be cooperative and helpful.)

*Building a Bridge*

How do you demonstrate respect for others? (For example, be courteous to others, don't badmouth religions or ethnic groups, and so on.)

What is your present association with the other parent? (Examples: hostile, every conversation turns into trouble, friendly but stressed, businesslike.)

Do you presently have a connection with your child(ren)? If so, how do you stay connected? (For example, through calls, letters, time together?)

What changes do you need to make in your life to improve yourself – for yourself – and for your child(ren)? (For example, be a better listener, be more open-minded or other ways.)

What example are you setting for your child(ren)? (For example, hard worker, enjoy the outdoors and work to keep it clean, or other ways.)

How do you show your children that you love them? (For example, call, write, think about them a lot, keep their pictures in my wallet, pay the child support and other ways.)

How do you feel about using prayer, meditation and/or visualization? (For example, day dreams seem like something I could do, but I am not interested in prayer.)

Are your pictures (mental or physical) of your child happy pictures? List some of your favorite memories of your child. (For example, the time we made Valentine sugar cookies together, when we went to Sea World, Christmas at mom's house three years ago.)

Affirm: I am one of God's children. He supports me in my efforts to participate and contribute to the lives of my children. I am grateful for this support.

**Additional reading suggestions:**

*You'll See It When You Believe It* by Dr. Wayne Dyer

*Creative Visualization* by Shakti Gawain

*Building a Bridge*

*Imaging: The Powerful Way To Change Your Life* by Norman Vincent Peale

*The Practical Guide to Prayer and Meditation* by J. Douglas Bottorff

*Bible Scripture & Prayer for Child Custody Litigants* compiled by Charlotte Hardwick

*Prayer Is Good Medicine* by Larry Dossey, M.D.

*Guide My Feet: Prayers and Meditations for Our Children* by Marian Wright Edelman

*The Prodigal Father* by Mark Byran

*Illuminata* by Marianne Williamson

*One Day My Soul Just Opened Up and In the Meantime* by Iyanla Vanzant

*Killers & Boosters for Child Custody Cases* compiled by Charlotte Hardwick

### *Anger*

**Anger is "a strong feeling of displeasure and usually antagonism (an active expression of opposition.)"**

At the onset of custody proceedings, each parent has an opinion as to what the outcome of custody should be. Rarely do these opinions become manifest in the exact fashion the individual parents were hoping for. Consequently, one or both parents will feel displeasure over the judgment that is given them to live by. The intensity of anger is developed depending on how different the judgment is from the mother or father's opinion. If the parent(s) are not able to accept the custody decree, expressions of opposition become apparent in their dealings with one another and any parties involved in the children's lives.

*Building a Bridge*

Charlotte Hardwick, author of *Win Your Child Custody War*, explains the difference between getting justice from the system and getting a decision from it with these four points:

1. Justice is the action, practice or obligation of awarding each person his just due while remaining free from improper influence. Each person sees justice from the influence of who they are, where they have been and what they need – that includes each person involved in the dispute as well as the one obligated to make the decision.

2. The court is the branch of government, which is responsible for the resolution of disputes arising under the laws of the government. A place or a person entrusted with and assembled for the administration of the law. The court is set up to render a decision in a dispute using the laws as they exist. Each law is passed to address a specific challenge. The problems arise when the solution for one problem impacts other situations that could not be anticipated.

3. As parents we each see the welfare of our children through our own needs and desires. The only way we will feel there is justice is if we are allowed to take the best care of our children in the way we know how. We see any deviation from that as an injustice.

4. If we are unable to work out our differences with others (the other parent, the other driver, or anyone else) we are punished. We are punished by having to go to court. By doing this, we become like children again. The court, like a parent, with its own agenda, will make a decision or ruling about our differences. As children we did not like it when our parents made the decisions because often we felt they were unjust. We don't like the courts making the decisions any better.

*Building a Bridge*

Our need to stay in alignment with what we deem as acceptable parenting generates anger. We each have a parenting standard by which we want to operate. When that standard is threatened by a custody decree, we feel the need to defend ourselves. We are defensive because we cannot see how we can appropriately parent outside of the standard we know and are comfortable with. Anything outside what we consider "normal" creates fear within us, therefore; we act from anger.

Richard Carlson, author of *Don't Sweat the Small Stuff for Teens* says, "If you can't handle your own small setbacks with grace, there is no reason to expect that your kids will. The difference between a together person and a crazy person lies in the way they put their angry feelings in perspective."

The children, too, often act from anger. That same desire for normal that parents want exists in the children as well. They may exhibit angry behavior, although they may not be clear what they are angry about. This aggression can be demonstrated towards anyone regardless of the connection or involvement with the family. Often the children will express anger with the parent they are closest to. While this may seem odd, it is actually not odd at all. Children will express anger toward the parent they are closest to because they have the security of knowing that they will be loved regardless of their behavior. The child feels internal security, knowing this parent will show compassion towards them, or at least allow them to vent their feelings, without serious consequences.

These harsh words from our children can be immensely painful to hear. They can cut into our souls deeper than any physical atrocity. Our human instinct to react must be overridden by our spiritual impulse to respond.

When your child acts out angrily towards you:

- get to eye level.

- be still and really look at your child.

- ask yourself these questions:

*Building a Bridge*

- Can you look into this child's face and see the precious baby you created?

- Can you recall the day the child was born?

- Can you re-embrace those incredible feelings of love and joy at this gift from God?

- Can you look into his eyes and see the fears he has faced while watching his parents at war?

- Can you look into her heart and feel the frustrations she endures while being caught in the middle of the battle zone?

- Can you understand why the world must be a confusing place for him when his own parents act in confusing and conflicting ways?

- Can you reach within your soul and find enough compassion to honestly answer her questions, to diffuse her angers, even if the answer is "I don't know?"

- Can you be vulnerable enough with your child to say you need his love as much as he needs yours?

More than our words, our children need our love. Demonstrate your love through tenderness, compassion, honesty, understanding and vulnerability. We do this when we:

- Speak with kind words in a caring tone.

- Live without prejudices or stereotypes.

- Reach out to help others.

- Don't tell lies.

- Don't cheat others.

Apologies are often in order. Apologize for what? We need to apologize for behaving poorly. We know when we have not behaved well because that little voice within us keeps reminding us of those

*Building a Bridge*

times. I have on many occasions been in need of apologizing to my children when they have called me on my words or behaviors. Apologizing, especially to our children, takes courage, but it is worth the risk. The steps for apologizing are:

- Acknowledge our behavior to those involved

- Apologize for our inappropriate actions or words

- Amend our behavior so we don't repeat it

### Release the Anger

Anger perpetuates itself. Like energy attracts like energy. If we have anger within us, we will draw angry energy to us – it becomes a vicious cycle and the anger never stops growing. We must consciously choose to cease holding anger within ourselves. Begin releasing anger by getting to the root of it.

- Write a letter. Write down everything that you are angry about, no matter how petty or insignificant it may seem. Write a letter to every person you are angry at ... the children's other parent, the children, the attorney, the judge, the system, God, yourself. Get all the anger on the paper. Hold nothing back. Let it rip!

  Once written, hold the letter in your hand – own the anger on the paper. Now, release the anger by shredding it, burning it, ripping it to bits – whatever method you choose is fine, but release the thoughts and feelings it contains. Make certain that you truly release the anger. Do not hold onto the letters or mail them to anyone! That will only continue and accelerate the cycle! Do not keep the letter – the point of the exercise is to **release** the anger.

- Go on a run or a walk. With every step you take, leave the anger behind you.

- Have a private temper tantrum. Sark suggests that you jump up and down and shout "I've had enough and I won't take it anymore!" Slam pillows against a wall. Throw stones into a lake or the ocean. Beat your fists into the couch. You will be amazed at the hurts that are released as you shout out your anger. As you

*Building a Bridge*

verbalize you will discover what your real fears are and be able to address them.

- Evaluate the boundaries you have set for yourself. Often times I feel angry because I feel someone has taken advantage of me. When this happens, I need to ask myself this question: "If I love myself, what would I do in this situation?" Your answer will show you where you might need to establish or redefine boundaries. If you do not have healthy boundaries set for yourself, not only are you exposing yourself to potential problems, you are also enabling an abusive personality an opportunity to be abusive.

- Make a list of the things that upset you. Find new, positive ways to deal with the challenges. These new behaviors will help you feel better about the situations.

| Irritation | Solution |
| --- | --- |
| Waiting in check-out lines | Read magazines or people watch |
| Slow moving commuter traffic | Listen to favorite music or educational cassette tapes |

- See a therapist. If you feel that you are not able to get to the root of your angers independently, then talk to a professional counselor. Not only can he help you talk and work through your anger, they can recommend books and support groups that can also assist in the healing process.

    Work with a therapist for genuine healing. Seeing a therapist for the rest of your life without experiencing positive change is not a healing experience. A counselor worth his salt will help you work through the problems and create a more joyful life for yourself.

*Building a Bridge*

Don't automatically blame a counselor if you do not experience results. Ask yourself, "Am I being honest with the counselor? Am I following through on the exercises and suggestions he offered me?" If you feel you are doing your part, but not experiencing a positive change, seek another counselor. It is important that you have a bond with your counselor. Mutual respect is a critical key in making counseling work.

If you are looking for a counselor, ask for a referral from a trusted friend, contact a local college/university as most psychology departments offer counseling services (often at lesser cost), or contact the local United Way services as they too offer counseling services through various programs.

- Talk to your minister. Clergy are trained to help people with life's problems. He can offer insight, support and guidance. Your minister can also pray with, and for, you.

### Sense of Humor

In working on anger, we sometimes get caught up in the anger and do ourselves more harm than good. In an effort to keep ourselves from going insane, I suggest that we remember to value our sense of humor.

Since recorded time comedians have poked fun at life's most personal matters. They are often criticized for being insensitive or cruel; however, the essence of laughter is to lighten our perspective of a situation by finding some amusement in it. When we make fun of something and enjoy a laugh, we relax, we open up and the truth about the situation is allowed to surface. Do you remember the "I Dream of Jeannie" show? Do you remember how Barbara Eden used to emerge in a misty swirl when the cap was taken off her bottle? This is how the truth is revealed to us through humor. When we take the cap off our trapped thinking, the truth comes swirling out. While Jeannie bestowed treasures on her master, humor bestows on us the truth – truth we can use to set ourselves free.

I encourage you to engage in some humor and lighten up about those matters that are weighing heavy.

*Building a Bridge*

This recommendation is not intended for the purpose of being malicious, but merely to have you step back from the issues long enough to see them from a different perspective. Once directly removed from the problems at hand, you may see the way for transforming those burdens into blessings.

**"The one that cannot laugh is burdened."**

**Gary Zukav**

Humor can be, and should be, a part of our everyday lives. In our family we laugh a great deal and make jokes about all subjects. One way we cultivate humor is by having each person share the funniest thing from the day. At dinner we ask each other "What was the funniest thing that happened today?" Occasionally a person will skip his/her turn, but generally on that day someone else will have a hilarious story to tell which brings balance to all of us. By doing this each night, we have set up our subconscious thinking to find funny things throughout the day. It really keeps our funny bones greased and working well. We invite you to try this exercise in your family. If you live alone, encourage your co-workers to do this at lunch.

Other ideas for tickling your funny bone:

- Rent a video of a comedy show or comedic movie
- Listen to a comedic cassette
- Buy a comedian's book
- Visit a comedy club
- Write some jokes of your own
- Create a cartoon – draw the pictures and write the dialogue yourself. By the way, have you seen the new syndicated cartoon, "Shirley & Son" by Jerry Bittle? Shirley, who is divorced from Roger, has residential custody of their son,

Louis. The cartoon features scenarios all too familiar to divorced parents. Check it out for yourself.

- Log onto www.funone.com and see the fun pages available. You can enjoy a joke, send a card, read poems with great graphics and more!

- As I worked on this book, I came up with two alternative titles: *Get Off Your Pain and Use Your Brain* and *Get Your Head Out of Your Buts*. Can you think of any funny titles for your life situations?

At one point in my humorous endeavors, I decided to write a sarcastic thank you note to the children's father (written, but never intended for mailing!). It was a full-page letter of highly toxic and sarcastic communication. I assure you it was a clear indication of my level of anger. One (mild) sentence read, "Thank you for being a pain in the seat. I appreciate the frustrations."

Using humor to rid yourself of anger is like squeezing water from a chamois – you must wring the chamois many times before you really achieve moisture reduction. This note was another episode in wringing my anger. Although I had much work remaining with regard to my anger, when I sat back and reread the note, I took a long and careful look at my words. As I read, "I appreciate" a deep sense of genuine appreciation ran through me. The energy of gratitude flowed through me and I could feel the tingling sensation in my body and on my skin. I thought, "I really am grateful. While I have always looked at his behavior in a critical light, I now see that he has been an actor playing a role in my life. His lines have been carefully choreographed to lead me to healing. I have become a better person. I have grown and matured. I have even found my life's purpose and mission. I SHOULD BE GRATEFUL!"

Another beautiful thing happened from this awareness. He can stop playing the role! Now that I respect the gift he has given me, he, too, is now free to move onto other roles and learning opportunities. How wonderful for both of us! Whether he chooses a new role, or not, is not my concern. He has helped me and for that I will remain thankful.

*Building a Bridge*

Why would anyone choose to stay in a role when they wouldn't need to? When people play roles for a long time, they start to think that they ARE the character they portray. They forget that they are precious children of God – perfect, whole and complete. Many times the people around them forget this as well. How many television actors do you know by character, but not by name? For example, "Oh … you know … the guy who was Marcus Welby?"

Do you want to really go over the edge? I suggest a second letter (written with the intention to be mailed!) that expresses the genuine thankfulness to the other parent for her role in the learning process. NOW THIS IS OVER THE EDGE! (But when we go over the edge, we fly!)

Dear Name,

For the past two years I have been struggling with many aspects of our co-parenting arrangement. In nearly every situation I have found fault in the decisions you have made and in the manner in which you have handled the raising of our children. Quite honestly, I have thought and said many unkind things about you.

I have come to understand that my hateful thoughts, harsh words and mean-spirited actions are doing more harm to me than you and even more damage to our children. This is not the example I want to be for our daughter and son.

I have given your position as their custodial parent a great deal of consideration. I am sure you put tremendous energy and effort into caring for the children on a daily basis. When I see them, I know that they are fed properly, safe and overall well cared for. For all you do for them, I want you to know that I am genuinely grateful.

I am working to get my life in order. I want to be happy and live in peace. I sincerely want these things for you, too. While we were not happy together, I pray that we can find happiness individually. We both deserve a good life – for ourselves and for our children.

*Building a Bridge*

If you don't understand anything I have said in this letter, please know this one thing – I appreciate all you do for the children.

Sincerely, name

Once you begin to release anger, God can start to show you creative and constructive ways to parent in your new role. When you begin to contribute in these positive ways, the need to be angry will dissolve.

One exercise that will eliminate anger in a hurry is the practice of appreciation.

- Make a list of the things you are thankful for – people, places, small things, big things, opportunities, memories and so on. Make sure you include those aspects you appreciate about yourself.

- Make a habit of saying, "Thank you."

- Learn to look for the goody in every moment and say "Thank you!" even when the goody doesn't look yummy.

*****

Personal Reflections

What aspects of the custody decree have you not been able to accept? (For example, the amount of time you have with the children, amount of child support, or other matters.)

Is there anything you need to apologize to your children about? (For example, the way you treat the other parent, things you said to them in anger, encouraging them to be loyal to you at the other parent's expense.)

Are you working through your angers? How are you doing that?

*Building a Bridge*

Do you need help in working through your anger? If so, list resources that can help. (Examples: counselor, minister, books, friends, group therapy, or journaling.)

Is your funny bone working? Do you have humor in your life? What do you laugh about? (For example, yourself, humanness of people, silly pet tricks.)

Can you write a humorous note to help release your angers and frustrations? Start your letter by making some notes. (REMEMBER: THIS IS FOR YOUR OWN HEALING PROCESS – NOT TO BE MAILED!)

Are you ready to write a "real" letter? If so, make some notes about What you will say in your letter? (MAIL THIS ONE!!)

Do you express appreciation? List the ways you express gratitude. (For example, saying "thank you," by taking care of your belongings, showing love to the people in your life.)

Affirm: I release my anger. I do not need to be afraid of parenting beyond what I have known. I trust the power of God to give me creative parenting ideas.

**Additional reading suggestions:**

*The Dance of Anger* by Harriet Goldhor Lerner, Ph.D.

*Facing CoDependence* by Pia Mellody

*The Little Soul and the Sun* by Neale Donald Walsh

*Simple Abundance* by Sarah Ban Breathnach

*Building a Bridge*

## *Arrogance*

**Arrogance is "a feeling of superiority manifested in an overbearing manner or presumptuous claims."**

- Have you ever flexed your parenting muscles in front of the children in an effort to influence their vote that you are the better parent?

  "No one can care for you the way I can. Just look at the healthy meal I prepared for you."

  "Son, you better just stay here with me. I have a steady job and provide you with a good home. You don't appreciate how good you have it with me."

- Have you ever suggested that "your" way is the "right" way and any other way is "wrong" or unacceptable?

  "This is the church our family has worshipped in for five generations."

  "I can help you with this problem. You do not need to discuss this matter with your other parent. This happened while you were with me. We will handle this."

- Have you ever accused the other parent of something based on your assumption?

  The other parent is late in bringing the children home, so you assume he/she does not respect your agreement. Reality is that they got caught in traffic due to an accident.

  You see that the residential parent has a new car. You assume the child support check is being used for the payments, then you learn that the car is a benefit of the parent's job.

- Have you ever bad-mouthed the other parent in an effort to establish a superior parenting position?

  "Your mother knows nothing about handling money."

*Building a Bridge*

"Your father is selfish. He does not even know the definition of consideration."

When we use these types of statements, we are trying to manipulate or brainwash our children's thinking. This is a very dangerous game. We must get a handle on our thinking so we can clean up our comments.

In *Healing Hearts, Helping Children and Adults Recover from Divorce*, Elizabeth Hickey and Elizabeth Dalton, outline seven areas where parents attempt to program or brainwash their children. They are as follows:

1.  Denying the existence of the other parent.

- Never talking about the other parent.

- Not allowing photos of the other parent in the child's room.

- Not relaying messages to the child from the other parent.

- Blatantly ignoring the other parent at social functions.

- Refusing to acknowledge good times with the other parent.

- Making the child feel guilty for talking about the other parent.

2.  Attacking the other parent's character and lifestyle.

- Criticizing the other parent's family.

- Attacking the other parent's career, or steering the child away from that career.

- Remarking that the other parent is living in a relationship outside of marriage and is therefore an immoral person.

- Refusing to allow interaction with the other parent.

- Attacking the other parent's choice of friends or new spouse.

*Building a Bridge*

3. Placing the child in the middle.

- Speaking to the child about issues that should be discussed privately with the other parent, such as visitation schedules, money matters, and child support.

4. Manipulating circumstances.

- Not informing the other parent of school performances, sporting events, and recitals.

- Embarrassing the other parent when she/he attends educational, religious, or social functions.

- Listing a stepparent at school as the parent of record.

5. Exaggerating differences.

- Instigating an argument with the other parent in front of the child, later telling the child that you were just trying to have a nice conversation.

- Snickering or making faces in reaction to the comments of the other parent.

- Taking minor issues and blowing them out of proportion in front of the child.

6. Making the child serve as an ally.

- Involving the child in adult issues and asking for his sympathy and support. Saying things such as, "Do you think your father should have all the money?" Or, "Now that I'm sick, do you want to be with your father instead of me?" Or, "Your mother is taking me to the cleaners!" Or even, "If you were the mother, what would you do?"

- Making the child feel that the other parent is not sincere. Saying, "If she really meant what she said, she would … "

*Building a Bridge*

- Creating an image in the child's mind that you will be left poor and homeless if she doesn't stay with you. Saying things such as, "If I didn't have you, I don't know what I'd do."

- Telling the child that your life has been stolen by the other parent, and you won't let him/her steal the child, too. Saying, "He got the house and car, he's not getting you, too."

7.   Threatening to withdraw love.

- Making the child feel that is she loves one parent, she will lose the other.

- Phoning the child at the other parent's house asking him if he misses you and wants to come "home."

- Encouraging the child to disobey the other parent.

- Threatening the child with punishment unless she tells you everything that happened during a visit with the other parent.

8.   Rewriting reality for the child.

- Telling the child that the way the other parent cares for him is inappropriate.

- Creating events to demonstrate that the other parent is either inadequate, unworthy, or inferior.

- Telling the child she is wrong when she makes positive comments about the other parent.

Do you recognize any of these arrogant behaviors? Arrogance develops when an image is threatened. We believe that we must establish a superior position because we believe in competition. In our desperate attempt to assure ourselves that our children love us, we don't feel it is enough to have their love. We feel we must have their love over and above the love they have for the other parent.

Any strategy used to influence the children's thinking toward one parent at the expense of the other is brainwashing.

*Building a Bridge*

This is an extremely dangerous approach to take in an effort to "win" your child's favor. In communicating to our children that the other parent is "less than," the children feel an uncontrollable urge to defend the other parent – although they may know that what you are saying about the other parent is true. This urge is natural. This person that you are demeaning is the other half of the child. It is survival skill for a child to protect who he is. When we attempt to negate the other parent, we are in essence telling our children to disregard a part of themselves. This holds a very destructive potential for your relationship with the child and for the child himself. Ultimately, your child will see through this charade and recognize your self-serving purpose. Is it any wonder that our children search for a sense of who they are?

### *Self-Respect and Appreciation*

This arena of competition occurs because we do not respect or appreciate our own talents and creative energy. We attempt to do the same things the other parent is doing and we try to do it better or sabotage their efforts because we are intimidated by their levels of personal maturity, inner security and creativity.

Take time to appreciate yourself. Stop comparing yourself to the other parent. When we compare ourselves to others, we disrespect our individuality. Why would a child need two of the same thing? You and your uniqueness are a gift to your child. Your disregard for yourself clearly indicates you do not appreciate your own value.

Have you ever watched the "Antiques Road Show" that is broadcast through PBS? Each time I watch that program I am amazed at the value of some of the pieces. At first viewing, many of the articles look tacky or crude. When the appraiser details the item, gives its origin and history, and highlights its features, I suddenly have a new outlook and attitude about the object. We need to have an appraisal of ourselves! Take a careful and considerate look at who you are. With great care reflect on your origins and life to date. Highlight your accomplishments – both personal/private and public. If you find you are having trouble doing this, solicit the help of a friend or family member. We can be so critical of ourselves we do not see our own qualities and strengths.

### *Building a Bridge*

Second, take time to show respect for your contribution to your children. Michael Oddenino, attorney for The Children's Rights Council and author of *Putting Kids First*, writes, "Children receive unique contributions from each parent and neither parent's role can be minimized."

- Make a list of what you do for the children that no one else can do. What special gift do you offer them? Examples might include:

    - As a biological parent, you have given your child the gift of life. If you are an adoptive parent, you have given your child the gift of family and home.

    - Your personality, experiences, philosophies, spiritual ideas, political views, and aspirations are all aspects of you – unique gifts that only you can offer your child.

- How do you uniquely show your love to them? Examples might include:

    - Through your way of sharing love, thoughts, ideas, inspiration and humor.

    - Through your hobbies, interests, and talents.

    - Through the activities that you enjoy together – such as camping, fishing, crafting, baking or others.

If you are having trouble making this list, go into meditation and allow your mind to open. Ask God to show you what you have to offer.

While on this topic of "what we have to offer," we need to address an issue that can got out of control in our minds ... "The Hero Complex." The hero complex is what I call a long-distance parent's "need" to become bigger than life for his children. Because we are not with our children on a daily basis and providing for them in a constant hands-on manner, we begin to think that our offerings of love through letters, cards and calls are not important enough. We start to think that we must do something big and public and impressive in order to offer our children the kind of parent they deserve. The long-distance

*Building a Bridge*

parent sets a lofty goal and decides that when it is accomplished he can contact his children and say, "Hey, I'm your dad. Yeah, I'm the guy that found the cure for cancer. Are you proud of me? Are you glad I'm your dad?" Sometimes long-distance parents get so caught up in this thinking they stay out of touch for years. What we have to offer our children right now, in this very moment, IS important and valuable. Let's demonstrate self-respect and self-appreciation and love our children – now that's heroic!

Here are some ideas for demonstrating self-respect and self-appreciation in our lives:

- Setting healthy boundaries

- Owning our own behavior

- Following our dreams

We need to take good looks at ourselves and understand that we individually have powerful opportunities to guide our children toward fulfilling and satisfying lives. This look at ourselves does not suggest that we limit ourselves to our current talents or abilities. As we grow, we will have new contributions to make. This personal growth is necessary if we are to help our children grow and challenge themselves.

Children need the contribution of both parents. When each parent stays focused on what he or she can do to genuinely serve the children and their growth process, we blanket the children in security.

*****

Personal Reflections

Do you have an arrogant attitude? Do you think you are better than other people?

Do you obey the laws and follow the rules/policies at work?

Do you attempt to program/brainwash the children?

*Building a Bridge*

Do you appreciate yourself? How do you demonstrate that appreciation? (For example, do you take care of yourself, do you have dreams and work to make them come true, do you take time for yourself?)

Do you compare yourself to the other parent or stepparent? How? (For example, do you compare your finances, education, career to the other parent's?)

Do you have a "hero complex?" Have you been waiting to contact your children in hopes of having some sensational news to share with them?

Affirm: I have an awesome opportunity to contribute to my child's life. I use my talents and abilities to teach and guide my children. I am grateful for what I know now and what I will learn as each day unfolds.

**Additional reading suggestions:**

*The Simple Abundance Journal of Gratitude* by Sarah Ban Breathnach

*Attitudes of Gratitude* by M. J. Ryan

*Gratitude: Affirming the Good Things in Life* by Melody Beattie

*Gratitude: A Way of Life* by Louise Hay

*Blame*

**Blame is "to find fault with; to hold responsible; an expression of disapproval or reproach."**

When the custody outcome does not equal our expectations, we fear what others will think of us or say about us. Although we may have made the decision that the children should live with the other parent, we find it difficult to accept responsibility for that choice. Because we fear being fully responsible, we find someone to blame. In a custody proceeding there are plenty of people to point the finger at – to blame. "It is my ex's fault!" "We have a lousy legal system!" "I had a crummy attorney!" "The children were manipulated to say things they really don't mean!" "The conciliator works for the county so why should I expect him to advise anything the judge doesn't want to hear?"

### Act Responsibly

When we exercise blame we are not acting responsibly. We literally give our personal power to another, so is it any wonder that we feel helpless and hopeless? Taking responsibility for our own life and its experiences is one of the most empowering steps we can take. Blaming others is self-defeating. It robs us of our energy, strength and creativity. *In You Can Heal Your Life*, author Louise Hay teaches that we need to be "100% responsible for everything in our lives, the best and the worst. Every thought we [I] think is creating our [my] future.... If a thought or belief does not serve you, let it go! There is no written law that says that because you once believed something you have to continue to believe it forever." Using the teachings of Louise Hay, ask yourself:

- Have I been making responsible choices based on my decisions, my thoughts?

- Do I have faith in myself when it comes to acting responsibly?

When I studied responsibility, I focused on my role – my ability to respond to life. Ownership. I own all the steps that work together in the formation of my life. Just as an artist is responsible for each brush stroke that she makes in creating a painting, we create our lives one thought at a time. When things happen or people say things that we do not like, we are responsible for our responses.

As adults we can deal with direct hits of hurt from the other parent because we understand, emotionally and spiritually, the other parent's desperate attempt to injure us and make us weak. However, when the other parent attempts to harm us by using the children, we waver in acting responsibly. The other parent entices us to neglect our boundaries and make choices that are less than responsible, less than wise. When they see us cringe, they know we can be coaxed into a manipulative web and tangled. Since they do not want to act

*Building a Bridge*

responsibly, they certainly do not want us acting responsibly. This is so because they know that the children will eventually see the honor and integrity in responsible behavior and be drawn to it. The only way they can stay in their small-minded fear-based space is to keep us there as well.

Deciding not to blame and accepting responsibility for self is a choice. A choice made a thought at a time. We need to remind ourselves that it is OK to take time when making a decision. We need to respond, not react. Responsive behavior is thoughtful and wise. Reactive behavior is impulsive – emotional and foolish.

Acting responsibly also works to clarify our boundaries. As we accept responsibility for our lives, we free ourselves from the need to accept responsibility for things that are not ours. When we act responsibly, we raise the standard of behavior for other people and call them to now act responsibly as well. It is their turn to step to the plate.

When we choose to be fully responsible for our lives, we choose healing for our souls. This healing also opens the door for others to heal as well because the positive energy released in acting responsibly moves out from within us to others. When we are not engaged in blaming others, they are more relaxed to receive this positive energy. We heal ourselves and we contribute to the healing process of all.

*****

## Personal Reflections

Have you been blaming others for the outcome of the custody decree? If so, who are these people/organizations? (For example, lawyers, family therapists, the legal system, and/or your family/friends.)

What was/is your role with regard to each of these parties? (Did I seek their advice for the custody proceedings? Did I trust them more than I trusted myself? Did I continue to let them work for me even if I felt they were not doing the job I wanted/expected? Did I give them my power in this situation?)

## *Building a Bridge*

While you cannot change the past, how can you change your thinking about these parties to reclaim your power and be responsible? (For example, did you trust them too much or give you power to them?)

Do you react or respond to situations? Describe how you handle problems? (For example, do you verbally explode, ignore the situation or evaluate problems and brainstorm for solutions?)

Do you have healthy boundaries set for yourself? Explain what you have done to establish those boundaries. (For example, I discontinue conversations that are hurtful. I say what I need or want for myself. I respect other people's privacy and expect them to do the same.)

Are you ready to work for personal healing? Write a note to yourself stating that you are ready.

> Dear Me,
>
> I have been hurting inside for a long time. I have not valued myself and therefore others have not valued me either. I am ready to get to know myself and discover who I am. I am ready to make the changes necessary to become the person I want to be.
>
> Me

Affirm: I have the power to make my own decisions and own those decisions. I accept full responsibility for my life. As I grow and learn I know that my decisions will become more and more perfect each day.

**Additional reading suggestions:**

*You Can Heal Your Life* by Louise Hay

## *Despair*

**Despair is "to lose all hope or confidence."**

When we experience change in our parenting job by becoming long-distance parents, our self-confidence is challenged. We are in uncharted territory, not sure of the local customs, and afraid to say too much for fear that it will be translated incorrectly. We are not really sure where we are or where to go next. All aspects of our lives seem to be unclear. Because we can't see down the road as far as we would like for our own comfort, we become even less confident about where we are going or how we are going to get there. We despair.

When we are uncertain, a child will also be caught up in uncertainty. Out of a need to find some clarity in life, the children often go along with the residential parent's thinking. They may agree with the residential parent's comments, philosophies and lifestyles because they have nowhere else to call home. Perhaps they aren't yet sure what they think and what the residential parent says seems right, so they accept that as the truth. If the children begin to question the long-distance parent's love, they may draw back as a protective measure. When the long-distance parent experiences withdrawal from his children, insecurity sets in. Because the long-distance parent is already on unfamiliar parenting ground, this withdrawal creates a deeper lack of confidence. The parent, too, begins to question whether the child wants to hear from him or not. Because we are not sure what to do, we make less contact. Because we have less contact, the children's doubts grow, and so the downward spiral is created.

### *Focus on Contributing*

- Stay focused on your contribution to the children.

- Do not absorb any negative communication from the other parent. Consider their comments and discern for yourself whether those comments are valid or not. (If the other parent called you a car, would you be a car? So why are you a jerk, just because the other parent says so?)

*Building a Bridge*

- Give the situation some time, but stay in touch with your children. Children go through many growing phases and change their minds often. Your consistent, loving behavior will be a powerful testimony to them that your love is genuine. Don't focus on the results – stay focused on your efforts. Practice unconditional love.

    Unconditional love sounds good, but practicing it takes effort. Stop yourself whenever you start thinking that your children should do this, or should not do that, or should be different in their appearance or behavior, or that they should demonstrate their love to you more effectively. Release any traces of criticism. Love your child without conditions – without "shoulds."

- Pray. Meditate. Visualize. Show some faith. How can we demonstrate faith in our daily lives?

- Be confident that the God that entrusted you to be the parent of this child is still working on behalf of your mutual relationship.

- Stop worrying.

- Trust your judgment and follow your inner guidance.

- Believe that everything will work out.

- Journal. Write about your fears. Write your hopes and affirmations. List what you have to offer the children.

    With regard to journaling, I want to share with you some journal pages I wrote on a flight to Chicago. The children had been moved from public school to private school without my prior knowledge or consent. I was clearly troubled about this situation. When I contacted the new school to make arrangements for meeting the principal and teachers, they were extremely cold toward me. I felt the new school was prejudging me based on my long distance. Having come from an awesome relationship with the staff and faculty of the public school, the cool attitude and behavior really hurt me. I wanted to communicate and cooperate with the children's educators. The following are some of the notes. These notes are messy and scattered, but they are the real deal. I hope by opening my journal, you will be encouraged to use journaling in your own life.

*Building a Bridge*

9:16 notes for school

- I am concerned for Sarah and Jason.
- I want to contribute to their education
- You can't dislike me — you don't know me
- You can be uncomfortable with the situation — it is unfamiliar + nontraditional
- I want to act w/ integrity w/ my children's best interest in mind and heart — hopefully others will too
- My love for Sarah and Jason is powerful. it cannot be bound by limits or rules. it transcends boundaries and distance.

I am sure you have preconceived ideas about me — a long distance mother — but I am not the stereotype "out of sight out of touch" mom. I care deeply about my children and put

I AM:
- constructive  • helpful  • contributive
- participating  • creative  • cooperative
- encouraging  • supportive

My support of this school and its programs + people can help Sarah + Jason be comfortable and then focus on their work. They need to know that we are working together towards their quality educational development.

MESSAGE TO SCHOOLS:
everyone would be better served if you would hold your judgments of me until you know the situation better. what you may think of me or have been told about me may not be true.

when you see me as Sarah + Jason's mom — not a long distance mom — you will see countless ways for me to contribute. This is about changing your thoughts on long distance.

*Building a Bridge*

I know you are at a disadvantage right now. You have a big job to do and this situation probably looks like trouble and work. But I assure you I will not be trouble. My goal is to be an asset.

I am worried about this school because it has lots of rules. Healthy boundaries are a good thing, but rules, limits, restrictions - these concern me. They are fear-based. They are controlling. How does the creative spirit soar? Where does compassion fit in?

What about these blue slips? Will my children grow up + hate blue paper? Will they feel scared when they see it?

S + J: While these childhood experiences look and are difficult, know that in your adult life they will be the tools you can use to carve out the you you choose to be.

Fear distorts images. Have you ever woke up in the middle of the night and seen something - a weird shape and thought, what is that? Shadows. That is what fear does to us. It shadows reality and truth and confuses us.

I also want to say that I don't want our relationship to be about the candy you want or your ridgedly defined Christmas list or what we will pay for. There is so much to life to share. Books, music, movies, friends, funny stories. What are we learning and experiencing together?

Building a Bridge

Either you are not telling me of your life or you are telling me of your real life. And if you are telling candy your soul must truly be starved for sweetness in life.

I want you to know that I went to your new school today because I needed and wanted you to see and feel my endorsement of your education. When you see the hall where I stood, I hope you will remember the embraces I gave you.

Remember: If you need me — close your eyes.

You are allowed:

- To be true to yourself
- To dance in the rain
- Make up new recipes
- Make mud pies (or fruit pies or pudding pies.)
- Get a chocolate milk mustache
- Wake up with messy hair, bad breath and crinkles on your face
- Wear fun clothes and silly shoes
- Sing on the potty or in the shower
- Play music you like
- Create a kid band and sing, sing, sing .... Sing!

Now I understand why you spend so much time bldg your lego fortresses and refuse to disassemble them. I get it and will protect it for you because now I too see how precious they are. (By the way, I love what you did with the garden, darling!)

Building a Bridge

> I also understand why you are so anxious to grow up. Freedom to choose for yourself. & I always want you to enjoy TODAY - NOW, and I am frustrated when you constantly talk of years down the road. What can I do to help you see the beauty of today?
>
> I am learning too. I am not arrived. No, no. I am growing. There are no arrived people on the planet. If they say so - RUN! No one knows everything. There are very smart, very awesome people but they will tell you they do not know it all. Life is all about learning - so learn, laugh, love and live.
>
> Mom

*****

## Personal Reflections

Do you feel uncertain about how to long-distance parent your child? If so, list your concerns. (For example, I don't like to write, we don't have a good time for telephone calls or I cannot afford to call very often – I have limited financial resources for anything long distance.)

Have you been making less contact (or any contact) with your child? Are you avoiding your child for any reason? Make some notes on why you think you have not been in touch. (For example, I never have any thing to say, the other parent and I don't speak to each other so when I do call it becomes a huge argument.)

What can you do for your child long-distance? (If you have no ideas, do not panic. There are lots of ideas in Chapter 8.)

Do you let the other parent's comments affect you? List the comments the other parent makes that effect you. (For example, "Your work is more important than your children" or "If you loved the children you would not have taken an out-of-area career move.)

*Building a Bridge*

Why do the comments you just listed affect you? Do you feel they reflect on you negatively? Do you feel there is truth in those statements – truth you may not want to acknowledge?

Do you parent your child with "shoulds?" List some expectations you have for your child. (For example, my child should belong to my religion because my family has been this faith for generations or my son should play this sport because I did.)

List some judgments you have about your child. (For example, boys shouldn't wear pierced earrings. Or girls shouldn't play sports.)

Can you put these expectations aside and love your child unconditionally?

Affirm: I am confident that all in my life and all in my child's life is in Divine Order. I send my child love.

**Additional reading suggestions:**

*7 Habits of Highly Effective Families* by Stephen R. Covey


### *Envy*

**Envy is "painful or resentful awareness of an advantage enjoyed by another joined with a desire to possess the same advantage."**

For the long-distance parent there is a belief that the residential parent has stolen the opportunity to have a loving relationship with the children. We think that because the residential parent is "hands-on" he has a stronger position of influence on the children. Often we perceive only the advantages of their position.

### *Do Not Compete*

This thinking is parallel to competitive thinking. We must stay focused on our opportunities to connect with and contribute to the children. The task of long-distance parenting is very different than parenting historically, but our mission is no less important.

### *Building a Bridge*

We must savor and cherish those precious moments when we are physically together and not waste time bemoaning our situation. It is not what we receive, it is what we do with what we receive that matters.

The area where we engage in the most competition is for the address of our children. In our complete selfishness we manipulate and coerce our children to live with us until we wear them down or out. We apologize for our lack of parenting and pledge we will do better if they give us the chance. We throw shiny, valueless promises at them or buy them things in an effort to seduce them into our houses. Sometimes our actions are not this blatant. Sometimes we operate so subtly we nearly fool ourselves. But there is no deceiving ourselves, we know when we are working from fear. The children agree to live with us because they are afraid of hurting us or because they feel sorry for us. They think that if a parent needs them this much certainly they must honor the request. After all, what loving child would abandon his parent when he is so needy? This is pathetic. This is disgusting. This is not love. This is a pitiful attempt to validate our lives.

Children want to have a meaningful relationship with both parents. When we put a child in the position of having to choose a parent, the child will often feel he must choose the parent who is more likely to revoke their love if not chosen. In this case, the children are not choosing to live with that parent because they honestly want to, but because they feel they must in order to maintain favor with that parent.

This is a painful, ugly game. Our actions speak louder than our words. If we are playing a game, our children will eventually see that. What respect can a child have for a parent who engages in such activity? What do we want for our children? Do we want to show them that we are game players? Or do we want them to see a wise parent who can lead them safely into adulthood?

If leading our children is our genuine objective, we must absolutely surrender any self-interested desire to have the children live at our home. We must allow our children the right to choose where they want to live and school. I am not suggesting we permit them to live in an abusive or neglectful environment. I am suggesting

*Building a Bridge*

that we open our hearts so our children can have the experience of living without our constant pestering about their address. It is our responsibility to make sure they understand that we love them regardless of their address.

Children in divorce situations have a great deal on their minds. They worry about everything.

- What's going to happen to my parents?
- Where will we live?
- Will we have enough money?
- Will we have enough food?
- Can I make my parents happy?
- Did I cause this divorce?
- Am I lovable?

Along with their concerns, Charlotte Hardwick, author of *Win Your Child Custody War*, reminds us that our children have their own agendas. She outlines twelve concerns of our children:

1. Make sure the parent I am with now does not get angry with me.
2. Do not cause either parent any pain.
3. Maintain contact with both parents.
4. Have assurance that I may give love and get love from both parents.
5. Know who will take care of me if something happens to my parents.
6. Maintain contact with extended family.
7. Know I will have a safe secure place to live.

*Building a Bridge*

8. Know what will be happening in my life in the future.

9. Know my possessions will be safe in my absence.

10. Maintain contact with neighborhood and school friends.

11. Have consistency in education and religious training.

12. Be assured I am not responsible for the conflicts of my parents.

Hardwick cautions parents about their children's hidden agendas as well. She writes, "Children also have hidden agendas. Agendas will change as the custody case drags on and the children tend to become alternately victims and manipulators of their parents. When adults use children as pawns in a custody battle, the children parrot an adult's agenda. Psychologists, mediators and guardian ad litems watch for indications of parental propaganda and specifically alienation messages when they speak with children and explore the children's agendas."

Parents need not be engaged in a custody proceeding for children to activate hidden agendas. If parents are handling the business of co-parenting in a hostile or war-like fashion, the children will follow suit.

Often children will decide they want to change residences and live with the other parent for a while. Maybe during high school a boy would like the opportunity to live with his father. Maybe an adolescent daughter wants to live with her mother during her teen years. Maybe a child wants to live with the other parent out of simple curiosity – what is my other parent really like? A change in residence for children is not uncommon. It is, however, critical that children have a sense of stability during their childhood.

The children should not go from one household to the other in an attempt to dodge responsibility or discipline. Do not allow children to play one parent against the other. Children of divorce learn early the opportunity they have for potential parental manipulation … "Mom said no, so I'll just leave and hang with dad." Or "Dad is always on me about stuff, but Mom rarely asks about anything, so I'll say I want to live with her."

*Building a Bridge*

When making the decisions about the residence of children, parents must be careful to communicate to the child that he may not jump back and forth from one household to the next. This may not be an issue if both parents live in the same town, but when the parents live in very different locations, children need to be more established.

When children want to move to live with the other parent, share conversation about why, the positive and negative aspects of such a change, how the parties involved will handle communications and other potential problem areas. When handled in this fashion, children learn that the parents will not be party to being manipulated.

About two and a half years ago Jason asked to live and school in Houston. We had many long discussions about the matter, and consulted a family therapist, prior to making the decision to change his residence. This decision was not made easily by anyone. It took a great deal of courage for Jason to speak from his heart and even more courage for his father to honor his request. But the result of respecting Jason and his request has meant he has a healthy self-esteem, is doing well in school and is making positive friendships. These benefits are in addition to the love he feels from both his parents.

One element of this change in residence that I want to point out has to do with the individual choices of our children. When Jason was expressing his desire to relocate, his sister made it clear that while she would not interfere with Jason's decision, she wanted her wishes respected as well. In fact, she said to me "I don't care what he wants, just as long as it does not affect me." Sarah is happy at her Illinois home. She too does very well in school and has strong healthy friendships. These are indicators of happy children and need to be weighed heavily during a decision-making process.

Although your child may make a decision about where to live, being separated from those you love is never easy. When your children are with you, they miss their other family. When they are with the other family, they miss you. Help your children to focus on what they do have and not what they are missing. This is the old dilemma of the glass being half full or half empty – which is it? Both, but it is all in how you look at things. Teach your children to appreciate each day and enjoy the people they are with, otherwise, they will waste all their

*Building a Bridge*

time bemoaning their situation and never learn to enjoy anything or anyone. Remind them of all the ways they have to stay in touch with those they are not with – telephone, email, letters, and so on. If you do not help them with this, each day will be torment for them and for you.

Another matter regarding a child choosing a place of residence that must be discussed – but one that might be considered a conversational taboo – is knowing that separation between you and your child is mutually healthier for your relationship. There is a great deal of truth to the saying, "Distance makes the heart grow fonder." Sometimes a parent and a child will find that they cannot live in harmony under the same roof. Maybe the relationship is not that strained, but is still healthier for the distance. I mentioned this as a taboo because not many parents want to admit that they and their child are better off by being distanced. If this is your situation:

- Work toward greater respect for one another

- Focus on one another's strengths

- Work to be more patient with one another's lesser attractive aspects (habits, mannerisms, expressions, opinions, and so forth)

- Find ways to stay in touch that you both enjoy

- Find ways to enjoy one another's company when together (make happy memories for you both)

*****

Personal Reflections

Do you compete with the other parent? List those ways you compete. (For example, do you try to earn more money solely for the purpose of being more financially stable than the other parent? Do you join clubs or organizations simply to show-up the other parent?)

Do you try to persuade your children to live with you to serve your own interests rather than their needs?

*Building a Bridge*

Have you done anything that might indicate to your child that you want him/her to choose between the other parent and you? (For example, make your home sound better than the other parent's, make unrealistic promises about how life would be if your child lived with you, criticized the other parent's disciplinary procedures and promise more freedom if your child lives with you.)

What do you do to support the other parent in creating a stable environment at their home? (For example, do you encourage the children to respect the other parent, do you respect the other parent's right to make his/her own decisions, do you pay your child support?)

What do you do to create a stable environment at your home? (For example, do you work to have a quality relationship with your partner, do you keep your home safe and inviting, do you have a space created for you children to call their own when with you?)

Affirm: I appreciate the role I play in my child's life. I contribute to my fullest potential. I am an important person in my child's life no matter where I, or my child, reside.

**Additional reading suggestions:**

*Mom's House, Dad's House: A Complete Guide for Parents Who Are Separated, Divorced, or Remarried* by Isolina Ricci


*Greed*

**Greed is "excessive or reprehensible acquisitiveness (a strong desire for acquiring and possessing.)"**

Our desire to acquire and possess the children in our residential household is fear expressed as greed. We create this fear internally, but are also influenced by external factors.

The internal factors are those questions we ask ourselves, but are often afraid to answer.

*Building a Bridge*

- Without my children, who am I?

- How do I fit into my children's lives?

- What do I think of myself?

- What do others think of me?

- Why do I care what others think of me?

Since we are feeling unsure internally, we have low resistance to the external factors. The external factors are the attitudes of parents, family, friends, co-workers/business associates and society.

Here are some important factors to consider:

1. Release the need to please your parents/family.

Often this need becomes so intense that decisions are no longer made in accordance with what you feel is personally right, but are based on how you think the parents/family are going to react. If you are caught in this thinking, give it up! As adults, we must be responsible for our decisions. We must determine what is right for ourselves and our children. Sometimes those decisions will not please our parents.

Asking those close to us for input and ideas can be a benefit to our situation. Seeking outside counsel can offer us new perspectives and approaches. However, when those people we solicit counsel from pressure us with their fears and prejudices, we need to step back. Sometimes the people we ask to guide us have their own agendas in the custody situation and therefore give us information based on what they want, rather than what might be best. When this happens, we need to seek new counsel or trust our own instincts to guide us.

When seeking counsel about long-distance parenting from parents/family, be aware that these folks may feel a long-distance parenting situation is a negative reflection on them. The grandparents may be worried about the affect long-distance will have on their relationship with the grandchildren. Their concerns about their opportunity to grandparent are legitimate and need to be addressed. Extended family may have these same concerns. Any other issue regarding the long-distance situation must be made with personal integrity and conviction.

Friends and co-workers/business associates can also place stress on us about long-distance parenting. While these people are a part of our inner circle, they are also a part of society.

2. Remember that society is a collected group of individuals.

Within this group exist patterns of thinking on a huge variety of subjects. Families, and family structure, are among the subjects. How are the patterns created for subjects? Traditional ways of handling matters are generally at the root of our ideas.

With regard to families and parenting, our ideas might go back to The Garden of Eden. First there was Adam, then Eve, then they had numerous children. (We know Cain and Abel best. They had a great deal of drama in their lives, which has been written about fairly extensively.) So we have a father, a mother and children who live together in Eden. The pattern is now set. Throughout history, society has used this pattern for family structure. However, in modern times families have deviated from this pattern, which has caused uncertainty. Anytime we move away from established patterns or ideas, fear moves in. These patterns are the stereotypes we hold onto because they are familiar – they form our comfort zone.

3. Do not limit yourself to established patterns.

In our society, we use these patterns to describe the roles people play. Unfortunately, we are so anal about detailing the descriptions that people are forced into spaces so tiny they have no room for diversity. People are complex, so getting a person to be the description is impossible. Regardless, we continue to maneuver ourselves in hopes of fulfilling a stereotype.

*Building a Bridge*

As an example, we believe in the pattern of parents being hands-on in order to be effective. This has resulted in divorced parents taking the address of their children very personally. In our prejudice we have a higher regard – a parental superiority if you will – for the parent who maintains residential custody of the children. This esteem transmits itself into an emotional validation of highest value for the residential parent. The residential parent becomes a winner. This pressure mandates the desire to gain custody – at minimum – residential custody. When a parent maintains residential custody, although they may have legal joint custody, there is the appearance of having more power and authority. The appearance of fulfilling the family pattern is highly esteemed in society. We must detach ourselves from the need to adhere to these appearances.

4. Be responsible for yourself.

How do we do that? Don't blame society for our status. In fact, we must take responsibility for thinking of ourselves as a "less-than" parent because of the distance between ourselves and the children.

Long-distance parents have been stereotyped. What is a stereotype? *Webster's Dictionary* states that to stereotype is "to repeat without variation." Society mirrors the image that parents away from their children have been projecting. We have stereotyped, or "represented an oversimplified opinion or critical judgment," of ourselves. We think we must be hands-on in order to be effective, and we pass that lie onto the public. They throw it right back into our faces, and we run with our tail between our legs desperate to find a place to hide. Out of sight and circulation, we become absent. Once absent, we don't fulfill our role as a parent. So if we created this negative image for ourselves, what is stopping us from creating a positive image using the same "to repeat without variation" system?

We have been afraid of long-distance parenting because it is different. Different seems scary. Long-distance parenting doesn't fit into any of society's pre-established, acceptable patterns. We have been taught that we need those patterns to keep things safe and predictable. We like knowing what is expected of us, although we frantically attempt to comply.

*Building a Bridge*

Society has skewed the definitions of traditional and normal by making them synonyms. They are not! Long-distance parenting, which is a part of our current culture and will be a part of our future culture, requires new and innovative methods for communication which fear-based thinkers find terrifying because it moves away from the traditional patterns – the comfort zone – that which is considered "normal."

Since there is a level of acceptance for residential parents, how do we view the non-residential parent? As a loser? As a junkie, an alcoholic or whore? As an irresponsible and selfish person? As a "deadbeat dad"? Much evidence exists that many non-custodial parents have done a poor job of providing support (financial, emotional, or otherwise) for their offspring. Using Webster's "repeat without variation" definition, what long-distance parents need is a role model from which they can pattern positive parental behavior rather than the negative representations which are currently in the forefront of society's thoughts.

My relocation and long-distance parenting started simultaneously. I was still numb from the separation when our new neighbors inquired about our family. Asking if children are a part of a household is a natural question. Those who were asking meant nothing by the inquiry; no one was digging for dirt. But my heart was hurting, so their interest felt like a courtroom inquest. When their questions fell on my ears, my heart stopped beating. Certainly my oxygen was gone; I could not breathe. I honestly did not know what to say. My mind raced, "Should I lie and say no for now and then explain later?" or "Should I come clean and put myself in a position of being judged? If I do that, they may suspect me of terrible things." I felt as if I was playing the life-or-death version of tag and was on the brink of being "it." I couldn't find the tree we were using for "SAFE." Panic was setting in. I did decide to be honest about the children living in another city, but I did so sheepishly. Because I was not yet comfortable with the matter, I found myself babbling out certain legal details, which I felt would pardon me from the judgment that I assumed was to follow. The need to defend myself was overwhelming. Fear was everywhere. I could feel intimidation engulfing me.

Once I was working at a restaurant and needed honey from the stock room. The jar stood on an upper shelf, but thinking I could

*Building a Bridge*

stretch and get it without a stepstool, I managed to tap the jar enough to have it come tumbling down. As luck would have it, the person who had used it before had not placed the lid on properly, so when the container hit my shoulder I became instantly covered in the sticky substance. That entire shift I had to work with honey all over me, not to mention that I was getting it on everything I touched. Nothing works in removing honey but full immersion. Once home, I could strip down and shower.

So it is with publicly stating my long-distance situation. I needed to strip down to my soul and allow myself to cleanse my thinking. I needed to release myself from the intimidation. I needed to stop being my own worst enemy.

When you are confronted with difficult questions, you may feel unprepared about answering. Here are some tips to keep in mind:

- Answer the question honestly, but do not feel the need to elaborate on the answer.

- Remember that this is your life and you are entitled to make decisions independent of the judgments of others.

- Stay calm. Do not allow others or their questions to make you feel inferior or insecure.

- Politely decline responding to the question by saying something like, "Thank you for your interest in my family. I prefer to keep those matters private." Or "I am in the process of working through my family matters and at this time prefer not to discuss them."

Here are some sample questions you might encounter. I offer these answers only as suggestions.

Q: Why don't your children live with you?

    A. The other parent and I made a decision regarding the children's residence based on what we felt was in their best interest.

*Building a Bridge*

A. The other parent and I had trouble coming to a mutual understanding regarding the children so we asked a mediator to assist us. He recommended the children reside with the other parent and I accepted that decision.

Q: Are you going to take the other parent back to court so you can get your kids?

A: I will do what is in the best interest of my children.

A: I do not need a court to "get" my kids. I am working toward a cooperative association with the other parent. As a result, I am able to maintain a healthy relationship with the children even though they live with the other parent most of the time.

Q: How can I help you with your custody situation?

A: You can support my efforts to cooperate with the other parent.

A: If you see any articles or books about long-distance parenting, I would appreciate knowing about them.

A: You can pray for me.

### Exercising our Current Rights –

### Appreciating the Opportunities Wc Do Have

1. Focus on your rights – right now.

Society is a collection of individuals. As we long-distance parents confront our own thinking, society, too, will get a more accurate image of who and what we are. The deal isn't that we don't have rights, it's that we don't exercise the ones we do have. We are tip-toeing in a place where we are allowed to tap dance. We spend our energy wanting different rights or more rights. We need to take

*Building a Bridge*

action with what we have. As we do, more opportunities will open up for us.

Long-distance parenting throws those hard questions into our face. Once we have looked within ourselves for the answers, we will feel confident about moving forward in our own lives, in creating a relationship with our child, in helping society to heal. Long-distance parenting is a dark issue. By working to connect with our children – transcending the miles – we begin to light the way. Can you recall the experience of getting up in the middle of the night and turning a light on? How did your eyes feel? Could you see right away or did it take a minute? It is the same with society looking at long-distance parents. Even when we do respect our current abilities, it will take time for people to see straight. We need to stay focused on what is right for ourselves and our children. In time we can expand the parenting pattern and it will look and feel comfortable.

2.  Act like a first-class parent.

When we stop acting like second-class parents, we will stop being treated as such. By educating the public about long-distance parenting, we must work toward improvement of ourselves while simultaneously building bridges to connect with all other involved parties. Only then can we help to heal our misinformed society. When we have something important to say, society will listen. While fear would like to strong-arm us into timid behavior and feelings of low parental-worth, experience has taught that confronting the matter strengthens us. This strength enables us to grow and advance.

3.  Put effort and ambition into parenting.

Our collective lack of real effort in parenting has caused these unfavorable images. This old, traditional pattern of how parenting must be done – hands on – has created illusions, which have lured long-distance parents into thinking they cannot be good parents: "Since we are not in the traditional parenting role, we must not be of value." We must embrace our new situation as an experience to customize parenting to meet the specific needs of our own children rather than positioning ourselves in a stereotype that confines and constricts. We get caught up in the cultural nonsense and deny we have any redeeming quality. Breaking free from these stereotypes is

*Building a Bridge*

not our effort to conspire against the other parent or society. Stepping away from the pattern enables and empowers us to meet our own needs as well as the needs of our children. We do society a huge favor when we honor our responsibilities, regardless of the location from which we orchestrate that achievement.

4.     Be patient – keep working.

Societal opinions change slowly. Our parenting position is foreign to the traditional thinker. It is different. Different does not mean wrong. As long-distance parents we are not released from our responsibilities as parents. We are challenged by the incorporation of distance. Our job is not impossible, but does require more intent and determination. It takes work. Perhaps society has been bitter towards us because it has seen so little accomplished. We need to shed the shackles of stereotype, dig our heels in and begin to work.

**"Progress demands progressive thinking and new ideas."**

**-Michael Oddenino**

5.     Promote change within your personal circles.

The work we have to do starts within our personal circles. When we talk about changing society's views, we think, "How can I – one person – change all of society's views?" The answer is to encourage change in one person at a time. Sometimes our progress is more appreciated by those viewing us from outside our personal circles than it is by those closer to our situation. Why does this surprise us? Jesus said, "A prophet is honored everywhere except his own hometown and among his own family." (Matthew 13:57)

This message came through to me loud and clear with my own mother. About a year after I became a long-distance parent, a close friend of mine was in a custody dispute. During a telephone visit with my mom, she inquired about the status of this friend's legal proceedings, which I told her. Mom exclaimed, "She had better be careful or she'll end up just like you!" While I was feeling that my work on long-distance parenting was going well, it was painfully obvious that my mother was not seeing the situation with the same optimism.

6.     You will be known by your actions.
*Building a Bridge*

While I do not want to further influence stereotypes, the truth is a tree is known by the fruit it bears and a person is known by his actions. Therefore, I want to clarify the difference between long-distance, absent parents and the "deadbeats."

Long-distance parents are parents who live apart from their children, but maintain relationships regardless of the miles. Fully aware of the challenges, they have remained steadfast in their commitment to parenting.

Absent as an adjective means, "not present or attending; missing; not existing." Absent as a verb means: "to keep (oneself) away." While the absent parent chooses, for a variety of reasons, not to be present in the lives of the children, many absent parents financially support the children.

The infamous "dead beat dad" must also be listed. (Which includes some moms.) These are the absent parents who do not communicate with the children nor do they contribute to their financial well-being.

When evaluating my relationship with my children, I do not find myself "not present, missing or not existing," nor am I "keeping myself away." I am not an absent parent. I am a long-distance parent. There is a huge difference.

*****

Personal Reflections

Do you feel a need to have your children live with you in order to fulfill an image?

Do you still try to please your parents at the expense of your own integrity and what is best for your child? If so, list some instances when you honored your parents instead of honoring yourself? (For example, following the religion of your parent's choice rather than following your heart, working in a career chosen by your parent's, not allowing yourself to create new traditions because your parent's would be insulted if you did not follow their traditions (holidays).)

*Building a Bridge*

Are your parents concerned about their opportunity to grandparent? If so, is this concern legitimate? What can you do to help connect them with their grandchildren? (For example, let them know in advance when the children will be with you so they can plan to visit also, keeping them supplied with updated photographs, send them school papers so they can see what your child is studying.)

Do you blame any one for your long-distance parenting status? If so, list those parties you hold accountable. (For example, your work, the judge, your attorney, the other parent, your parents or others.)

What hard questions have you been asked? List them.

Write one or two responses to each question. Once written, say the responses aloud until they become comfortable for you to say.

How do you contribute to society's views of long-distance parents? List both positive and negative contributions.

| Positive | Negative |
|---|---|
| Pay child support | Bad mouth the other parent |
| Talk to children once a week | Don't communicate with school |
| See the children twice a year | Don't know anyone in my child's life |

What can you do to create a more positive image for long-distance parents? (For example, correct those negative aspects listed in the previous question, work within your support group to encourage other long-distance parents.)

Take some time to brainstorm for new ideas on long-distance parenting. For example, do you have an imagination for creating a new school system? A new travel system? How about redesigning the calendar? If so, start from scratch and fill in all 365 days so they ideally work for you and your children. Allow yourself to be creative.

Describe yourself as a parent? (For example, loving, caring, unprepared, confused, frustrated, scared.)

*Building a Bridge*

Has your description of yourself changed with the incorporation of distance? (For example, frustrated, discouraged, afraid.)

Are you intimidated about discussing your long-distance status? Can you recall an experience when you felt this intimidation? If so, describe your thoughts and feelings from that time.

Do you exercise your custody rights to the fullest as outlined in the custody decree? How do you accomplish this? (Reread your custody decree, list your rights as outlined and then note how you exercise that right.)

| Your Rights | How I Exercise This Right |
| --- | --- |
|  |  |

Do you act like a secondary parent or do you act like a co-parent? Do you genuinely participate with the other parent in making decisions about your child? How do you do this? (For example, do you stay focused on your child and the issues rather than on your dislike for each other?)

Are you willing to put effort and energy into long-distance parenting your children? What effort are you currently demonstrating? (For example, write, call, email, send care packages, plan trips together, have a room/space for your child at your home.)

Are you familiar with the Child's Bill of Rights and the Parent's Bill of Rights? List what you think are your rights.

*Building a Bridge*

## Child's Bill of Rights

- A Child has a right to a name, a nationality, and special protection regardless of race, religion, sex or disability.

- A Child has the right to love each parent without being subjected to the other parent's hurt or anger.

- A Child has the right to develop an independent and meaningful relationship with each parent and to enjoy the uniqueness of each parent and each home.

- A Child has the right to be free from involvement in parent's personal battles and/or from being used as a spy, messenger or bargaining chip.

- A Child has the right to have adequate nutrition, education and personal security.

- A Child has the right to extended family relationships, which include siblings, grandparents, aunts, uncles, cousins, and to appreciate the unique differences of each side of his family and not have these differences referred to as "better" or "worse."

- A Child has the right to be free from questions about the other parent's private life.

- A Child has the right, whenever possible, to maintain a degree of contact the child requires with both parents.

- A Child has the right to see his/her parents treat each other in a courteous and respectful manner.

- A Child has the right to develop and maintain activities and friends without fear of losing time with a parent.

- A Child has the right to be a child without having to assume adult and/or parental roles or duties.

*Building a Bridge*

## Parent's Bill of Rights

- A parent has the right to love and nurture his/her child without harassment from the other parent.

- A parent is entitled to access all school records of the child directly from the school, as well as from the other parent. School reports should be photocopied promptly after receipt and supplied to the other parent.

- A parent has the right to receive respect and courtesy from the other parent and the obligation to show respect and courtesy to the other parent.

- A parent has the right to be notified promptly of all child-related activities, which encourage or allow parental participation.

- A parent has the right to access his/her child. Child support and access, while they may be emotionally connected, are separate legal issues. The law in most states provides that parental access may not be denied due to the inability or failure to pay child support.

- During parenting time, each parent has the right to follow the standards, beliefs and style of child rearing they think is proper without interference from the other parent.

- A parent has the right to the knowledge of the other parent's address and phone number(s) in order to maintain contact with the child.

- A parent has the right to encourage the child to initiate telephone and/or mail contact, on a regular basis.

- A parent has the right of daily telephone contact with the child during the child's normal waking hours.

- A parent has the right to a separate and private life.

Affirm: I accept my responsibility for parenting. I know the creative energy of God supports me in parenting my children. By sending out positive, loving energy for my children, society will learn that different is not wrong.

**Additional reading suggestions:**

*Pulling Your Own Strings: Dynamic Techniques for Dealing with Other People and Living Life as You Choose* by Wayne W. Dyer

*Yesterday, I Cried: Celebrating the Lessons of Living and Loving* by Iylana Vanzant

*Grief*

**Grief is "a deep and poignant distress caused by or as if by bereavement; a cause of such suffering; mishap; annoyance; an unfortunate outcome."**

As parents we become accustomed to various routines with our children, some of which go back to their birth. We have our own ways of demonstrating love and affection to our children. When those opportunities on a day-to-day basis are interrupted, we feel a real sense of loss. As a result, we feel that the outcome of the custody proceeding is unfortunate or a mishap – a mistake. We try to make sense of it by analyzing the entire situation, everyone involved, and of course, ourselves. All this does is stir feelings of annoyance, distress and grief. Grief is normal. The stages of grief are shock, denial, bargaining, anger, guilt and finally, acceptance.

The onset of long-distance parenting is particularly painful. As with a serious muscle sprain, you encounter tremendous pain. Often it is said that a sprain is more painful than a break. At first my thinking about long-distance parenting was that I had been severed from my children. As I worked toward inner peace, my visualization changed from severed to stretched. A severed relationship with my children would have occurred if their lives had been taken.

*Building a Bridge*

I was feeling my parenting put to the test – stretched – by the long distance between us. My emotional muscles were definitely screaming with pain. As I worked toward peace, I experienced the muscles becoming more comfortable and familiar with the new situation. Just as physical muscles need to be exercised and limbered, my emotional muscles needed stretching.

Everyone involved experiences grief. The residential parent may feel distress over the new, and perhaps larger, parenting role. Often residential parents feel they are now only living to comply with the non-custodial parents' visitation rights. The children may be annoyed that they cannot see the long-distance parent whenever they wish. The grandparents, especially of the long-distance parent, fear they may lose contact with the children and miss their opportunity to enjoy grandparenting. Other family members and close friends also experience an uncertainty about when, or if, they will ever again share time with the children.

### *Draw on Creative Ability*

We must draw on our creative ability to find new and innovative ways to communicate with our children. Evaluating our talents, abilities and hobbies is a great place to start. Ask yourself, "How can I use what I already know to contribute to my children?" If you don't feel that you currently have a talent, ability, interest or hobby to offer, you need to open yourself up to the possibilities. I guarantee that you have something you can offer. Consider also those interests you and your child share together, for example, collector dolls or muscle cars.

- If you have any art supplies (crayons, markers, glue, glitter, construction paper) available to you, get them out. Start doodling, drawing, cutting, or pasting until something inside of you starts to groove.

- Meet with a creative friend and ask for help in brainstorming. Teachers, Sunday school teachers, day care professionals and other parents are great resources.

- Go to a crafts/hobby store and look around – something might click. These businesses also have many creative people on staff that can help you. If you see something that interests you, give it a try or take a class.

- Explore children's activity books and magazines.

- Subscribe to Together Time! Activity Club Magazine. Write to The Creative Learning Institute, 7 Indian Hill Avenue, P.O. Box 208, Portland, CT 06480. You will receive a monthly kit, which will contain all the materials necessary to complete at least three craft projects. These kits are fabulous for stimulating your creative juices!

- Take a look at the book, *Family Fun Crafts: 500 Creative Activities for You and Your Children*. It is a Disney editions book.

- You can definitely help family members (grandparents, aunts, cousins and other extended family) by being the conduit of information to and from the children. Pass along letters, cards, photographs, school papers or art projects to keep everyone connected.

- Read books on stimulating your creativity. Sark's book, *A Creative Companion, How To Free Your Creative Spirit*, is awesome. So is Julia Cameron's book, *The Artist's Way*, which is also available as an activity box.

- Demonstrate a desire to be creative in your daily life by:

- Trying new foods

- Reading a book different than your normal choice

- Listening to music other than your normal choice

Long-distance parenting may be a detour, but it certainly is not a closed road. In the book, *My Mother Is the Best Gift I Ever Got*, author David Heller quotes Jenny saying, "The best thing about motherhood [parenthood] is nobody ever makes you quit. You can do it as long as you want." Good words to remember!

*Building a Bridge*

## *Acceptance*

Acceptance works to heal the grief. We grieve in part because we hold the thought that things should be a different way...our way. Acceptance allows us to take our situation and work with it in a fashion that brings peace to all concerned.

During the time when I was working toward acceptance in my own situation, I was at the library reading randomly through a poetry book. This was one of those times when you know that guidance and instruction are coming from God, but you wonder how He ever managed to connect you to that instruction! The words I needed to hear and concentrate on were found in this beautiful poem by Ella Wheeler Wilcox.

### *"Whatever Is – Is Best"*

I know, as my life grows older, and mine eyes have clearer sight,
That under each rank wrong somewhere there lies the root of Right;
That each sorrow has its purpose, by the sorrowing oft unguessed;
But as sure as the sun brings morning, whatever is – is best.

I know that each sinful action, as sure as the night brings shade,
Is somewhere, sometime punished, tho' the hour be long delayed.
I know that the soul is aided sometimes by the heart's unrest,
And to grow means often to suffer – but whatever is – is best.

I know there are no errors, in the great Eternal plan,
And all things work together for the final good of man.
And I know my soul speeds onward, in its grand Eternal quest,
I shall say as I look back earthward, whatever is – is best.

We demonstrate acceptance in our lives when we:

- Unconditionally love ourselves

- Unconditionally love others

- Release our expectations of situations

*Building a Bridge*

## Personal Reflections

Are you grieving over the loss of the ways you formerly parented your child? Make a list of those activities you miss. (For example, helping with homework or tucking your child in bed.)

Evaluate the list you made and find ways to modify for long-distance parenting.

| **What I Miss** | **How I Can Modify** |
|---|---|
|  |  |
|  |  |
|  |  |

Make a list of your talents, hobbies, abilities and interests. (For example, woodworking, baking, gardening, and so on.) Think of ways to use your list to connect with you child. Consult others for ideas as well.

What additional resources do you have for developing creativity? (Teachers, craft stores, magazines and others.) Check with as many of these as possible to generate new ideas.

Have you fully accepted the custody decree and your long-distance parenting situation?

What is keeping you from accepting it? (For example, anger, resentment, fear.)

Affirm: I accept this situation as an opportunity for me to not only expand myself, but also stay in touch with my child in creative and constructive ways. I do this for myself and for my child.

*Building a Bridge*

**Additional reading suggestions:**

*Love Yourself, Heal Your Life Workbook* by Louise Hay and Glen Klob, editor

*Healing Grief: Reclaiming Life After Any Loss* by James Van Praagh

*The Grief Recovery Handbook – The Action Program for Moving Beyond Death, Divorce, and Other Losses* by John W. James and Russell Friedman

*Guilt*

**Guilt is "the act of having committed a breach of conduct especially violating law and involving a penalty."**

Holding onto guilt about the failure of the marriage and/or the things you did or did not do in the past is a useless waste of energy. The past is the past. It is over. Finished. Nothing can be done about the actions of yesterday. Do not hold yourself to yesterday's behavior and do not judge others by their old behaviors.

I say, "Don't hold onto the past" and your reply might be, "Oh, I've let go of the past." But have you? If we look at our lives we will quite possibly see the ways we punish ourselves. While we may say we have given up the behaviors of old, our actions indicate that we think we must forever pay mental, emotional and spiritual penalties and thereby we keep ourselves imprisoned in the past.

Consider what you are feeling guilty about and know that whatever it was in the past that you deem unacceptable, can be changed. The thoughts you held in the past can be released in this moment. As an example, if you have felt that you were not a good parent in the past, release the guilt you hold. Today is where your power lies. TODAY be a good parent.

If you are stuck in the past, are you really living or just existing? I think you must be in a void because the past is over, but its hold on you keeps you from the present. If you don't have a present, how can you have a future?

*Building a Bridge*

## *Release the Past*

Each day is a new opportunity to grow and become smarter and wiser. If we were given the exact same circumstances today that we were given ten years ago, wouldn't we make smarter and wiser decisions? If not, we need to take a careful look at ourselves and ask why we are in the same place as ten years ago! So if each day we pledge to do our genuine best, then nothing more can be asked of us. We are in growth processes and as life is lived we learn. Each day we make the best choices we can with the information we have at the time. Dr. Wayne Dyer taught me to not dwell on the past choices I've made, but to say to myself, "Now I know better!" Since I know better, I make better choices!

This is about self-forgiveness. Allowing ourselves to grow each day is about loving ourselves through that growth and not beating ourselves up for past mistakes or lessons.

Release the past by evaluating what it is you are feeling guilty about. As you think on these things, further study the experience(s) to determine what you learned. Every moment in life offers us powerful learning opportunities. Ask yourself:

- What good came from this experience?

- Given the experience again today, what would I do differently?

Once this is figured out, you will be free to release the guilt and embrace the present.

Releasing the past for most of us is a slow, reluctant process. It does not need to be, but old patterns are familiar and we resist relinquishing that familiarity. Old habits are like layers of wax on the floor. Over the years we have allowed the layers to build up even when we have occasionally recognized that we need to get to the bottom and do a refinish job. Or how many times do we paint an old house and think "Someday I'll go down to the wood, but this year I'll just spruce the place up with another coat." We think it is easier to wait, but in the end, it is not.

In Pia Mellody's book, *Facing CoDependence*, she writes,

*Building a Bridge*

"The secret to your recovery is to learn to embrace your own history. Look at it, become aware of it, and experience your feelings about the less-than-nurturing events of your past. Because if you don't, the issues from your history will be held in minimization, denial, and delusion and truly be behind you as demons you are not aware of. And this situation will continue to make you miserable through your own dysfunctional behaviors. More directly I tell my patients, "Hug your demons or they will bite you in the ass." In other words, if you do not embrace what is dysfunctional, you are doomed to repeat it and stay in the pain."

Don't be afraid to put a little effort into doing the release work. Dig in and scrub down to the wood. When you do get to the bottom and release yourself from the attachment to the past, you will find an excitement runs through you. You will be anxious to share your new energy with others in an effort to help them free themselves. (It's like showing off our newly refinished floors or handsomely repainted homes!)

Once you share your excitement over the release process, you inspire others to do the same. We delight in our ability to inspire others. All others, except for the children's other parent, that is. We hold him to his old behaviors long after we have any real evidence that he behaves in such manners. Heck, we don't even need evidence – we assume he is what he has always been. We keep him in his box because we are comfortable with what we know him to be. We will even force him back into the box if he attempts to change.

- Do you hold him to the past because you want him to suffer as long as possible in order to make some restitution for his deplorable deeds during the marriage?

- Do you want to appear the stronger, wiser parent and by keeping your former spouse in the dark you think you can fool yourself and others to think you shine in the light?

How egotistical of us to think that we could keep any other person from growing and becoming the well-rounded person he was

*Building a Bridge*

created to be. Life does not assign one teacher per person. We learn from countless sources. If you are growing and moving from the past, consider the possibility that the other parent could be doing the same. As you work toward self-improvement, hold the other parent to the light of God and pray that he/she will seek the same. In attempting to keep anyone in the past, you only keep yourself there.

*****

## Personal Reflections

What feelings, experiences or problems of the past are you still carrying with you? (For example, anger toward the other parent for divorcing you, second failed relationship, financial burdens.)

Are you living life with joy and passion? Or are you existing by going through the motions each day?

Thinking of today only, finish the following statements:

> I wish I would have done ... differently.

> I feel great about the way I handled ... .

List those situation that have been burdening you – those situations you wished you had done differently – no matter how long ago they happened. (For example, the way you handled the interview at XYZ Corporation, comment to family during Christmas six years ago, marrying the children's other parent when you knew there were issues.)

Evaluate this list. What can you learn about yourself from this list? (For example, I need to stand up for myself or I need to trust my instincts or I need to stop listening at ABC's advice.)

As you review each listing, can you say aloud, "Now I know better?" If not, allow yourself to rethink each situation until you can say this.

With regard to these situations, are you able to forgive yourself for the role you played?

*Building a Bridge*

Now list those moments when you have been most proud of yourself. Use all the extra paper you need! ☺ (For example, taught your son to play baseball or ride a bike, handled major account at work that brought the company success, finished college or a training program.)

Write and/or draw a description of the other parent.

What colors did you use? Any? Dark ones? Light ones? Did you draw any ugly characteristics such as devil horns or evil eyes or fire coming from the mouth? Did you draw any nice qualities such as pretty hair or strong shoulders?

Are you holding the other parent to old behaviors? Think about and list ways you can begin to change your viewpoint of the other parent so it is more positive. (For example, talk nicer to other parent, make less assumptions about other parent, be more grateful for all the other parent does to contribute to your child's life.)

Affirm: Each new day I give my genuine best. In return, Life teaches me and I become smarter and wiser in every moment. Life is great!

**Additional reading suggestions:**

*Your Erroneous Zones* by Wayne W. Dyer

*How Good Do You Have To Be?: A New Understanding of Guilt and Forgiveness* by Harold Kushner

### Hatefulness

**Hatefulness is "being full of intense hostility and aversion usually deriving from fear, anger, or a sense of injury; extreme dislike."**

Those things that we intensely dislike, or hate, in others is really a reflection of the things we dislike, or hate, about ourselves. When we project our hostility onto other people or situations, we trick ourselves into thinking that these attributes are not or could not be a part of us.

*Building a Bridge*

Those things that we dislike will not go away because we hate them. When we send out the negative energy of hate, regardless of where it is directed, it comes back to us. Rather than contributing to the negative energy, why not take a look at yourself and see what qualities it is that you don't care for and find ways to heal those soul wounds? If you see behavior in others that repulses you, simply observe that behavior, go within and evaluate what you can learn about yourself from this encounter.

For example, if I say, "I hate the other parent who is so inconsiderate," I need to look carefully at my own actions and evaluate whether or not I demonstrate inconsiderate behavior. Since I am human (as are we all – regardless of what you think of the other parent) chances may be that I will have work to do in this very area of my life. However, if this is an area of my life that I honestly have in alignment with my Higher Self, then what I need to do is stop criticizing and judging the other parent. We are ALL learning. No one on this planet has "arrived." So, we can relax in knowing that we are all students. We can focus on our individual lessons (that means: mind our own business) because we have plenty of our own homework. While we are not all working on the same lesson, we are all working on lessons. If I have learned a lesson that the other parent is still working on, I must trust the Universal Teacher and be confident that the other parent will learn in his perfect time. Our responsibility is to be an example of the highest behavior. We must act in a considerate manner, as our pointing out any weaknesses will only create more hostile feelings, which will work against the objectives of communication and cooperation.

Here are some ways we can demonstrate communication in our daily lives:

- Talking **with** the other parent. (Not talking at or to the other parent.)

- Writing the school.

- Sharing positive ideas with your child and the adults in your child's world.

*Building a Bridge*

Cooperation is another critical element. Did you notice that cooperation is at the backbone of this book? (Flip the book around and look.) It is at the backbone of everything. Here are some ideas for demonstrating cooperation in your daily life:

- Be as willing to listen as you are to talk
- Be willing to compromise when it is for the greater good
- Taking your turn to help with a willing attitude

### Be Considerate – Focus on Our Own Growth Needs

Let's focus on ourselves. We are all quite ready to look at others and evaluate their shortcomings, faults, and problems. In particular, we are ever ready, even anxious, to point out what the other parent needs to do or not do. Our mission is to keep ourselves focused on our own evaluations. Let there be no misunderstanding on this one thing: WHAT THE OTHER PARENT DOES IS NONE OF YOUR BUSINESS. If the children are in real physical, mental or emotional jeopardy, then we, of course, must take appropriate action. More often the case is that we need to let go of our need to judge. Their journey in this lifetime is for them to travel. We have our own journey. Didn't you divorce this person so you would no longer be associated with his path? If some behavior is bothering you, then you must evaluate why this is happening and also learn to respond to the situation instead of react. The following is an example response chart of how I evaluated many of my feelings. Use this chart or design another for working through your own issues.

| Incident | Feelings | Response | New Response |
|---|---|---|---|
| Other parent tells the children bad things about me. | Anger and desire to retaliate. | I will fight fire with fire. | Stop caring about what other parent says. Live my truth.<br><br>Set the example by telling the children nice things about other parent. |
| Other parent is always after me about more money. | Used and unappreciated. | Abandon the situation. Let her figure out other ways to get more money – I'm not an ATM. | Discuss the children's needs and evaluate how they can be managed economically. |

We do not disarm hate with more hate. We disarm hate with compassion and understanding – expressions of love.

Ask yourself this question: If all around me is a reflection of me, what do I see?

*****

Personal Reflections

List the attributes in others that you dislike. (Example: selfish, inconsiderate, habitually tardy, excessively loud, or others.)

*Building a Bridge*

Take a moment to honestly consider your own behavior with regard to those attributes. Do you possess any of those habits?

What can you learn about yourself from this exercise? (For example, I need to be more considerate, I need to pay more attention to the time, or I need to be less angry and more patient.)

What can you learn about dealing with others? (For example, I need to be more compassionate or be more open-minded.)

Describe your life in adjectives. (Examples: negative, impatient, or creative, joyful, or abundant.)

Think about the words you used to describe your life. Then write your response to the following question: If all around me is a reflection of me, what do I see?

Affirm: Everything in my life is a reflection of myself. As I look into the mirror, I send myself love, compassion and understanding. I can then send it to all in my world.

**Additional reading suggestions:**

*The Power is Within You* by Louise Hay

*Your Sacred Self* by Wayne W. Dyer

### *Inferiority*

**Inferiority is "a feeling of a little less importance, value or merit; situated below another."**

Our feelings of inferiority are rooted in our belief that we are not good enough, that we are less important than others. Since our children are not living with us, we use this situation as proof that we are of little value and hold no merit as a parent. We swallow the societal stereotypes hook, line and sinker. These are our perceptions and we must work through them. Because we deem ourselves unworthy, we offer little-to-no input regarding the rearing of the children. Since we hold ourselves in low esteem, we think that others

*Building a Bridge*

will as well. We determine their opinion of us based on our opinion of ourselves.

> **"Remember, no one can make you feel inferior without your consent."**
>
> Eleanor Roosevelt

Remember the "hero complex" we discussed previously? We say to ourselves that we will contact our children when we have a great accomplishment to brag about or have become a hero is some fashion. Why do we insist that we have little or nothing to offer our children as we are? Why do we allow ourselves to be seduced by the worldly suggestions that only "the beautiful people" have something to offer?

Children, too, suffer with feelings of inferiority. They think that because they do not have the traditional family structure, they are not worthy of it. They question what role they played in the failure of the marriage and what they might have done or not done to influence the outcome of the custody decree. Because they have no real awareness of the bigger picture regarding their parents and the marital relationship, the children think that they must in some way be responsible. They punish themselves by getting into drugs, alcohol, gangs and other abusive behaviors.

Surgeon General David Satcher and Tipper Gore recently released their report, "Call to Action." In their report they beseech us to pay attention to the national crisis of suicide:

> The nation must address suicide as a significant health problem and put into place national strategies to prevent the loss of life and the suffering suicide causes. ... Suicide is now the third leading cause of death for young people between the ages of fifteen to twenty-four years old, exceeded only by homicide and accidents. It is the fourth leading cause of death among children ages ten to fourteen years old.

*Building a Bridge*

As parents we cannot turn our heads and say that it won't happen to our kid. Our children are hurting inside. Do you see that our children are begging for attention? Do you see that they have colored their hair a thousand shades and painted tattoos all over themselves in an effort to be noticed? They are crying out, "LOOK AT ME! LOOK AT ME!" When we don't, they go further.

Some of these situations may be self-expressive behavior. Some may be self-abusive. Hopefully you know your child well enough to make a determination, but if something has you puzzled, discuss it with your child from a curious point-of-view. If you approach your child by firing question after question with a demanding tone of voice, you will not get answers. If fact, all you will do is drive your child further from you.

Marian Wright Edelman, founder and president of the Children's Defense Fund writes, "Our "youth problem" is not a youth problem, it is an adult program, as our children do what they see us adults doing in our own lives. And they seek our attention in negative ways when we provide them too few positive ways to get the attention and love they need." Our children are looking for answers, guidance and adults to help. Our children need us. They need to know how special and precious and important they are. As the parent it is our foremost responsibility to tell them. We must focus on their value.

Can you rise from where you are sitting, right now, and take a photograph of your child into your hands? It does not matter how old of a photo it is – just get one. As you hold that picture in your hand, look directly into the eyes of your child. Can you see in those eyes the baby that you created? Can you look past the "problems" and see a soul that wants to be held and cooed to the way you did when he was born? Can you see the sweet little girl that twirled around in her party dress just as tickled as she could be when daddy told her how beautiful she was? The only thing that is different about your child today from the day he was born is the harsh experiences he has encountered. The neglect and abuse your son or daughter has suffered has taken a toll visible on the face – and you can see it in the smile – or lack thereof.

Now can you get up from where you are sitting, right now, and write a letter or a postcard or place a telephone call to your child? All

*Building a Bridge*

you have to say is that you love the child. Remind your child that he is important.

J. S. Salt has compiled a list of things kids want from their parents.

- Listen to me when I am talking.

- Be proud of me even if I didn't get all the answers correct.

- When I'm crying, say nice things.

- Treat me like you treat your customers.

- Give me things to look forward to.

- Please learn to respect my friends a little more, just as I respect yours.

- Let me get wet in the rain.

- Sometimes can you play with me instead of saying no?

- Take me somewhere special once in a while, by myself, without my sister.

- Say "It would help if you do it this way," instead of "You are doing it wrong."

- Don't spoil me and then later on yell at me for being spoiled.

- Never forget to kiss me good night.

**"If I could say just one thing to parents, it would be simply that a child needs someone who believes in him no matter what he does."**

Alice Keliher

*Building a Bridge*

## *Focus on Your Value and Your Child's Value*

Every person on this planet is valuable and important. We all have something valid to offer – regardless of who we are. We must stop focusing on our shortcomings and start focusing on our strengths. We must throw out the seeds of contribution and allow the universe to work its miracles. We cannot know what wonder will result from our smallest efforts. We must affirm that we are parents by Divine Order and we do have valuable input to contribute to our children's lives.

We must tell our children that they are not responsible for the divorce or outcome of custody. Stay focused on the children and encourage them to celebrate themselves. We do this by telling our children how wonderful they are. We need to applaud their successes – big and small. We need to tell them how grateful we are to have them as our child. We need to say this – often and abundantly – because they need to hear it.

Here is a list of things kids love to hear (in writing or verbally):

- I love you.

- I am glad you are in my life.

- You are a terrific kid.

- You did a great job on that assignment.

- I really admire the effort you put into your schoolwork.

- It is great that you help with your little brother.

- Thank you for helping me with the chores.

- Your letter really brightened my day.

- I like your friends.

- Have I told you lately how much I love you?

*Building a Bridge*

## Personal Reflections

Do you feel inferior to the other parent? Describe when you feel this way. (For example, at school conferences when the other parent knows all the teachers and friends and I do not know anyone.)

Do you feel inferior to other parents in general? Describe when you feel this way. (For example, all the time, during discussions about school or at church when other parents are fussing over their children.)

Make a list of what you have to offer your child – right now. (For example: love, encouragement, wisdom, child support.)

Do your children have the feeling or impression they are responsible for the divorce or hostility between the other parent and you?

Do your children use cigarettes? Alcohol? Drugs?

Do you know your children's friends? Fill out the chart below. Have your child help you, if necessary. Make a point of meeting those you do not know. Have you met the parents of the friends? Make a point to meet them as well. (Make a chart for each child, even if some of the friends are the same.)

| FRIEND/PHONE | MET? | PARENTS | MET? |
| --- | --- | --- | --- |
| Susie Brown 555-1212 | Yes | Jack and Jill Brown | Yes |
| Linda Green 555-4545 | Yes | ? | ? |

Have you ever thanked these people for being available for your children? Write a draft note of thanks.

*Building a Bridge*

> Dear Jack and Jill,
>
> I know that Jonathan spends a lot of time at your home. He tells me he really feels comfortable there and you are very good to him. I appreciate all you do because I want Jonathan to have caring adults in his life.
>
> Jonathan's dad, name

Have you noticed any self-abusive behaviors in your child? If you have suspicions about some behaviors, make note of those. (For example, never available to eat with family, has no interest in anything, tired all the time, has lots of symbolic tattoos, has money but you cannot determine how child has earned it.)

If you do suspect your child is involved with cigarettes, drugs, alcohol or others abusive behaviors, how can you address the issue without alienating your child? List some ways you might approach the subject. List some resources you might seek out for assistance. (United Way agency, minister, counselor or others.)

When was the last time you told your child how special he/she is? Write a paragraph about that time. If you cannot recall a time, write a letter to your child telling him/her how special he/she is. In your letter, share a fond remembrance you have of your child.

> Dear William,
>
> I was thinking about the time you and I went fishing at Taylor Lake. Remember how we got the line all snagged up and then snapped the pole trying to free it from the tree? We laughed so hard our sides hurt. Then we went to McDonald's for fish sandwiches and pretended we caught the fish! That was a great day together. You are a great kid. I love having you in my life.
>
> Dad

Draw a picture of your child.

What colors did you use? Dark ones? Light ones? Is your child smiling? Does your child look happy?

*Building a Bridge*

What causes you to think of your child? (Photographs around the house, a place, a song, a story, a program or movie, other children?)

Take a favorite love song and rewrite the lyrics so the song is from you to your child.

Tape a picture of your child(ren) to the inside flap of this book. It will be a powerful reminder of why you are reading this book and working through these exercises.

Read through the list of things kids want from their parents (page 129.) Do you give these gifts to your children?

Read through the list of things kids want to hear (page 130.) Do your children hear you say these things to them?

Affirm: I am on this Earth for very important work. I have valuable contributions to make. My life is worthwhile and I am worthy.

**Additional reading suggestions:**

*The Measure of Our Success: A Letter to My Children and Yours* by Marian Wright Edelman

*How To Raise Drug-Free Kids* available through the United States Department of Education, Washington, DC 20202-6123 or at www.ed.gov

*Laziness*

**Laziness is "disinclined to activity or exertion; not energetic or vigorous."**

Laziness is a habit that can rob us of precious opportunities. We lumber through days as if we are on a treadmill to no where. We don't plan ahead to participate in our children's lives. We miss their birthday by a few days and then are embarrassed to follow through with a gift or call. We don't order the airline tickets early enough. By the time we call, the fares are outside of our budget. Laziness

*Building a Bridge*

demonstrates a lack of ambition. Laziness can turn a day into a week and a week into a month and a month into a year and by then our child is so distant, we think that a relationship is not possible.

Ask yourself:

- Am I using laziness as an excuse not to connect with my child?

- What fears hide behind my laziness – Rejection? Commitment? Not wanting to face truth?

Have you seen the movie, "Fly Away Home?" When Amy moves into her dad's house, she asks him why she has not heard from him in many years. He says that he has been busy. She replies, "Lame excuse."

- Are you using laziness as a lame excuse for connecting with your child?

### Focus on Today – Get to Work!

We only have today. This talk about "someday I'll do this" or "someday I'll do that" must stop. We cannot know what our life span will be. We do not know how much time we have on this earth. Once a day and its potential have passed, it is gone. Do you ever look at the obituaries? Do you feel shock or disbelief when you read of a young person's death? We must claim TODAY – THIS DAY – and get to work!

**"Opportunities are usually disguised by hard work, so most people don't recognize them."**

**Ann Landers**

Long-distance parenting takes effort, energy and ambition. It takes planning ahead. Get out the calendar. Look ahead to when the next school break is or how long before the next birthday. But don't wait for "big" occasions to contact your child. Any day is a great day to celebrate the birth of our children. Create good habits for calling, writing, sending treat bags and planning for times together. Establish

*Building a Bridge*

communication routines as they keep us on track and help us to avoid laziness.

Whatever you do to connect with your children, do it consistently so they can count on you. Your consistency will build trust and strengthen your relationship. We demonstrate consistency in our daily life when we:

- Communicate with our children on a regular and consistent basis so they learn to trust us.

- Show our children that we are committed to them with a consistent effort for communication.

- Do what we say we will do. Make our word our bond.

- Ask yourself, "What is more important than my child?"

If you must break a promise, your child should be the first to know. Inform him as soon as possible. Discuss the matter. Reschedule, but do so with conviction. Do not make an empty promise.

Residential parents, too, experience laziness. They miss sending information about school or doctor/dental check-ups. While sometimes these are done deliberately to keep the long-distance parent out of touch, it can also be a result of laziness. It can be a result of too much to do. When a residential parent has full hands, something is bound to get dropped.

When this happens, don't you be lazy! It is our responsibility to get the school event list or calendar, regularly communicate with the school principal and teachers, plan trips to attend important events, and get the sports schedules and talk to the coaches. Write, call, email – do whatever it takes to get the information you need and want.

Take your calendar and mark it for the next year. (Having a master calendar is important. Having a calendar for work and another for home is plan for disaster. Keep everything together so you can see how it all fits together.) List birthdays, school schedules, important

*Building a Bridge*

events, holidays, your time with the children, and so on. If you don't have this information available, get it.

*****

### Personal Reflections

Do you have a regular time selected for calling your child? Does this time work for both of you? When you call, do you ask if it is a good time to talk?

Do you send mail (letters, cards, treats) regularly?

Determine when you will see your child. Start gathering the necessary information for the reunion. Do you need travel arrangements? Evaluate your needs. Make a list of them and get as much information as possible so you can make the best decisions at affordable prices. (See Travel, Chapter 8)

Are you being lazy or is something else keeping you from connecting with your children? If you are using laziness as an excuse for something else, write a letter to yourself. In the letter express the hurts, fears and feelings that are keeping you from your child.

> Dear Me, I don't call you because I feel like a failure. Your life seems together and mine does not. I love you but feel like my love is not enough. When I call you to say, "I love you" I feel stupid. I think you will say, "That's all – you just love me? Nothing else?" Then I will feel worse than now – if that is possible.

Affirm: I have lots of energy for my life and for loving my children. I am a good manager of my time and therefore, always have time to accomplish my goals.

**Additional reading suggestions:**

*First Things First: To Live, to Love, to Learn, to Leave a Legacy* by Stephen R. Covey and A. Roger Merrill

*The Complete Idiot's Guide to Overcoming Procrastination* by Michelle Tullier

*Building a Bridge*

*Living Without Procrastination: How to Stop Postponing Your Life* by M. Susan Roberts

### Loneliness

**Loneliness is "a state of feeling sad or dejected as a result of lack of companionship or separation from others."**

Oftentimes parents use their children as their companions, relying on them for conversation, friendship and support. While we all want meaningful communication and relationships with our children, looking to them to fill voids in our lives is not healthy. In fact, it indicates dependency, making the child co-dependent. This dependent behavior can often go undetected until the separation of parent and child. Separation from our children forces us to look at the difference between 1) being a complete person alone or 2) living through our children, which is exhausting for the child.

The most important quality to develop in ourself is the joy of our own company. Being alone is not a punishment to be avoided. It is a wonderful opportunity to get to know yourself better. Learn to embrace the quiet times you have. Don't zone out in front of a television set. Become childlike by being open to learning, being amazed by life. Investigate life's mysteries without reasons (fatigue, worry, money, time) not to. Laugh, play, enjoy your food or don't eat it. Celebrate the pleasure of your own company!

When the children are away from home – whether at the other parent's home or elsewhere – use the time to focus on other children at home. If you do not have other children at home, focus on your significant other or spouse. This does not mean that you don't miss the children. It simply offers you an opportunity to direct some of your time and energy to other relationships that also need attention.

### Reach Out to Others – Celebrate Your Connectedness

Feeling loneliness indicates that we are not recognizing or appreciating our connectedness to everyone and everything on this planet. Rather than engaging in self-absorbed behavior, reach out to

*Building a Bridge*

others. Remember that someone else's long-distance is our "right next door." While your children may be too far away for you to spend time with them this afternoon, there is someone down the street or around the corner who could use your love and compassion. The energy we send out flows through the universe. Dr. Wayne Dyer reminds us that the meaning of universe is: uni, one and verse, song. Let us all join the in the melody and harmony of life.

> "We cannot live for ourselves alone.
> Our lives are connected by a thousand invisible threads,
> and along these sympathetic fibers,
> our actions run as causes and return to us as results.
>
> **Herman Melville**

Here are some ways we can connect:

- Introduce yourself to your neighbors.

- Find a church that gives you a sense of family – attend regularly and participate in the activities.

- Attend the local school sporting events and theatrical productions. School teams and drama clubs always need fans.

- Order magazine subscriptions (or wrapping paper or candy or whatever) from students working toward a better school.

- Volunteer to teach the Sunday school or youth group class.

- Volunteer at the local school. PTA groups are ALWAYS in need of workers!

- Volunteer at the library. Sign up to teach someone to read.

- Sponsor a child through the Big Brothers/Big Sisters program or Boys and Girls Club.

*Building a Bridge*

- Volunteer for Girl Scouts or Boy Scouts.

- Volunteer at a hospital or nursing home.

- Call the local volunteer center through the United Way – they have many other suggestions they can share with you!

**Note:** Because there are people in this world that have not behaved well, you should be prepared for a personal interview or investigation prior to your participation in organized programs.

Whatever positive energy we send out into the world will come back into our lives. It will also flow into the lives of our children. Any time spent helping others keeps us connected with all of life and is time well spent. When we love any child, we send out love to every child. Reach out to those children within your arm's reach and show them the support and encouragement that you want for your own children.

While there are times when we miss our children, there are also times they miss us. Children often struggle with these occasions. If you share a telephone call during this time, talk with your child patiently. Don't rush the call. Ask them if you could send anything to help ... a photograph or something homemade (perhaps a batch of their favorite cookies) or a second copy of a book that you could read at the same time and talk about later. Don't underestimate the power of real listening – it is a great comfort. Be honest about missing them and what you do to work through those times. Spend time writing your child a follow-up letter. Also, write in your journal and acknowledge your own feelings.

### *Listening Skills*

When you talk with your child, be sure to really listen and hear what they say. Authors Elizabeth Hickey and Elizabeth Dalton offer these tips in their book, *Healing Hearts: Helping Children and Adults Recover From Divorce*:

*Building a Bridge*

- Pay attention. Notice when your child needs to talk. Take time to give one hundred percent attention to your child.

- Make eye contact with your child when you ask questions.

- Use reflective listening skills. Acknowledge the child's statement by repeating what you believe he said. Say: "It sounds as if you are worried about trying out for the team because you think you might not make it."

- Be specific when you ask questions. Ask: "How do you think you did on your spelling test today?" "Did it help to do all the practice tests last night?"

- Don't forget to give physical affection when the child needs comforting. Children of all ages need affection. Young children like to cuddle in the parent's lap, while older children appreciate a pat on the back or a hug.

- Schedule one-on-one time with each child as often as you can. This can even be time to do chores together. The point is that you are spending time with the child to listen to his concerns, his interests, and his joys.

When you are listening to your children, pay particular attention to her words that describe her feelings, frustrations, worries or other problems. Our children often give us more information than we realize. If he uses words that cause you to suspect he is more concerned than he is elaborating, compassionately request that he share more with you on that topic.

When we respond to our children, we must be thoughtful in our word choices and tone. Consider the following examples:

- Poor choice: "Poor baby."

- Good choice: "I hear what you are saying."

- Poor choice: "Your dad should not have done (or said that.)

*Building a Bridge*

- Good choice: "I know you are frustrated. What would you like to tell your dad about this experience?"

- Poor choice: "Your mother is so selfish."

- Good choice: "We cannot always know why people make the choices they do. Sometimes all we can do for others is be compassionate." Or "We can also learn how to conduct ourselves by observing what behaviors we don't like in others. What can we learn from this experience?"

In Adele Faber and Elaine Mazlish's book, *How To Talk So Kids Will Listen & Listen So Kids Will Talk*, they note the ten different methods adults use in communicating with their children. I have expressed each of the ten aspects with dialogue we might have used ourselves or encountered during conversations. As you review each, take a moment to feel how each might relate to you. Review the list a second time to consider how these comments might affect your children?

1. Blaming and Accusing

    "What's the matter with you anyway?"

    "How many times do I have to tell you ...?"

2. Name-calling

    "You have to be a slob to keep such a messy room."

    "Look at the way you eat. You're disgusting."

3. Threats

    "You had better .... or else ..."

    "If you don't ... by the time I count to three ..."

4. Commands

    "You had better do as you are told – right this minute!"

*Building a Bridge*

"You must" or "You will" or "You have to"

5. Lecturing and Moralizing

   "It is your responsibility to …."

   "Do you realize …"

6. Warnings

   "Watch out!" or "Be careful!"

   "Don't do that, you'll hurt yourself."

7. Martyrdom Statement

   "Don't do that again or you'll give me a heart attack!"

   "I have gray hair because of you. You will put me into an early grave."

8. Comparisons

   "Why can't you be more like your brother?"

   "Other kids your age know how to …., what's wrong with you?"

9. Sarcasm

   "Wow, that was a brilliant move. You are really the smart one, aren't you?"

   "Oh, yea. That outfit really looks great. You should get lots of compliments – I mean comments – on this look."

10. Prophecy

    "All you ever do is complain. You just can't find anything good to say about this family, can you?"

    "You will never amount to anything – you're just like your …."

*Building a Bridge*

### "The first duty of love is to listen."

### Paul Tillich

On the subject of communication, I also want to note a common practice used in dialogue exchange – the practice of slurring words or shortening phrases of speech. For example:

- 'jeat? translated fully means "did you eat?"

- 'jou? translated fully means "did you?"

- 'snough translated fully means "that is enough."

If we hear these phrases frequently, we generally understand what is being communicated to us. However, when we aren't familiar with them, they can cause real misunderstandings. This happens with our children as well. Trendy expressions or slang words that are popular with young people mean nothing or very different things to "old fogy" parents. When communicating with one another, if you don't understand what is being said, ask for clarification. Otherwise you will not know what each other is saying and miss important messages.

Allow your child to share his feelings with you without being grilled for information. Sometimes the children will want to discuss a problem from their other home. While we want to have information to work with in helping them sort situations out, we should not abuse the children using them as spies to report on the dealings of the other parent. Keep in mind that what the child is saying is a child's perception of the problem and may not be a true picture of the situation.

As parents, it is our responsibility to teach our children how to handle problems in a responsible manner. We must tell our children that problems are a normal part of life. They need to understand that problems will not just go away. We don't outgrow problems, and though many try, we cannot buy them away. The only solution to problems is to solve them.

*Building a Bridge*

## *Problem Solving*

Eleanor Reynolds, author of *Guiding Young Children: A Child Centered Approach*, offers these suggestions for teaching children problem solving techniques:

1. Encourage your child to talk about his problems when he is ready.

2. If your child is pre-verbal, guess at what she is trying to tell you and keep trying until you find the answer.

3. Bend down and make eye contact; keep your voice and facial expressions warm and accepting.

4. Reflect what you think he is saying, using such phrases as, "I hear you saying…."

5. Give names to your child's feelings. Learning a variety of feeling words will help your child tell you how she feels.

6. If identifying your child's feelings is not enough to solve the problem, proceed to the next step.

7. Trust your child to find his own solutions. Ask questions such as, "What's your idea?" and "How can you solve the problem?"

8. Be patient. Give your child plenty of time, and offer ideas if you are sure she needs help.

Once you have worked through a problem solving conversation, ask your child, "Do you feel better now that you have talked about this?" This will help you determine if your child needed to vent frustration or really solve a problem.

These eight steps in problem solving can be used in any conflict situation. Problem solving is an extremely valuable tool to teach your children and will benefit them in all their personal interactions and life circumstances.

Other resources for teaching your child problem solving skills are available through:

*Building a Bridge*

- *Raising a Thinking Child* by Myrna B. Shure, Ph.D.

- *Raising a Thinking Pre-Teen* by Myrna B. Shure, Ph.D.

- *What Do You Stand For?* by Barbara Lewis

- *81 Fresh & Fun Critical Thinking Activities: Engaging Activities & Reproducibles to Develop Kids' Higher-level Thinking Skills* by Laurie Rozakis

From my own experience with my children and problem solving, I have learned that there are no bad ideas in brainstorming. I am excited about staying open to all ideas as the most outrageous suggestion often turns out be a marvelous solution – once refined.

Occasionally after we have gone through the problem solving steps, the only solution we can find is to "agree to disagree." People often find they have differences of opinion. In those cases we need to learn to respect each other's choices.

Sometimes problem solving at home is not enough to help your child through his difficulty. If your child needs counseling, get it. You should not feel any shame or embarrassment in needing to talk to a professional about life's problems. Counselors can help children to handle the problems that they face in being from a divorced or blended family. If your child is hurting, do not brush her pain under the rug and think that she will work it out. Get help for her and show her through your actions that you are concerned and do not want her to hurt.

### *Holidays*

Our loneliness can often lay silent until the holidays. Like a sleeping dragon within us, we slumber through loneliness until the holidays aggravate us and we rise up and spit fire. When this happens, the holidays are literally burned. Who wants to partake of a burnt holiday? No one! It has lost its appeal, flavor and nutritional value.

We need to get our thinking cleared on holidays and avoid "holiday hell."

*Building a Bridge*

First of all, December 25$^{th}$ is a date. We must understand that holidays can be celebrated on any day you can be with your child. This goes for birthdays and other life celebrations as well.

Holidays are crazy enough without adding the logistic nightmares of who the children will be with, on what days, for how long, and other scheduling problems. Consider the following tips:

- Refer to the decree to confirm your allotted time.

- Coordinate with the other parent in accordance with the decree. Do this PRIOR to making travel arrangements or other plans. If your relationship is under a great deal of strain, you might write a note confirming the dates allotted to you.

- Preplan schedules for parties or family get-togethers. Almost any arrangements can be satisfactory if the days/times are set early enough for plans to be made.

- Don't overwhelm the children with lots of parties with friends, neighbors, or others unless these are people that the children know and want to see.

- Do not attempt to please everyone on the planet. You cannot do it. While you and your children will have many family members and friends you want to see, trying to visit with everyone you know in a few days is a recipe for disaster. It will cause resentment and frustration and create negative memories. Ask your family members to assist you by planning reunions. Suggest to your friends that you all take your children to a favorite pizza/arcade restaurant for dinner. If there are some who cannot attend these prearranged get-togethers, send them your love. Do not be caught up in guilt.

- Don't over gift the children because you miss them.

- Discuss plans with the children and make sure they are as excited about the arrangements as you are. It is a bummer when you put lots of energy into arrangements only to find out the kids were not the least bit interested in them.

*Building a Bridge*

- Don't get caught up in whiney dialogue about missing the children at the Midnight Mass or Sunrise Service or at Aunt Nelly's annual Christmas Eve buffet. Enjoy them when you have them.

- Do not save big news for the holidays. For example, you and your new wife are having a baby, you are going to marry Susie-Q whom they met five minutes ago, or you are moving to another town in two weeks.

If you do not have the children for a particular holiday, create a beautiful occasion for yourself. Think about this holiday and what it really means to you (rather than swallowing what we have been fed through commercialism to think it means.) Once you have evaluated this holiday for yourself, decide what plan of action fits your heart.

- Plan your own holiday celebration. Invite neighbors, co-workers, or others for a potluck holiday meal. This does not have to be fancy or elaborate. Many people are looking for a place to enjoy the holidays. Be the catalyst that brings these folks together.

- Find out what charity organizations need volunteers for serving the elderly or homeless.

- Visit a nursing home. Pass out flowers or a small gift to the residents as you extend holiday greetings to them. (Be sure to get the OK from the nursing home administrator before passing out any gifts.)

*****

Personal Reflections

Are you dependent on your child? Do you look to your child to be your best friend?

Do you avoid opportunities to be by yourself?

List those activities you do when alone. (For example: read, journal, or garden.)

*Building a Bridge*

Do you like yourself? List the qualities you like about yourself. (For example, hardworking, fun to be with, good sense of humor, intelligent, compassionate.)

How do you redirect your "kid energy" when you are not with your own children? (For example: play ball with neighbor kids, volunteer at youth center, or another way.)

When your child misses you, how do you help him/her? (For example: call and listen, write, send a care package.)

When you miss your child, how do you help yourself? (For example: journal, work on a scrapbook, look at pictures of your child.)

Are you a good listener? Sharpen your skills with these two exercises:

- Ask a friend to share a story with you. Listen for words expressing how your friend feels. When your friend is done sharing the story, say those feeling words to him/her. Ask if you heard the story correctly.

- The next time you are in an unfamiliar area, ask for directions to your destination. Repeat them for accuracy.

Think about how you view problems. Are they "out to get you" or here to help you learn something? List your methods for problem solving.

Do you put emphasis on the actual day of a holiday (December 25) or do you celebrate the spirit of the season? Write your thoughts regarding holidays.

Write a paragraph about your favorite holiday memory. (For example: your child's first Christmas or the third Christmas when your child discovered presents under the tree or an Easter egg hunt.)

List the holidays you share with your children.

Write a paragraph describing an ideal holiday with your child.

What do you do for holidays when you do not have your children with you? (For example: plan a group get together at your home, volunteer to help others who are alone.)

*Building a Bridge*

Affirm: I am an integral part of the human race. While I might be alone at times, I never need to feel lonely.

**Additional reading suggestions:**

*No More Holiday Blues* by Wayne W. Dyer

*Heaven on Earth: 15-minute Miracles to Change the World* by Danny Seo and Marian Wright Edelman

### *Regret*

**Regret is "to mourn the loss or death of; to miss very much; to be very sorry for; an expression of distressing emotion (as sorrow or disappointment.)"**

Why me? Why this? Why? We mourn the loss of our children as if we have lost them forever. Of course, we miss them very much. Of course, we are sad to be away from them. We could spend an entire lifetime outlining scenarios on what might have or could have happened if this or that or something else. We must not spin our wheels on those things that are in the past, but confront the question of why. Do not confront the question of why on the mental plane of, "Why didn't the courts support me?" or "Why didn't the attorney do this or that?" We need to confront the question of why in our hearts and souls. We must consider the possibilities of what this situation can teach us. If you do not thoughtfully and prayerfully do this, you will continue to re-live the painful experience repeatedly until you understand the lesson you need to learn.

In *Conversations with God*, Neale Donald Walsch writes:

Your world would not be in its present condition were you to have simply listened to your experience. The result of your not listening to your experience is that you keep re-living it, over and over, again. For my purpose will not be thwarted, nor My will ignored. You will get the message. Sooner or later.

*Building a Bridge*

I will not force you to, however. I will never coerce you. For I have given you a free will – the power to do as you choose – and I will never take that away from you, ever.

And so I will continue sending you the same messages over and over again, throughout the millennia and to whatever corner of the universe you occupy. Endlessly will I send you My messages, until you have received them and held them close, calling them your own.

Let's say that we take a careful and critical look at the situations in our lives. During this observation we see a pattern in our behavior or experiences. Now that we acknowledge it, what do we do with it?

Practice forgiveness.

## *Forgiveness*

WHAT?! You must be wondering what forgiveness would have to do with your life lessons. After all, isn't forgiveness an act of generous spirit that we bestow on others when they have wronged us? Isn't forgiveness our effort to forget the hurtful behavior of others? Forgiveness has been a very confusing concept for me because I always had this feeling that when I forgave someone, they felt they were off the hook – like they had been given a pardon from accountability. Since this was confusing to me and stayed in my mind, I had difficulty with forgiving and forgetting. Forgiveness must be more than what we do for the other guy.

Let's take our eyes off "the other guy" for a moment and look at forgiveness with ourselves in mind. When we keep repeating an experience in life, we do so because we keep thinking about the situation in the same way, therefore, we behave towards it in the same way as well. In order to learn from the experience (and thereby stop the need for the lesson) we must change our thinking about the experience. We become the responsible party rather than "the other guy." Can you see that forgiveness is changing our thinking about situations, which opens us to learning?

The act of NOT forgiving ties us to these three elements:

*Building a Bridge*

1. Our judgment of what is right and wrong. Our judgment does not mean that the situation was right or wrong – it means that we have an opinion about it. In not forgiving, we attach ourselves to that opinion, even when it harms us. Is your opinion that important, or is your pride at stake?

2. Our past behavior. Why do we hold ourselves to the past? Our goal for each new day should be to grow beyond yesterday. Can you say to yourself, "Today I know myself better than I knew myself yesterday?" Binding myself to the past keeps me from growing. Life is growth. Growth is change. Forgiveness allows growth. No forgiveness – no change – no growth – no life?

3. The past behavior of others. Are you holding grudges? If you want to grow, how can you deny another person the same right? Do you expect others to be completely perfect?

So what are the answers to these questions? What are the steps we must take to understanding?

1. We must get to the root of what is happening.

In his book, *Radical Forgiveness*, author Colin Tipping writes,

*Building a Bridge*

"Seen from a spiritual standpoint, our pain and discomfort in any given situation provides a signal that we are out of alignment with spiritual law and are being given an opportunity to heal something. This may be some original pain or perhaps a toxic belief that stops us from becoming our true selves. We don't often see it from this perspective, however. Rather, we judge the situation and blame others for what is happening, which prevents us from seeing the message or understanding the lesson. This prevents us from healing. If we don't heal whatever needs to be healed, we must create more discomfort until we are literally forced to ask, "What is going on here?" Sometimes the message has to become very loud, or the pain extremely intense, before we pay attention. A life threatening illness, for example, provides a loud message. Yet, even when facing death some people don't get the connection between what is happening in their lives and the opportunity for healing that it provides.

We always create our reality according to our beliefs. If you want to know what your beliefs are, look at what you have in your life. Life always reflects our beliefs. ... We're not taught to look at what is going on in our lives and to say, "Look what I have created in my life? Isn't that interesting? Instead, we are taught to judge, lay blame, accuse, play victim and seek revenge."

2. Choose to heal or not.

Colin continues his steps in the healing process by teaching that once we have acknowledged what we are bringing into our lives through our belief system, we need to make a conscious choice for healing. If we do not choose healing, we will experience another learning opportunity in our lives. Much like a required course in school, we don't get the degree unless we pass the core classes.

Whether we take the class once or ten times is up to us, but why take a class ten times?

3. Choosing to heal means choosing to forgive.

*Building a Bridge*

Choosing forgiveness means "to radically shift our perception of the world and our interpretations of what happens to us in our lives so we can stop being a victim." Colin continues by stating, "Radical forgiveness takes the position that there is nothing to forgive."

Do you remember when I wrote the "humorous" thank you letter to the children's father? Do you remember that after I wrote it, I experienced the overwhelming sense of appreciation and gratitude? That was my shift in perception; a change in my thinking. I moved from blaming him and being a victim to thanking him and being a victor. I experienced radical forgiveness!

We need to make a serious evaluation of our lives, paying close attention to those experiences we regret, but repeat. Sitting in a dark room and mourning the day-to-day loss of our children serves no one. We do not benefit. Our children do not benefit. Our only accomplishment is assurance that we will once again live an experience that will offer us this same learning opportunity. So look deeply into your life and find the goody…the silver lining. When we begin to exercise radical forgiveness, we will stop being sad and mournful – we will be free to live joyfully.

**"You can be as happy – or as miserable – as you decide to be."**

**Ben Dichter**

We will also experience soul satisfaction. Can you close your eyes and recall that wonderful feeling of physical satisfaction you experienced after partaking of a delicious meal? We can enjoy that same nourished feeling in our souls. Dr. Wayne Dyer tells a beautiful and powerful story that can be used to illustrate forgiveness and how spiritually satisfying it is.

*Building a Bridge*

…The man who was given a tour of heaven and hell. This wonderful guide was taking him through and showing him heaven and hell. First, they went to hell and he saw this large kettle of soup. The only utensils were just a series of very large spoons. However, the handles were all longer than the arms of the people making it impossible to feed themselves. Everyone was in various stages of starvation since they couldn't bend their arms. And here was the scene, a large kettle of soup, these large spoons and all these people unable to bend their arms – and all starving. This was hell. Then he said, "Let me show you heaven." So he took him to heaven and the man saw the same identical scene. All these stiff-armed people with these large handles on these long spoons with a large kettle of simmering soup in the center of the room. But in heaven people were all healthy and smiling and they were obviously all well fed. When the man inquired about this, he was told by the guide, "Oh, in heaven the people have learned to feed each other."

We too must learn to feed each other. We must understand that we are all connected and our Divine Purpose is to feed and nourish each other. Can you see how forgiveness nourishes both the soul of the giver and the soul of the receiver?

**"Without memory, there is no healing. Without forgiveness, there is no future."**

**Archbishop Desmond Tutu**

*****

Personal Reflections

Look at your long-distance situation as a movie. Put yourself on the screen. Watch your parenting story. Observe each person involved

*Building a Bridge*

and decide how you would instruct each one for the best outcome of all. What would you say to the ...

Father? (For example: be more considerate, plan more times together, stop bad mouthing the mother.)

Mother? (For example: be less angry, don't influence the child, stop thinking that you can be everything in your child's life.)

Children? (For example: don't be afraid to speak your heart, don't manipulate your parents, try to get along with your stepparents.)

Do you have a pattern in your behavior? Do you always play the bad guy, the abuser, the disciplinarian, the victim, the rescuer or the peacemaker?

What are your thoughts about forgiveness?

How do you demonstrate forgiveness in your daily life?

Is there anything you need to forgive yourself about? List any/all of those things. (For example, old relationship issues, handling of the divorce, refusing counseling when it was available.)

What did you think of Colin Tipping's approach to forgiveness? Did you immediately reject it? Did you contemplate his ideas? Did you consider how you could use his ideas to help yourself?

What negative experiences in your life have you been repeating? (For example: troubled relationships, dissatisfaction with career choices, no long-term friendships, or encounters with the law.)

What positive experiences in your life have you been repeating? (For example: strong friendships, satisfaction with career and career growth, peaceful living, abundance both spiritually and materialistically.)

List the ways in which you feed or support and encourage those around you. (For example: being a good listener, offering a helping hand, donating time or resources, offering sound advice or creative ideas or by praying for others.)

*Building a Bridge*

Affirm: I forgive by changing my view of situations from one of burden to one of blessing. I am grateful to those individuals and situations that have offered me the opportunity to grow and love myself more fully.

**Additional reading suggestions:**

*Real Magic* by Dr. Wayne Dyer

(The story of heaven and hell was taken from the cassette program of *Real Magic* available through Nightengale-Conant. Tape 5: Taking the First Steps to Miracle Making.)

### Resentment

**Resentment is "a feeling of indignant displeasure or persistent ill will at something regarded as a wrong, insult, or injury."**

If the children are not living with you, you probably think some huge cosmic error has been committed. Not only do you consider that you have been wronged, but so have the children. You may even feel that your quality of parenting has been insulted, and as a result you suffer a grave emotional injury.

If this is the case, you are still stuck in the rut of thinking that things should be a different way – your way!

Evaluate your resentment.

- Is it based in fear?

- Old thinking?

- An isolated situation?

- Assumptions?

- Some or all of these?

*Building a Bridge*

The truth is that everything in this world happens in Divine Order. Whether we choose to look at the experiences of our life as negatives and wrong-doings or as positives and opportunities is our free will. We cannot know the universal purpose for all happenings and experiences. We must accept what each day offers us as it unfolds. We must embrace every experience as tailored specifically to meet our spiritual growth needs.

### Practice Letting Go

Letting go of our opinions about the way things should be is called surrender. As soon as we hear the word "surrender," we shut down because we associate surrender with defeat. Military movies portray the side who surrenders is a loser.

Spiritual surrender is a very different action. Surrendering to God is yielding our free will to His guidance and handling of the matter. We think it is a risk to trust God, but the real risk occurs when we do not surrender to His guidance. In Marianne Williamson's book, *A Return to Love*, she writes, "The truth is, of course, that the more important it is to us, the more important it is to surrender. That which is surrendered is taken care of best. To place something in the hands of God is to give it over, mentally, to the protection and care of the beneficence of the universe."

I used surrender. It was a painful decision to stop the legal proceedings, but not nearly as painful as continuing them would have been. I say the decision was painful because at the time I could not see how I could possible maintain a quality relationship with my children. I was also concerned about the relationship my parents and extended family would have with the children. Since we cannot see tomorrow, we are asked to walk by faith. When I surrendered, I felt the protection and care Marianne writes about.

How can we demonstrate surrender in our daily lives?

- Obeying the laws.

- Living with an attitude of cooperation.

- Respecting other's rights to grow and learn in their own time.

*Building a Bridge*

- Practicing patience.

When we open ourselves to guidance, we are given guidance. It can come from a sense of knowing, a thought that pops into your head, a book that lands in your hand, someone that comments out of the blue, or any other of a zillion ways God has to communicate with us. I felt this guidance also. Each day presented me with new ways to connect to the kids, sort through my "stuff," and create a healthy life.

This ancient Japanese fable, passed along to me by a friend, is just such guidance. Rich in wisdom, the story calls us to let go of those we love – to release them so they can live their own life.

### "Holding With An Open Hand"

From An Ancient Japanese Fable

Once upon a time, a boy found a sparrow with a broken wing in the woods outside his home. He took the bird inside, made a cage for it out of sticks, and patiently nursed it back to health. It wasn't long before he came to love the little creature and began to think of it as "his."

Within a month or so the bird's wing had healed. Soon, it began to try to escape from its cage, flapping its wings and hurling itself against the bars. Seeing this, the boy's father said, "Son, you have to let her go. She is a wild thing, and could never by happy in a cage. If you keep her, she will only hurt herself, and may try to hurt you as well."

They carried the cage outside, and the boy gently lifted out the sparrow. Sensing freedom, the bird spread its wings and tried to fly. Reflexively, the boy closed his hand, suddenly afraid of losing his pet forever. The bird squawked and flapped.

"My son," said the father softly, "open your hand. I know that you love her, but see how she struggles. In a moment her fragile wings may break. If you squeeze her tightly enough to prevent her escape, you will hurt her, perhaps kill her."

"But if I open my hand, she'll fly away!" cried the boy.

"It may be so," answered the father. "On the other hand, if she flies, someday she may return. If your fear of losing her causes you to cripple or kill her, you'll lose her for sure.

*Building a Bridge*

The only way one can ever hold something wild and free is with an open hand."

### Legal System

Before I elaborate on my opinions of the legal system, I acknowledge that many divorced parents return to court for a variety of legitimate reasons. If you are in a hostile parenting situation and are still seeking legal counsel, I recommend you read the following books before you proceed.

- *Win Your Child Custody War* by Charlotte Hardwick

This book is highly acclaimed by attorneys, mediators, counselors and parents. It offers a vast wealth of information as well as wisdom earned through experience.

- *Healing Hearts: Helping Children and Adults Recover from Divorce* by Elizabeth Hickey, M.S.W. and Elizabeth Dalton, J.D.

Elizabeth Hickey is a family counselor and mediator and Elizabeth Dalton is an attorney and mediator. Their book offers valuable professional advice as well as personal insight from their own divorces and custody arrangements.

- *Putting Kids First* by Michael Oddenino

Michael Oddenino is a family law attorney as well as the attorney for the Children's Rights Council. His words are genuine, caring, and provide wise counsel. He understands parents' needs while protecting children's interests.

*Building a Bridge*

You do not have to look very far to see that our legal system is overwhelmed with family dispute cases. Is it possible for our judicial system to carefully look at every case? Is it right to ask them to? To the courts, if both households provide the necessary elements for growth (shelter, food, clothing, schooling), why should they spend more time on the case? In the system's opinion, the children must live somewhere – with the mother or the father. If families live in close enough proximity to one another, sometimes the children have the freedom to move between homes. However, in the case of long-distance parenting, a clear residential decision must be made.

If the physical needs of the children can be met by both parents, then shouldn't the courts look at the emotional and spiritual opportunities for the children as determiners for quality parenting? I don't know if it is conceivable that our system is really capable of handling such a job. I don't know if it is qualified for such a task. The courts have assigned counselors to evaluate families, which has done a good service to many children. What if the psychologist involved does not see a clear difference in the maturity of the parents?

It is the personal responsibility of the parents to rise to the highest level of parenting. Whether the children live with you or not, no one can keep you from providing the children with the emotional and spiritual example they need. Since these qualities exist above the physical realm, we cannot be blocked in our efforts.

- Be an example.

- Pray, meditate, visualize.

Demonstrate responsible behavior in your life by:

- Following the custody decree.

- Being a participating co-parent.

- Acting like an adult.

Our legal system is an easy target to blame, but I had to seriously evaluate my contribution, or lack thereof, to the creation of this system. I had to ask myself some questions:

*Building a Bridge*

- When I vote, do I really know the candidate I am voting for?

- Have I attended debates and asked the candidates questions about family law practices?

- Have I read the campaign literature? Do I know this candidate's biography and career history?

- Do I exercise my voting right every time I have the opportunity to do so?

The very foundation of our country was designed to give the voters the right to express their voice in government. Along with this privilege, we have a responsibility as citizens of the United States to know who our candidates are and what they intend to do if elected to office. If we surrender or neglect to fulfill that responsibility, what right can we possibly have to complain?

We must start paying attention to the candidates. We must attend their speaking engagements, listen to their agendas, and ask questions. We must follow them when they get elected and make them accountable for keeping their campaign promises.

While I have personally felt disappointment in our legal system, I must also confess that I have on many occasions gone to the polls to vote and not had a clue who the judicial candidates were or what their stands were on any subject, let alone family law. I now understand how critical it is to express my opinion through my vote. I am not suggesting that we all become political warriors. I am suggesting we all become responsible citizens and informed voters.

If you do not have a voter's registration card and wish to exercise your voting rights, contact the Voter's Registrar Office in your area

*Building a Bridge*

If you feel that your participation in committees or political study groups can work to make better known the needs of long-distance parents, then join and offer valid ideas for dealing with the matters of our children. In the meantime, pay your child support, work at home, at school, at church, and in your neighborhoods to promote positive environments for our children. We cannot expect government to do the jobs we are called to do. As parents we must fulfill our obligations to provide for our own.

In America lawsuits have become a sport. We get involved in these dramas because we cannot communicate and cooperate. When the legal system works effectively, it evaluates the entire family situation and assists in mediating our disputes. When we abuse the system by using it to defend our own personal agendas, no one is served. If we insist on using the legal system to exercise our rights, we will prolong doing right. Our hope lies in the changes in us – not those mandated by a court. Genuine change comes from the soul – not the bench.

Are you bound by a legal agreement or mandate that you feel is unjust or unfair? Have you considered why? Does your life evidence that the document is accurate in what it says? If you feel that the court order is absolutely inaccurate, are you willing to use it as a catalyst to promote change – for yourself and other parents?

We need to embrace "The Serenity Prayer."

> God grant me the serenity
> to accept the things I cannot change,
> the courage to change the things I can,
> and the wisdom to know the difference.

### *Money*

Putting the topic of money under the "Practice of Letting Go" section is no accident. I intentionally placed it here because second to our attachment to our children is our attachment to our money.

We face the issue of money at first base in a divorce, as there is child support to consider. Before a divorce is official, child support is often ordered. In our anger toward the other parent, we rarely consider that the money is used for the children's well being, but instead see the check with the other parent's name on it, and resentment wells up in us. If you have an agreement to pay child support – pay it. Your financial contribution to the residential parent provides shelter, food and clothing to your children. This is the very least we can do for our sons and daughters.

Sometimes the residential parent sees the long-distance parent enjoying success in work/business and figures she can get more bucks, so goes to court and gets some. Often the long-distance parent will intentionally keep himself poor to protect himself from this very abuse. Are you holding yourself back to get even with the other parent? How smart is this? I encourage you to look at the bigger picture. If you pay twenty-five percent to child support, can you see that you are keeping seventy-five percent? Can you see that when you grow professionally, you give yourself the opportunity to also mature personally? If you are feeling resentment when paying your child support or when you need to send money to the other parent, try emotionally distancing yourself from the situation.

- Have the child support taken directly from your paycheck so you can concentrate on the funds going directly into an account that will care for your child's financial needs.

- Write checks directly to the school, doctor, dentist or elsewhere.

- Take your child on a shopping trip yourself so you can assist in the purchase decisions.

- Have you really considered how much money it takes to care for your child?

Make a list of expenses that apply to your children. Beyond their need for a food and shelter, consider the many additional expenses associated with raising a child.

*Building a Bridge*

| ITEM | $ |
|---|---|
| Clothing, shoes, seasonal wear and accessories for a growing child. | |
| School expenses: tuition, books, supplies, lunches, projects (such as science), activities, clubs, sports, photographs, field trips, or events (such as dances or plays). | |
| Dental examinations and/or orthodontic costs. | |
| Eye care examination, glasses or contacts. | |
| Counseling or therapy. | |
| Personal grooming (hair cuts). | |
| Day care expenses – include any additional costs for summer care. | |
| Lesson expenses such as lessons for musical study, sports, dance, and so forth. | |
| Birthday party costs, holiday expenses, social life expenses | |
| Entertainment such as movies or outings. | |
| Allowances | |
| Special needs | |
| Savings for future expenses such as a car, the insurance for the car, college or trade school expenses | |

- When you have finished making the list, evaluate the expenses of caring for your child(ren) to see if your child support is really meeting the needs of growing children.

*Building a Bridge*

If you feel there is a surplus, discuss with the other parent what possible expenses you may have overlooked. If there truly are extra monies, discuss how these funds might be invested for future expenses such as college tuition or an automobile. If there is a deficit, you can research creative ways to manage the money more effectively or teach the children about budgeting and spending. This exercise is meant to help, so do not use it as an opportunity to find fault with the other parent.

- When evaluating expenses, do not begrudge the residential parent a safe place to live or a reliable vehicle. Your children need a secure place to call home and dependable transportation.

- For a year, record the amount you spend – both incidental and planned – on your children. Sometimes our projections are different than the reality. This exercise may also help you to be more compassionate to the residential parent who is probably faced with incidental expenses on a daily basis.

One reason we resist allowing ourselves abundance is the fear that we will be taken advantage of. We have worked hard to achieve our success and the goodies that go along with it. We feel that the residential parent has the same opportunity available to her. While we may be willing and wanting to extend more to our children, when we are ordered to through the courts, we become obsessively possessive. Often we feel that if the residential parent would have merely asked us to meet a need, we would have been glad to do it. By using the legal system to put demands on our finances, we feel that the goal was not to provide for the children, but to get into our pockets as a means to further hurt us.

Could our courts help in this matter? How could we curtail support abuses? What if residential parents were periodically required to report a budget to the courts and be accountable for the expenditures for the children? Would there be fewer parents abusing the system? On the other hand, if residential parents witnessed the other parent being more generous and less resentful, would there be a need to pursue the legal route? Food for thought.

Another way we abuse money occurs when we attempt to buy our children's affection. If you have engaged in this game, you soon learn that your only value lies in the most recent gift or outing or whatever it was that pleased the children last. This will cause an empty feeling within you. Respect yourself by creating a genuine relationship with your children. Use your money as a way to broaden your opportunities for mutual enjoyment.

Don't allow your children to abuse your generosity. Is there a parent on the planet – residential or long-distance – who hasn't felt taken advantage of at some point? I doubt it! Set healthy financial boundaries for yourself and communicate to your children what those are. This is a fabulous opportunity for us to teach children about choices and options. It is also a fantastic way to tap into our creativity. If you have $25 to spend for a weekend of fun, you can have a blast finding ways to stretch the dollars.

Even if the availability of money is not an issue for you, teaching children to handle money responsibly is a worthy endeavor. Practice saving coupons for your favorite items at the grocery or discount coupons to your favorite attractions. Learn what restaurants offer "kids eat free" nights. Shop early for gifts so you are not subjected to "last minute lunacy" and in frustration pay higher prices or select more expensive items because you are under pressure.

Another way we abuse money is by trying to fill our wounds with stuff. Material possessions cannot fill the void in your heart. No amount of trinkets or bobbles or toys will make you feel better if you are hurting inside. Work on the interior issues and the outer items will be for your enjoyment rather than your attempt at fulfillment.

*****

### Personal Reflections

With regard to your custody decree, do you feel you have been wronged? Explain. (For example: the judge was too harsh on the child support, judge did not allow me enough time to be with my children.)

What would it take for you to feel justified? (For example: feel that the money really helps the children or be allowed more time together.)

*Building a Bridge*

Was there anything you could have done differently? (For example: listened to counselor's advice, focused more on children's needs and less on my own needs, been less anxious to hurt the other parent.)

Are you open to guidance on how to connect with your children? (For example: this book, other books, counselors, support groups, ministers.)

What did you expect from your attorney regarding the custody proceedings? (For example: to "win.") Is this what you received?

What did you expect from the courts regarding the outcome of those proceedings? (For example: to "side" with you.) Is this what you received?

Do you keep an attorney on retainer or speed dial? Why? (For example: so other parent is less likely to "mess with you." So you feel safer or more in charge.)

Do you vote? Do you know who you are voting for?

What are you personally doing to improve your relationship with your children? (For example: pay child support, support other parents, call regularly, send small tokens of your love, plan for times together.)

List some ways you might get involved (committees, organizations or other ways) to improve relations between long-distance parents and their children.

What are your thoughts on child support in general? (For example: kids need money to live, money is the other parent's problem.)

What are your thoughts on child support as related to your personal situation? (For example: feel the other parent uses child support to hurt me or the other parent uses money wisely and stretches every dollar.)

Do you pay your child support? Why or why not?

Have you kept yourself poor to avoid paying support or more support? How have you done that? (For example: refused opportunities for advanced positions, stopped attending continuing education classes,

*Building a Bridge*

change jobs frequently to avoid additional responsibilities, do as little as possible at office so promotions aren't offered.)

Do you ever feel taken advantage of financially? List the times when this has occurred. (For example: I feel I am only as good as the last outing or only needed to buy toys or eat out or pay for new clothes.)

How can you create healthier financial boundaries? (For example, do you set an amount for spending, or set a budget for clothing or give your children some of their own money to use for incidentals. Don't give in – allow your children to learn about money and how to manage it.)

What are your ideas for improving the child support system? (For example, make residential parents accountable for funds by showing receipts or reporting the use of the money.)

Do you buy things for your children to replace the time you do not have together or to avoid working on a genuine relationship with them?

Do you buy things for yourself to fill a void? Can you think of a time when you made a purchase to fill that void?

Affirm: I know that all happenings in this life are in Divine Order. I accept my life experiences as powerful learning opportunities. My job is to stay centered in love and call on that love to help me learn.

**Additional reading suggestions:**

*The Language of Letting Go* by Melody Beattie

*The Courage to be Rich* by Suze Orman

*Don't Worry, Make Money: Spiritual and Practical Ways to Create Abundance and More Fun in Your Life* by Richard Carlson

*Building a Bridge*

## *Self-pity*

**Self-pity is "a self-indulgent dwelling on one's own sorrows or misfortunes."**

This is the "poor me" syndrome which is also known as "the victim complex." We carry our long-distance parenting saga around with us. At the slightest invitation to share something about ourselves with others, we bring out our story and painstakingly elaborate on every detail of the custody proceedings, our opinions of the other parent and her new family, our critique of the system, and so forth. While we may fool ourselves into thinking we are justified in our behavior, we are only keeping the past alive and preventing ourselves from experiencing the power of the present. To continue in the victim mode is draining – for ourselves and our support network. Soon people get weary of rescuing our feelings.

### *Stop Being a Victim*

Give up the story. Stop being a victim. When someone asks if you have children, be honest. If they ask where they go to school, be honest. You can tell them the children live with the other parent if you like, but you don't have to. You can decide how much or little you want to share with the party to whom you are speaking. However, your honesty is critical. Do not deny the existence of children that you want to have a relationship with and love. This sends out a mixed message to the universe and therefore, it does not know what you want or how to respond to you. If you are sending mixed messages, you will receive mixed responses.

If you find that you have less people in your support network, you need to make a serious evaluation of your victim status. Others giving up on you may be the indicator that you need to give up your "poor me" position.

*****
Personal Reflections

When do you feel like saying 'poor me?' (For example: on your birthday, during the holidays, whenever you can?)

How often do you tell your parenting story?

*Building a Bridge*

When do you tell your parenting story? (When you meet new people? When someone asks if you have children? Whenever you can?)

How do you feel when you are sharing the story? (For example: inferior, victimized, stereotyped, or do you feel at peace or empowered?)

Do you have a strong support network? List those you turn to for support and encouragement.

Have you thanked these individuals for the support they give you? Write each person a thank you note for helping you. If writing a note will delay the expression of appreciation, pick up the telephone and call those people.

> Dear name,
>
> I want to thank you for being supportive of my efforts to strengthen my relationship with my children. Your encouragement has been a real blessing.
>
> name

Affirm: Self-pity does not serve me. I cease being a victim. I choose to live in the now! I choose to concentrate on the positives in my life ... which make me a victor!

**Additional reading suggestions:**

*Transformation: You'll See It When You Believe It* by Wayne W. Dyer (This program is available in book and cassette program.)

*Transformation Soup* by Sark

### *Spite*

**Spite is "petty ill will or hatred with the disposition to irritate, annoy or thwart; offend."**

Spiteful behavior is generally demonstrated toward the other parent. If you feel that you have been wronged, you may also feel that

*Building a Bridge*

you are justified in taking a jab at the residential parent. You may think that the burden you bear entitles you to cause that parent irritation or to be offensive toward him.

Spiteful behavior only undermines any hope for a cooperative relationship between you. While you do not have to be friends, you need to be friendly. Spitefulness can also be very subtle, but hurtful just the same. Sarcastic comments about the parent and/or his new spouse will cause anxiety in the children. Because the children already have a plateful to handle, they will not welcome or appreciate additional problems that are generated by spitefulness in you. It will also work to put them in the defensive mode of protecting the other parent.

The residential parent may engage in spiteful behavior as well. Sometimes the residential parent feels the long-distance parent has a "cushy" life by not having the day-to-day child-rearing responsibilities. Maybe the residential parent is jealous that the long-distance parent has had time to go to school or take a better career position. If the residential parent conducts business with you in a spiteful fashion, diffuse the behavior with kindness – genuine kindness can be demonstrated by our tone of voice and choice of words. This does not mean that we should abandon our integrity or be dishonest or phony. You need to acknowledge to yourself that while this spiteful behavior is unnecessary, the other party has chosen to act in such a manner. Their choice does not mean that you need to respond likewise.

Other ways to demonstrate kindness in your daily life are:

- Offering a helping hand by opening a door for someone, or holding the elevator door for another passenger or letting an older person take your cab while you wait for the next one.

- Speaking respectfully to others – in word choice and tone.

- Writing a note of encouragement to someone who needs a boost.

- Discreetly and gently telling someone he has toilet tissue stuck to the bottom of his shoe or mustard on his chin.

*Building a Bridge*

## *Release Emotional Attachment - Be Professional and Pleasant*

Our behavior is our choice. Choose to behave in a fashion that makes you feel genuinely good about yourself. If conversations or communications between you and the children's other parent create emotional ill will, you need to take a look at why you are still emotionally connected to this person. Why are you still allowing your "buttons to be pushed?" Why are you reacting to this person, instead of responding to the situation regarding the children?

When we have a legitimate need to contact the other parent, we need to prepare ourselves with dialogue as to how we will address the subject at hand. What information do I need? What questions may he ask of me? Keep the conversation non-emotional. Handle the matter as you would a business situation. Be courteous, professional and pleasant.

*****

Personal Reflections

Do you feel you have the right to take a jab at the other parent? Why? (For example: you think they have wronged you, you think you are the better parent.)

Think about ways you behave spitefully toward the other parent. List some situations/experiences you can recall. (For example: using a belligerent tone of voice in conversations, choosing words that accuse or suggest the other parent is "less than.")

In your opinion, does the other parent behave spitefully toward you? List some situations/experiences you can recall. (For example: calls during office hours for petty reasons and creates an argument, give "evil eye" when you pick up the child, creates "rules" that are impossible to follow.)

How did you handle these situations? (For example, consult an exorcist, retaliate, disregard other parent's behavior so it isn't fueled.)

Do you allow the other parent to "push your buttons?" Why? When does this happen? (For example: when in public together – school functions, or in private – during telephone conversations.)

*Building a Bridge*

How do you handle your dealings with the other parent? (For example: telephone calls, emails, and/or letters?)

Are these dealings done with hostility or are they conducted in a business-like manner?

Affirm: I choose to respond to situations in my life. Reacting only creates negative energy. I can handle every situation in a professional and pleasant manner.

**Additional reading suggestions:**

*How To Win Friends and Influence People* by Dale Carnegie

*Mary Kay on People Management* by Mary Kay Ash

### *Superiority*

**Superiority is "an exaggerated opinion of oneself."**

Superiority complexes, according to Pia Mellody, author of *Facing Codependence*, are generated in two fashions: 1) by being critical of others for the purpose of making them feel they are beneath you or 2) by actually believing that you are better than others.

If a parent engages in criticism of the other parent in an effort to elevate her own position with the children, that parent will only work to destroy her own credibility. While you may think you are criticizing the other parent, you are also criticizing the children because they are as much a part of the other parent as they are of you.

If a parent actually believes he or she is better than the other parent, be patient and prayerful. This parent is in for a rude awakening. People who believe they are better than others will soon find that life offers them an opportunity to learn compassion and understanding ... the old-fashioned way ... through experience!

*Building a Bridge*

*"Pride cometh before a fall."*

## King Solomon

Residential parents often think that they are above fulfilling their responsibilities as outlined in the custody decree. Sometimes their actions indicate that they think they do not need to behave civilly toward the long-distance parent. They start to think that they alone offer the children the highest good. We must stop looking to physical factors as determiners of what is best for our children and also consider the spiritual offerings we have for them.

### *Focus on Integrity and Spiritual Values*

What is important to consider? Rather than focusing on a superior attitude, let's put our energy into superior living – living with integrity and spirituality at the forefront.

Suggesting we live in a superior fashion opens a can of worms because everyone has a different opinion or standard for quality living. What is the yardstick for measuring superior living? We need to ask ourselves:

- How does my example teach my child integrity and ethics?

- How do I demonstrate the love of all people?

- How is my child learning the difference between rights and doing the right thing?

- How is my lifestyle a demonstration of reverence for the earth we live on?

- How am I cultivating my child so he can find his divine purpose on this planet?

*Building a Bridge*

Our forcing our children to live in the hometown of our youth, or to enter a profession of our choice, or profess a religion of our ancestors does nothing to serve the evolution of their souls. In attempting to manipulate our children into our ways of thinking, we drive them away from us. This type of parenting does not come from love, but from fear. If we need our children to be younger versions of ourselves, all we are doing is attempting to validate our own lives. "If it was good enough for me, it is good enough for them" creates suspicion that maybe "it" really isn't good enough for anyone.

Are we thinking about what is best for our children, or simply repeating our parent's actions? Perhaps we need to take some time to think back to our childhood experiences. Were there times that we wished our parents had put a little more thought or compassion into their decision making? Of course those times existed!

So let's take our childhood experiences as our lessons. Let's take time to carefully consider each child before making decisions. Let's make choices that are appropriate for their individual developmental needs. We must offer our children spiritual guidance – not religious rhetoric – so they can become the beautiful, perfect souls they were born to be. This is the way to superior living.

*****

Personal Reflections

Are you critical of the other parent? When? (For example: Always, sometimes, about specific things.) Why? (For example: You want to look better than other parent, you want the children to like you more, you want to hurt the other parent.)

Do you think you are better than the other parent as a parent? (For example: you have more experience with children, you spend more time with the children.) As a person? (For example: you have more education, you live with higher standards.) Explain why you feel as you do.

Are you living in a superior fashion – with integrity and spiritual growth? (For example: are you honest on your tax returns, do you "borrow" little things from the office, or do you seek out wise people for advice, do you tell the cashier when she has given you too much change or forgotten to bill you for an item?)

Did you answer the five questions on the good-enough-for-me philosophy? Why not?

Do you parent based on the good-enough-for-me philosophy? In what areas of parenting have you adopted the ideas of your parents without questioning their decisions? (For example: education, religion, or prejudices.)

With regard to the previous question, are there any of those areas you would like to rethink and perhaps handle differently? List which areas you might want to reconsider. (For example: education, religion, or prejudices.)

What in your childhood would you have liked your parents to have done differently for you? List some experiences you recall from your childhood. (For example, the way they disciplined you, the amount of time you spent together, their level of interest in your friends/activities.)

Have you ever asked your children what they would like you to do differently? If not, would you consider asking them now for their input?

Affirm: Many people contribute to the development process of the child that has come to the planet through me. While I have a very important role in my child's life, I know that others, too, make valuable contributions to his/her growth. We are all working together.

**Additional reading suggestions:**

*Spiritual Literacy: Reading the Sacred in Everyday Life* by Frederic Brussat and Mary Ann Brussat

### Building a Bridge for Your Children

Creating a healthy relationship with our children requires us to build a bridge between ourselves and the other parent for them to cross.

*Building a Bridge*

In Diagram 1 you can see that during the marriage while you and the spouse were still existing as a married couple, there was a separation between you. This represents the breakdown of the relationship. The children are the dotted line running down the middle – between the two of you. While there is a definite separation between you and the spouse, you may still be physically living together which allows the children access to either of you at any time. As time passes, you and the children's other parent are moving farther and farther apart, but the children are still in the middle. The corner turns represent the individual choices and changes we make in our lives. As you grow more distant from each other, the children are more obviously in the middle.

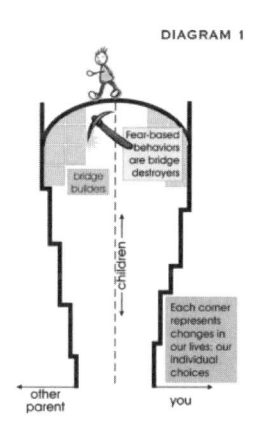

DIAGRAM 1

*Fear-based behaviors are bridge destroyers*

*bridge builder*

*children*

*Each corner represents changes in our lives; our individual choices*

*other parent*   *you*

As you distance yourself from the other parent, the children need a secure, safe way to move between you. In Diagram 2, you can see how love, faith in God and in yourself, form the support beams for the bridge. The stones that secure the structure are the loved-based behaviors that we have been reviewing in this chapter: respect, kindness, friendliness, courtesy, compassion, creativity, surrender, cooporation, self-worth, spiritual development, trust, acting responsibly, acceptance, forgiveness, and honesty.

*Building a Bridge*

**DIAGRAM 2**

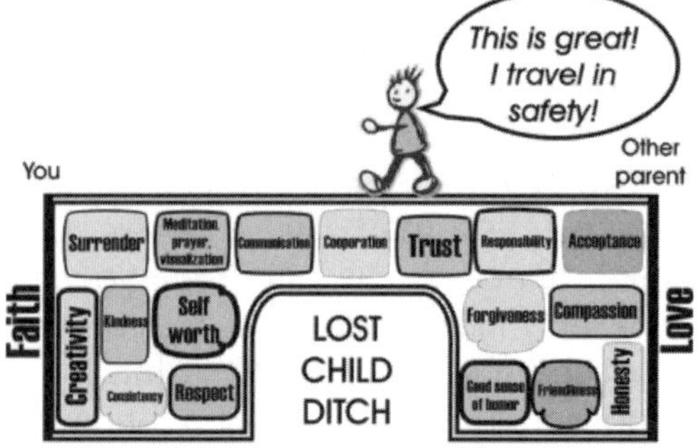

What eats away at the stones and weakens them are the acts of alienation, anger, arrogance, blame, despair, envy, greed, grief, guilt, hatefulness, inferiority, laziness, loneliness, regret, resentment, self-pity, spite and superiority.

Everything I have been sharing with you boils down to choice. In every encounter we have the free will to choose between fear-based behaviors or love-based behaviors. The consequences of our choices will either strengthen the bridge or weaken it.

If the bridge weakens to the point of falling apart, the children drop into the emotional ditch that lies below. In this emotional ditch they experience the fear-based aspects and project those fears onto both the parents and the world through acting out. Our children become lost, uncertain, untrusting. They feel unloved and unworthy of love.

It is our responsibility as parents to put aside our fears and rear our children well. Our actions teach our children how to behave. Whatever experiences our children embrace in their childhood will be those that they take into their parenting opportunity. We are all products of our experiences. Dorothy Nolte's poem, "Children Learn What They Live," should call each of us to choose the higher road.

*Building a Bridge*

## "Children Learn What They Live"

If a child lives with criticism,
He learns to condemn.
If a child lives with hostility,
He learns to fight.
If a child lives with ridicule,
He learns to be shy.
If a child lives with shame,
He learns to be guilty.
If a child lives with tolerance,
He learns to be patient.
If a child lives with encouragement
He learns confidence.
If a child lives with praise,
He learns to appreciate.
If a child lives with fairness,
He learns justice.
If a child lives with security,
He learns to have faith.
If a child lives with approval,
He learns to like himself.
If a child lives with acceptance and friendship,
He learns to find love in the world.

All efforts to assess the fear-based aspects of our lives and move to the love-based aspects are ongoing work. We are never done. We must work on these endeavors by using the situations that are presented to us each day.

On difficult days I sometimes feel like a fraud because I have not mastered releasing the fears. Sometimes I do not automatically demonstrate love. In those moments I wonder how a fraud can write a book. Then I think to myself, "I am a parent in process of becoming a better parent like those I am sharing with. We are all learning and growing. This is honest. Everything I share in this book I have been through or tried – and found success. So writing this book is a good and honest endeavor." In Sark's book, *Succulent Wild Woman*, she writes, "It isn't easy for any of us to transcend the past, or pain we might have suffered. Yet, there are gifts in those pains, and we can choose to let light into the dark places. We are not alone!" I encourage

*Building a Bridge*

myself and I encourage you to always be true to yourself and always aim to be the best you can be.

In our effort to cooperate on behalf of the children, there will arise times when we need to act lovingly even when we don't feel loving inside. "Fake it 'til you make it" does not mean to be phony. It means that we are to put our best foot forward as we move toward our goal of communication and cooperation. This is the process of transcending. Let's work together to create strong, safe and secure bridges that our children can travel on their journey to adulthood.

*Building a Bridge*

## Chapter 4: Worst Case Scenarios

This is "the worst" section of this book. Does it sound strange that I would be offering this to you?

While I have been outlining various situations for you to evaluate your fear-based thoughts and behaviors, release them and move towards love-based thoughts and behaviors, I fully appreciate that each person who experiences long-distance parenting has their own unique set of circumstances to deal with. I want you to address your own personal issues.

So much of our fear lies in the "what ifs?" in life. In our parenting experiences we find times when we bite the inside of our mouths or hold our breath in anxious anticipation of those things that might happen…circumstances created by the other parent that leave us in dismay. Those situations that sting our souls the most and longest are the ones that we did not see coming.

To that end I want you to work through your "what if?" situations. Write down all your "what if?" fears.

What if …. (the other parent kidnapped the children?)

What if …

*Building a Bridge*

What if ...

After you have listed the scenarios that you have the highest level of anxiety about, take each situation individually and work through it. Develop a movie in your mind of how this experience will play out. Become the writer, actor and director of your life. You have full charge of this experience. Ask yourself:

- What are my first thoughts in this situation?

- What am I really angry about in this situation?

- What are my greatest fears? For myself? For my children?

- What is your gut instinct for taking action?

- Do you need to talk to anyone?

- Who has been through this to offer sound advice or insight?

- What resources do I have for figuring out a response (not reaction!)?

Go through the situation in detail. Make notes if you like. Analyze the physical, emotional, mental and spiritual aspects of the situation. Figure out how you will deal with the matter in a responsible and wise fashion. As the director of this production, you have the right to cut the scene whenever you like and redo it for a different ending if you are not pleased with your role in it. Trust your inner guidance to lead you into right action.

The point of this exercise is to prepare you for the worst. In the process of preparing ourselves for these situations, we strengthen ourselves. This strength is then available to us when the real life situations are thrown into our face. Dr. Susan Jeffers, in her book *Feel the Fear and Do It Anyway*, encourages us by stating, "All you have to do to diminish your fear is to develop more trust in your ability to handle whatever comes your way!"

*Building a Bridge*

Two notes of caution:

1. Be aware of transferred fears. These are fears that you do not hold within you, but are communicated to you by others. Someone tells you a horror story they heard, and you start thinking about their nightmare. Then the story churns inside you until you are sick. Do not absorb the garbage others pass along. Stop the fear fungus before it spreads!

2. Do NOT dwell on these scenarios. The more energy you put into these "what if" situations, the greater the chances are that you will create the experiences. Stay focused on working to strengthen yourself in the event of unexpected events.

As you think about the handling of each situation, say over and over to yourself, "I will handle whatever happens." Think: Plan, Practice, Prepare. This instills in you a powerful vote of confidence – you build trust in yourself. This trust remains within you and is always available for you to draw on when needed.

For you skeptics who are reading and saying, "What if I didn't think of the worst thing?" My response: It doesn't matter! It truly does not matter because the result of this exercise develops new strength and wisdom inside of you. The by-product of this exercise is a sharpness within you that will be immediately available to you when you need it – regardless of why you need it. You can truly handle whatever comes down the pike. Remember that you are working through your worst fears, so whatever the future hands you will be manageable.

Affirm: "I am now handling my fears. I am becoming more confident every day." - Dr. Susan Jeffers

### Additional reading suggestions:

*Feel the Fear and Do It Anyway* by Dr. Susan Jeffers

*What to Say When You Talk to Yourself* by Shad Helmstetter by Ph.D.

*Building a Bridge*

*Building a Bridge*

# Chapter 5: Step Four: Our Greatest Mission: To Be a Living Example

In the previous chapters of this book we have discussed working through fear-based aspects and embracing love-based aspects. In doing this we not only work to create communication and cooperation with the other parent, we are also creating a healthy and beautiful life for ourselves. While it should be obvious that we need, and should want, a healthy life, too often we live otherwise. Creating a healthy life for ourselves does not mean that we become self-centered or self-absorbed. It means exactly the opposite. It means that we value our own life and act accordingly.

Our greatest mission as a parent is to be a living example for our children. Often parents talk the talk, but parents who are serious about leading their children will also walk the talk. The old saying, "Do as I say, not as I do," is garbage. Our children hold no regard for this thinking and when they challenge us about the contradiction between our words and behaviors, we retaliate by saying they are disrespectful. But is it not our disrespect for ourselves that we are most angry about? While we may cringe at the thought of verbalizing this – of being this honest – we know in our souls that our children are beseeching us to lead them by example.

*Building a Bridge*

> "Children are a great deal more apt to follow your lead than the way you point."
>
> **Anonymous**

You may doubt that this is true, but rather than elaborate on the point myself, I am going to call on the inspirational words of teachers and leaders to speak to your heart.

- Dr. Wayne Dyer, author of *What Do You Really Want for Your Children*:

    "Imagine going to your dentist and having him give you a lecture on the importance of oral hygiene, while all the time smiling at you through rotten teeth. Or, visualize yourself talking to your doctor and having him tell you about the evils of nicotine addiction while blowing cigarette smoke in your face. Your initial reaction would be "This person is a phony." The same kind of logic applies to the teaching of attitudes about life. If your goal is to assist children in developing an appreciation for life, and the ability to always enjoy life, then you must begin this task by first working on yourself and modeling this kind of an attitude in all your interactions…YOU MUST LIVE BY EXAMPLE!"

    "The principal goal of parenting is teaching children to become their own parents. You want children to rely on their own inner signals, to be able to think for themselves, to avoid costly emotional letdowns, and to know that they have the skills and the ability to use them, to lead happy and fulfilled lives without the need to consult you forever. You are to be their guide for a while, and then, you will enjoy watching them take off on their own."

- Marianne Williamson, author of *A Return to Love*:

    *Building a Bridge*

"We can't really give our children what we don't have ourselves. In that sense, my greatest gift to my daughter is that I continue to work on myself. Children learn more through imitation than through any other form of instruction. Our greatest opportunity to positively affect another person's life is to accept God's love into our own."

- Williamson addresses a parent's example again in her book, A Woman's Worth:

    "The key to mothering [parenting] is to visualize our children as the adults we would love them to become: strong, happy, serious, loving. Now imagine what kind of mother [parent] they must have had to grow into such fabulous grown-ups. And whatever that is, becoming it is the task that lies before us."

- King Solomon, the wisest man who ever lived, wrote in Proverbs 22:6:

    "Train up a child in the way he should go: and when he is old, he will not depart from it."

- Read again Dorothy Law Nolte's poem, "Children Learn What They Live." (Chapter 3, page 179.)

I doubt anyone would disagree that parenting is a critically important responsibility. Yet I wonder why we do so little to prepare for the mission. We need no credentials, training or even permission to become a parent. We can't drive a car without taking a course and obtaining a license, yet we can create a life.

In this day and age we are blessed with abundant opportunities to become better parents. Bookstores are filled with books on general and specific parenting topics, community colleges, cultural centers and churches offer seminars and workshops to develop stronger parenting skills. While these many facets are available to us, it is our choice to use them or not.

*Building a Bridge*

We are being called to rise to the occasion of our most important work. It is time for us to choose to become a quality parent by becoming a quality person.

Do you remember Dr. Martin Luther King, Jr.'s "I Have a Dream" speech? Dr. King had a dream for our country, but his dream was also for his children. Do you have a dream for your children?

We need to develop our dream for our children – for all children. We need to commit ourselves to the pursuit of that dream. It starts with you. It starts with me. I renew my commitment every Sunday as our church service closes with "Let There Be Peace On Earth."

### *"Let There Be Peace On Earth"*

Let there be peace on earth and let it begin with me
Let there be peace on earth, the peace that was meant to be.
With God as our Father, family all are we,
Let me walk with my brother in perfect harmony.
Let peace begin with me, let this be the moment now
With every step I take, let this be my joyous vow:
To take each moment and live each moment in peace eternally
Let there be peace on earth and let it begin with me.

Say these words. Allow them to penetrate your soul. Allow them to melt away the calluses of fear that have developed. Let your pride be dissolved so your self-esteem and self-respect can flourish. Pick up the task before you and **be** the person and the parent you have been created to be.

When I evaluate the example I set for my children, I use these two questions to measure my thoughts/behavior:

- Are my current thoughts/behaviors what I would be proud to see in my child?

- What kind of world would this world be, if every parent were like me?

*Building a Bridge*

## *The Steps to Personal Fulfillment*

So now we know what we need to do and why we need to do it. How do we accomplish this task? How do we become better people?

In Dr. Sonya Friedman's book, *On A Clear Day You Can See Yourself*, she writes that in order to live a full life we must strive for these seven goals:

1. To have marketable skills and be able to support yourself.

2. To feel fulfilled and happy – with or without a mate.

3. To acknowledge that you are the key player in your life.

4. To seek the company of people with whom you share mutual respect and appreciation.

5. To provide as best you can for the people who depend on you.

6. To help make the world a better place.

7. To make peace with your past – to forgive yourself for making mistakes and to go forward with your life.

Inside of each of us lies our ideal person. This is the person we want to become. The person we respect and admire. The pursuit of becoming this person is a day-to-day operation and the path to your ideal self is paved with these steps.

- Carefully consider each of these seven goals and how they are currently represented in your life. What steps must you take in order to move closer to your ideal self?

Here are some steps I have outlined:

1. "The List." Get a pad of paper. Find a quiet, comfortable location where you can think and write down your thoughts. Open your mind. Allow all your hopes, dreams, and fantasies to flow out onto the paper. Just make the list.

*Building a Bridge*

Do not judge it, evaluate it, critique it, or mock it. Write it. This will be an on-going list. A week from now you may think of something you want to add. Three months from now you may decide a previous listing is no longer important to you.

Keep the list moving. As you grow and change, it makes sense that the list will too.

---

**The List**

- pay off credit cards
- trade in car
- finish associate's degree at community college
- learn Spanish
- exercise daily
- find a church family
- and so on ....

---

Here are eight areas of development to consider when making goals for yourself:

| | |
|---|---|
| Career | Mental |
| Creative | Physical |
| Emotional | Social |
| Family | Spiritual |

*Building a Bridge*

Consider also T. Berry Brazelton's list of ten things to cultivate in our children. I suggest a review of this list, because we must set the example for our children. If we develop these traits, our children will be more likely to as well.

| | |
|---|---|
| Self-esteem | Leadership |
| Honesty | Responsibility |
| Resilience | Humor |
| Enthusiasm | Creativity, imagination |
| Sensitivity to others | Mediation |

**"You see things as they are; and you ask why?**

**But I dream of things that never were; and I ask why not?"**

**George Bernard Shaw**

2. Go through the list, item by item, and decide if this is something you want to work on now or later, or if this is a "someday" idea. Again, do not be overly critical as you work through the list. Allow your spirit to guide you in decision making. Look at the item and make the notation for it.

*Building a Bridge*

> **The List**
> 
> - pay off credit cards - NOW - create budget plan
> - trade in car - later this year
> - finish associate's degree at community college - maybe a fall class
> - learn Spanish - cassette tapes while commuting? Investigate.
> - exercise daily - NOW
> - find a church family - NOW - visit First Church on Sunday
> - and so on ....

3. Focus on your "now" listings. Evaluate how much time you have available. Take a sample calendar page and work through it for your normal week. Mark out the times you are currently unavailable. As you consider your schedule, also consider what activities you are engaged in that you think of as time wasted. For example, commuting time. Get a feel for how much time you have to work with. Do you have every evening available? Do you have every Saturday free? We generally have more available time than we recognize. Ask yourself how much time you are spending watching television or visiting with friends on the telephone or engaging in Internet "surfing." I am not suggesting you give up relaxation time or time with your friends. I am suggesting you look at all your activities and honestly determine for yourself how much available time you have to pursue the items on your "now" list.

Once you have taken a look at your overall monthly schedule, take a second look at your weekday schedule. Most people find that

*Building a Bridge*

they have some sort of routine during the workweek, but whatever your personal schedule is, outline it to see where your time is spent.

If you have three or four goals in the "now" category, ask yourself if you can really accomplish anything when attempting several new things simultaneously. You will experience more success by having one, possibly two, "now" goals.

4. Create a "Plan of Pursuit" sheet.

List the goal. List what considerations or commitments would come with pursuing this goal.

If you want to return to college, you will need to account for class and study time.

If you want to hike Mt. Rainer, you might need to have some supporting goals, such as getting into physical condition, and financially planning for the expenses of such an endeavor.

Then list what you can do today to start working on this goal. (For example, contact the local college for a schedule of classes or make an appointment with a counselor or inquire about hiking groups and local hiking locations.)

*Building a Bridge*

| Plan of Pursuit |||| 
| Goal | Considerations, Commitments, Financial Needs | Starting Place of Action | Progress |
|---|---|---|---|
| Pay off credit cards | Personal commitment to budget | Make a budget | |
| Exercise daily | Walk during lunch hour at work | Take walking shoes to work | |

5. Write the "now" goal that you are pursuing on an index card. Write with a marking pen so the writing will be big enough to see at a glance or use a large font size on the computer. Hang this card where you can see it every morning and evening. Better yet, make several copies and put them in places that you frequent...your desk at the office, refrigerator, bathroom mirror, dashboard of your car, or inside your daily calendar.

You can also make a collage of photographs and inspirational sayings to remind and encourage yourself about the goal. Take clippings from magazines, newspapers, or other sources that show someone else in pursuit of the goal. If they can do it, SO CAN YOU! Work each day toward these goals. Show respect for yourself and your life.

This powerful testimony will positively affect your children. They will see how a quality life is nurtured one day at a time and not landed by winning the lottery.

*Building a Bridge*

**"Life is a progress, not a station."**

**Ralph Waldo Emerson**

      Do you also understand that this practice of nurturing one day at a time is the same philosophy we need to embrace for development of our relationships with our children? Have you included in your goals a plan for cultivating your relationship?

      These are to be your goals, but when considering your goals, is it possible that your child might also want to pursue this goal with you? Would your teenage son like to rebuild an old car with you? Would your daughter also like to learn to use a potter's wheel? If your goals can also contribute to your time with your child, keep in mind how you can do some of these activities together.

6.    Mark your calendar as a reminder to check your progress. On the seventh day from your initial pursuit, what progress has been made? Did you actually see the counselor? Did you actually call the hiking group? At the one-month time evaluate where you are in your pursuit. Then again in three months, six months, one year. If you are not making any progress, you need to ask yourself why. Is this a goal you really want? If you really want to achieve this goal, why are you not accomplishing steps toward its completion?

      Do not be intimidated or overwhelmed by the steps you must take. If this is happening, you are too focused on the end goal. Make each step a mini-goal and keep your focus there. Did you look up the name of the hiking group? Did you locate the telephone number of the college? In handling goals in this manner, you will set yourself up for success.

      Often times our goals do not have a "completion". For example, a goal to eat healthy foods or exercise regularly is a lifetime goal. We don't accomplish these things once and move on. In these cases, monitor your ongoing commitment.

*Building a Bridge*

Consider options for attainment of your goals. For example, if your goal is to return to school, investigate the various ways you can work toward that goal. While evening and weekend classes are traditional, many colleges are now offering correspondence and Internet studies.

If you spend any time commuting to and from work, you can use this time for goal achievement. For example, if one of your goals is to learn to speak a foreign language, you can purchase (or check out from the library) cassette tapes. Listen to these tapes as you commute and make great use of your travel time. Tape programs are available for learning all kinds of subjects. For information about cassette (or CD) programs, contact these companies:

Nightengale-Conant, 800-525-9000 or www.nightingale.com

National Press Publications, 800-258-7248 or www.natsem.com

Our opportunities for development are endless. Give yourself permission to follow your dreams and pursue your ambitions. Allow your child to see that you are accepting challenges and changes with grace. This is an example worth flaunting!

As you work on your goals, do you see with your mind's eye the person you want to be? Close your eyes and get a good look at this person. Study his characteristics and qualities. Become familiar with him and give him permission to mentor you. This person you see in your mind is you fulfilled. Go to that person often for guidance and insight.

**"The me I see is the me I'll be!"**

**Dr. Robert Schuller**

*Building a Bridge*

Carmen Moshier's song, "We Make Our Own World," expresses these concepts:

### "We Make Our Own World"

We make our world wherever we are
Our happiness is of our own making
We make our own world wherever we are,
Our happiness then is for the taking.
Our world goes with us as we talk and walk along each day.
Our world can be a heaven or hell, our attitude will say.
We make our own world wherever we are
Let's make it happy, let's live in beauty.
We make our own world wherever we are,
Keep thinking happy, we'll make a new world!

Nothing can aid you in accomplishing your goals – in making your own world – unless you have the genuine intent and use your will power. In Gary Zukav's book, *The Seat of the Soul*, he writes,

> "With each choice that you make you align yourself with the energy of your soul, you empower yourself. This is how authentic power is acquired. It is built up step-by-step, choice by choice. It cannot be meditated or prayed into being. It must be earned. ... Each time you are tempted to become angry, or jealous, or fearful, and you challenge that feeling, you empower yourself. ... If you decide that you cannot beat a temptation, what you are really doing is giving yourself permission to be irresponsible."

Making our own world requires us to make and act on responsible choices. Choose to be responsible. Choose to be the awesome person you have been created to be!

### Volunteer Work

Keep in mind that a great deal can be experienced and learned through volunteer work. Charities are always willing to give people challenges and often times train them in the process. This is such a beautiful way to give and receive. Talk to a volunteer coordinator at a local United Way office or contact the Points of Light

*Building a Bridge*

Foundation at 1400 Eye Street, NW, Suite 800, Washington, DC 20005, 202-729-8000.

Another benefit of volunteering is in the fabulous connections you make with other volunteers. People who participate in charity work are people with big hearts and beautiful spirits. I have made many wonderful friendships through my volunteer work.

### Teachers

In the pursuit of your goals, if you know that you need help, get it. How do you know you need help? Have you tried to achieve this goal before and been unsuccessful? If you are trying to learn healthy eating habits, join a program. If you want to stop drinking, join AA. Do not be embarrassed by thinking that this indicates weakness in you. We all need to help one another on this planet. Use your resources to move toward your goal. I am not suggesting that you achieve the goal at any price. Any activity that harms rather than heals is not what we are working toward. For example, if you want to lose weight, do not engage in anorexic or bulimic behavior. Trading one problem for another does not work toward improving the quality of your life. The point is to show more compassion and care for your self, not less.

Often we set a goal to achieve something that we have previously attempted to achieve, but have not experienced success in accomplishing. If this is a real goal in your life, commit yourself to the goal and all that goes along with its achievement. Do not allow negative input from others (such as well-meaning relatives, friends or co-workers) to rain on your parade. Often we give too much value to the comments of others and too little value to our heart's desire. If you want to stop smoking and this is your third try, do not focus on the past experiences. Learn from them, of course, but do not tie yourself to those outcomes. Go within to the silence of your soul and ask God for the strength to fully accomplish the goal.

We live in times where nearly everything is instantly done. We have computers with high-powered modems, microwave ovens that can prepare full meals in a matter of minutes, overnight delivery services and fast-track college courses. We have lost our ability to be patient for anything. The idea of working toward a long-term goal nearly sends us over the edge. Because we have become

*Building a Bridge*

accustomed to everything being accomplished in the "right now," we have very little interest in patience. But patience is a key to achieving our goals.

Another key is perseverance. This, too, is a key we rarely want anything to do with. Our culture is not only focused on fast, it is also obsessed with successful finishes. But the reality is that in an effort to achieve fulfillment of our goals, we experience mistakes. We make mistakes, think of ourselves as failures and then proceed to beat ourselves up. John Maxwell, author of *Failing Forward: Turning Mistakes Into Stepping Stones for Success* writes, "Changing your perspective on failure will help you to persevere – and ultimately achieve your desires." He sites seven things about failure that we must keep in mind:

1. People think failure is avoidable – it's not

2. People think failure is an event – it's not

3. People think failure is objective – it's not

4. People think failure is the enemy – it's not

5. People think failure is irreversible – it's not

6. People think failure is a stigma – it's not

7. People think failure is final – it's not

Maxwell's book features story after story of people who we regard as successes. While he acknowledges the accomplishments of these people, the foundation of his accounts are the struggles each person faced in advancing toward fulfillment of their goals. People who have done something positive and constructive with their lives have all been through tough times. Evaluate what your "failure" is and use it to your advantage – turn it into a stepping stone.

If you are experiencing intense frustration with your goals, meditate on why you are drawn to the goal. Think back to your first memory of this goal. It is OK with God if we change our minds about a goal. Only you can make this decision and know when you are being honest about it or using it as a cop-out to quit.

*Building a Bridge*

For many years I had the goal of learning to play the piano. I had started lessons in a collegiate classroom environment. This proved to be a disaster for me, because learning music for me was like learning ancient hieroglyphics. I needed a slow pace, but many of my classmates were versed in music and able to follow the lessons quite efficiently. I, however, was struggling. It was like trying to swallow an orange whole. It wasn't working, and soon I was not enjoying the process. Thankfully, part of our overall grade was based on a written report about a live symphony performance we attended. This, coupled with weeks of laboriously practicing a very short song, allowed me to finish the class with a B grade. Years later I met a lovely woman who taught piano in the homes of her students. She was as patient as the day was long. I thought this would be the experience I needed to become a piano player. (I say piano player because my goal was to find some level of cooperation between myself and the instrument. I have never had visions of being a pianist. In my definition a pianist is a person who becomes one with the piano.) So I began piano lessons. Although I was much more familiar with the material, (having been exposed to it once before!) I was not experiencing success.

During a morning meditation I asked God to help me to step away from the matter and observe. What I discovered was this: as a young girl I knew several classmates who took piano lessons. In my mind there was something a little more special about them than me. I thought their families must be extra special to cultivate such talent in their children.

I realized that I was not taking piano to fulfill my hopes for myself, but to rise to a level that I had placed my classmates on because of my own judgments and perceptions. I was putting my energy into a task that I had no real enjoyment in because I had a need to fulfill an old stereotype. I no longer see myself as inferior to those classmates that did study piano.

I am now free to decide for myself if I want to study piano or pursue other goals. Regardless, I want aspirations that are in alignment with my true desires for myself. Take another look at your goals – are they yours or someone else's?

*Building a Bridge*

Life offers us teachers in every moment. A teacher can be a frustrated parent you observe at the grocery store, a disgruntled customer at the bank, a young person helping an elderly person carry a heavy object or a memory from your past. Teachers can be characters we see on screen or lyrics in a song. Self-help books can teach us directly and novels can unfold to teach us indirectly.

- Have you considered your own past a valid teacher?

- Who did you observe today that taught you something?

**"Learn from the mistakes of others. You cannot live long enough to make them all yourself."**

**Hyman G. Rickover**

In whatever goal we choose, success can only come when we stay focused. The accomplishment of any goal requires discipline. We hear the word discipline and automatically our skin crawls. As children we grew up believing that discipline was punishment. This thinking of punishment has led us to believe that if we want to accomplish our goals, it must be an up-hill battle of pain and suffering. This will only be so if we think it is. The meaning of discipline that we want to focus on is the "training that corrects, molds, or perfects the mental faculties or moral character." Learning to live in the moment allows us to focus on the beauty of the learning experience. As you watch your goal unfold, allow yourself the joy of being in process and progress. Stay in tune with the journey rather than being obsessed with the destination.

Do not discount your opportunities to learn from any source. The information we need for learning is always at our disposal. Often, when we are looking for it, we look too hard and we miss it. Relax and ask God to guide you to the teachers you need and are ready to accept

**"When the student is ready
the falling of the leaf can bring awareness.
When the student is not ready,
the falling of the tree won't help."**

**A Chinese Proverb**

*Building a Bridge*

## *Journaling*

Journaling offers us another opportunity to be our own teachers. Journal pages offer a sacred place for working through our thoughts, feelings, confusions, frustrations, dreams, desires, and hopes. The journals of today were the diaries of yesterday. Do you remember those little keys that came with our diaries? Do you realize that these are the keys for unlocking your soul?

There is no "way" to write a journal. Do you remember my chicken scratch journal pages from Chapter 3? It was written on notebook paper using an old pen from the bottom of my purse. Nothing fancy or sophisticated about this girl's journal!

If you want to make your journaling experience a bit more special, simply choose a notebook or blank book that you like and set aside a time each day when you can settle down and write. Now that doesn't sound so scary, does it? Well, maybe for some people it still does seem scary. If that is the case, here are some additional resources that might help you:

- Journaling Magazine

- http://www.writersdigest.com/journaling/

- *A Garden of Thoughts: My Affirmation Journal* by Louise Hay

- *Love Yourself, Heal Your Life Workbook* by Louise Hay

- *Sark's Journal and Play! Book* by Sark

- *The Handbook of Journaling: Tools for Healing the Mind, Body & Spirit* by Neil F. Neimark, M.D.

- *Journaling for Joy: Writing Your Way to Personal Growth and Freedom: The Workbook* by Joyce Chapman

Sark, author of *Succulent Wild Woman* shares these thoughts on journaling:

*Building a Bridge*

"The journal is a witness, an unconditional friend, a soul teacher. Sometimes, we just complain. Writing out the dark thoughts lessens their power. Having conversations with ourselves in journals gives us chances to work things out in private. We collect and form our own history with journals...It doesn't matter what you write in a journal. It matters that it is <u>yours</u>."

Other ideas for enhancing the journal experience are:

- Find a pen that allows you to write easily.

- Clip pictures from magazines and use them to enhance your ideas and dreams.

- Enjoy a favorite beverage or flavored coffee or herbal tea.

- Listen to instrumental music and allow your creative juices to flow.

### *Making Peace with Imperfection*

In our work to achieve goals, we must also allow ourselves to be human. Often we get so focused on the goals that we forget that we set the goals rather than vice versa. While working to accomplish our goals, we must be careful not to put too much pressure on ourselves. We are human and should give ourselves permission to be.

**"Our limitations, our imperfections, our mistakes ... these do not reflect our inferiority, but are part of being human."**

Joan Sheingold Ditzion

*Building a Bridge*

## *In Search of Balance*

Setting goals and working to achieve them are noble and worthy efforts, but sometimes we get a little obsessed; a bit over-focused. Balance is a critical element if we are to experience true success in our self-improvement plans. What does it benefit us if we achieve our goals at the expense of our families? How do we honor our families if we put our energy into a local charity and disregard the needs of our own children? Make sure your goals fit into your life – do not allow your goals to control your life.

Also, be balanced in your soul. Celebrate what you do and do not feel the need to seek the approval or applause of others. Do not be embarrassed to verbalize your goals if you are asked. It is most honorable to say that you are working to improve yourself, regardless of what work you need to do. Do not be duped into shyness about your dedication to your goals, although they may not be cutting edge or socially dynamic. If they are important to you, they are important – irrespective of the opinions of others.

**Additional reading suggestions:**

*How To Behave So Your Children Will, Too!* by Sal Severe, Ph.D.

*Manifest Your Destiny: The Nine Spiritual Principals for Getting Everything You Want* by Wayne W. Dyer

*Spiritual RX: Prescriptions for Living a Meaningful Life* by Frederic Brussat and Mary Ann Brussat

*Lanterns: A Memior of Mentors* by Marian Wright Edelman

*Live Your Dreams* by Les Brown

*Building a Bridge*

# Chapter 6: Our Relationships with the Third Parties

Parents are a child's primary caregiver and instructor, but many other parties play vital roles in the lives of our children as well. As long-distance parents we often feel very disconnected from these sources. We need to acknowledge who they are, give attention to these individuals and organizations, and show appreciation for the valuable contributions they make to the development of our kids.

## THIRD PARTIES

### The Residential Parent

From the vantage point of the long-distance parent, the residential parent is a third party. With this particular third party, it is obviously important that we have a working relationship without harboring a negative attachment to him/her.

Therefore, I want to encourage you to stop calling the other parent "your ex." If you call the other parent "your ex," you are indicating that you still have an attachment as the meaning of "your" is "possessor or relating to oneself." Refer to the other parent as "Johnny's father," or "Susie's mother," or simply by the other parent's first name. If you are sincerely working to create quality cooperation and communication, you will also need to stop using those little "pet" names you've grown so fond of ... jerk, idiot, creep, for example. (I am sure you have been more creative with names than I have, but you get the idea!)

The reason we maintain negative attachments to the other parent is because of unresolved issues from the past. Clearing the old air will require you to look at the past and your participation in it. It will require forgiveness, which will allow you to focus on your present life without the ball and chain of old hurts that you have been dragging around.

- What was I looking for in my relationship with _____ that I should have been looking for in myself?

- What was my level of maturity at the time of that relationship?

- What was the real issue that created the breakdown of the relationship?

- What was my role in this issue?

- Can I look back on the person I was then and see how afraid and hurt I was?

- Can I take that person into my arms and offer compassion and comfort?

- Can I forgive that person I was for the mistakes and misjudgments I made?

*Building a Bridge*

In honest reflection of the relationship I had with the children's father, I realize that when I married him I was looking to him to fill a void within me that I should have been filling on my own. I now recognize that I was feeling uncertain about my life and looking for stability and security. I saw a form of stability in his lifestyle and therefore, thought it would complete me. Oh boy, did I have to learn the hard way that it doesn't work like that!

As I became aware of looking within to meet my needs, I began to align with my Higher Self. Before divorce was ever a thought, I was starting to go my own direction, not fully conscious of how separated our lives were becoming. Yet each day we made our individual choices; choices very different from each other. As time passed, more individual decisions trenched a huge irreparable gap between the two of us. I can recall the frustration we experienced as we tried to influence each other's choices. Our weak communication skills made any attempt at conversation a confrontation. It soon became apparent that it was better to make my private choices in silence. Our individual levels of maturity and spirituality greatly affected our choices – all part of our growing process – a process that resulted in us growing apart.

I can look back on that time without the emotional turmoil I felt then. Removing the emotional turmoil comes from forgiveness. I have looked back on those days with compassion toward the person I was in those moments. I see the valuable lessons we offered one another – each of us was a teacher for the other. Though we played very different roles, I do not look back and see a "bad guy" in him or me. While that may sound odd, in the process of personal growth we are all at different stages of development. I cannot blame him or myself for the level of awareness – or lack thereof – that he or I had during that time. No one person is to blame. I am at peace with the decisions I made. I hope he can honestly say the same.

Once forgiveness has taken place, the emotional baggage of those marital experiences is released and we are free to move forward in life. However, as long-distance parents, it may be necessary to do a second cleansing process in order to make peace with the results of the custody proceedings.

*Building a Bridge*

When forgiveness is genuine, the other parent simply becomes a person. You will notice yourself observing the other parent with compassion. Without judgment or criticism you will look at him with spiritual eyes. What you see may surprise you. You might see a dynamic and talented individual who is enjoying the fruits of his genius. You might see a lovely woman who is uncovering her strengths and honoring her abilities. As a result of your growth, you will be able to celebrate this person and his accomplishments – genuinely celebrate them because forgiveness has freed you to do so.

Unfortunately, however, you might find a very sad man consumed with fear and making foolish choices in a desperate attempt to feel important. Or you might observe a woman trying to drown her pain and heartache in a bottle. When this happens, you need to offer a prayer of love and hold this person up to the God that created the person to be more than a wasted life. Nothing less than authentic compassion is called for under these circumstances. While it may be sad for us to look on the individual in this low state, can you imagine for a moment how painful it would be for a child to have to acknowledge the disappointing state of his parent? In our acts of compassion, especially toward the other parent, we honor our children.

Regardless of where the other parent is in his development as a person, we need to remain focused on our own status. To our intellectual selves, forgiveness is foreign because in our dealings with this person we no longer need to engage in hostile encounters. It is as if our minds say, "What? I don't have to be nasty?" Any communication or handling of matters with the other parent can now be done in a calm, courteous fashion.

While behaving in a human manner toward each other may seem odd, exercise faith that the other parent can grow and change. If you can do it, why can't he/she? Remember to focus on love-based behaviors although they may feel awkward.

### *Your Spouse or Partner*

No one gets married thinking about divorce (I hope!) In my case, the children's father and I tried to make it work, but it did not. I do not regret getting a divorce and moving on. But moving on to a

*Building a Bridge*

healthy relationship meant that I had to evaluate the previous marriage and learn from it. Having done that, I am now more emotionally and spiritually mature, able to handle differences of opinion and conflicts in my present marriage. My new husband, too, has found that life's lessons have enabled him to be a better husband. While we both would not have chosen divorce if we could have avoided it, we did learn from those previous relationships and are grateful that our marriage is now benefiting from those experiences.

Showing the children that we have a healthy partnership is important to us. We have made our marriage a priority. Since no one lives in Utopia and everyone deals with problems, each day we are given opportunities to demonstrate communication and cooperation skills to the children. They hear us speak tenderly and kindly, yet truthfully, to each other. They witness us confessing our shortcomings, which allows them the freedom to be human as well. They see us share in the responsibilities of home and family. They also see us laugh and joke and tease. These are priceless gifts they can use in their own relationships. I hope that they learn from us and someday luxuriate in beautiful spirit-filled relationships of their own.

As we work on our relationship with our children, our new partner or spouse will develop a personal relationship with the children as well. While we all dream that our children and our chosen love will get along in complete harmony, that relationship will need its own time to develop and mature. The older the children, the longer it may take. Regardless of your child's age, do not rush a new relationship by trying to force affection or respect. Do not insist the children call this person "Mom" or "Dad." Respect must be earned. Affection will be a result of trust and comfort. While most first marriages have an opportunity to create a foundation before embracing a family, stepfamilies are created instantly. These families have many issues to face from day one. So, the best thing you can do to cultivate the relationship between your partner and the children is keep your own relationships – marital and parental – in check. Be open and honest when the children have comments or questions. Above all, let them proceed at their own pace.

Sometimes the children will not like, or greatly dislike, the person you choose to be your new partner. The worst thing to do in this situation is try to force a friendship. The adults involved must

*Building a Bridge*

show respect for the child and exercise courtesy. The natural parent must also communicate to the child that the child's conduct needs to be respectful and courteous as well. There may be days (many of them?) when you walk a fine line. Words on this page make it sound easy, but when tensions build and emotions flare, it can become a long, hard day. You may need to distance yourself from the battle. Find a quiet place to think. Go for a walk. Write in your journal. Discuss valid options with your spouse. You may need to seek the advice of clergy or a counselor. But know this: if a hostile relationship between a stepparent and child continues, it can undermine the healthiest marriage. These tensions can chip away at us a little bit each day and soon we will find ourselves thinking that the marriage is not worth it. Find solutions!

While it is very possible your child and this person genuinely do not care for one another, it is more likely that the child would reject any person you choose to be your mate. Sometimes the child and the mate simply do not know each other and are making assumptions about the other's character. Time, honesty and respect can help to heal these wounds – if the members of the family are looking for healing. Have you seen the movie, "Man of the House?" It is worth viewing and available at your local video store.

If healing does not take place, many blended families find themselves in a "triangle tragedy." This occurs when the relationship between your spouse/partner and the child is not healthy. In this situation the natural parent is between a rock and a hard place, attempting to please a spouse and protect the child.

- How do I show support to my spouse/partner without alienating my child?

- How do I protect my child and keep peace in my marriage?

- Is my relationship with my spouse/partner healthy? Can I speak honestly about this situation or will the topic automatically create a hostile confrontation?

  - Is my child acting in such a fashion as to create ill will in my relationship?

*Building a Bridge*

In these situations counseling is highly recommended. Each person involved is probably contributing in some fashion to the problem. Although you may be intellectually aware of those contributive elements, the parties involved will receive them better from a neutral third party professional than from you. Verbalizing your observations of the matter may only contribute to further family problems.

If this triangular tug-of-war is not addressed, it can destroy a family member or result in another family breakup. At minimum, if not handled, the family will find itself in constant conflict, making respect and harmony forever unattainable.

Another situation many blended families face occurs when a child becomes a handful to manage. Sometimes this happens when the child does not have a good relationship with the stepparent, stepsibling or other family member. As a result, the child acts out. Sometimes this is simply a matter of childhood growth – a young person experiencing the trials of maturing. Sometimes jealousies exist. It is critical that you discover the root of the problem and evaluate solutions for handling the situation. Ask yourself, "Is my child really a problem child or is he screaming for attention and acceptance by his behavior?"

During this time it is critical that the parents not communicate the idea of "eliminating the problem" with talk of shipping the child to the other parent. Maybe a move to the other parent's household is exactly what the child needs; however, this decision must be made in a thoughtful manner. Expressing the notion that "no one wants to deal with this kid and his nonsense" will only further harm the child by deepening his hurts and thereby distance him from both parents.

How do you handle a child's request to live with the other parent? A wise parent will share real conversation with the child about this request. If there are no real reasons for your child not to go, and the other parent consents, let the child go. How could it possibly benefit the parents to deny this request? How could it possibly harm the child to honor the request?

A child who wants to make a move is in a tormented situation – he is in the position of choosing between one parent's home and the other parent's home. Because children want to love both parents,

*Building a Bridge*

they can't see how they can make a change of residence without hurting one of their parents. When a child wants to move to the other parent's home, it is not always an indication of rejection toward the present residential parent.  Perhaps the child simply wants an opportunity to spend more time with the other parent. Whatever the reason, a child may have trouble communicating the request to the parent.  In fact, the child may – consciously or subconsciously – create problems as a possible solution.  The child may think that by generating emotional frustration between the two of you, the chances of your saying, "Go live with your other parent" are more likely.  If this happens, the child is "off the hook" for making a choice – you've just done it for him.  If you suspect this situation exists with your child, here are some signals to watch for:

- child initiates arguments with you
- child presses you to expand boundaries that are not good for him
- child deliberately sabotages his school work
- child generates ill-will among friends and classmates

My son Jason had lived in Houston for two years when he began talking of a move back to Illinois.  I was deeply troubled by his comments.  In fact, I initially reacted to suggestions by blurting out facts that I felt would clarify why he should remain in Houston.  He was doing very well in school, he had a great group of friends, he was on a terrific basketball team and just joined swim team … I don't need to continue because I bet you are familiar with your own list.  Pointing out these positive aspects only caused him to be more defensive about his desire.  So, I followed the advice I offer you.  First, I stepped away from the situation.  Repeated attempts to hold conversations would have benefited no one since they probably would have escalated into arguments.  Second, I contacted two wise counselors – a respected lawyer and a trusted friend.  I poured out my heart, expressed my fears and concerns and then shut up so I could listen to their ideas.  For the next couple of days my husband Fred and I exchanged thoughts regarding the situation.  I also prayed – not that Jason would stay with us, but that I would have the courage to make a good decision and act with the highest integrity for everyone involved.  The conclusion was this: Jason was free to relocate if he chose to do so, but he had to wait until the end of the school year.

*Building a Bridge*

Legally, in Texas Jason is allowed to make a residential decision at age 10. In Illinois he can decide at 12 (which he will be just after the start of the new school year.) If I challenged his choice, as crazy as this may sound, the judge would probably reprimand me for interfering with his legal right. Additionally, the "facts" that I blurted out to Jason were in reality my opinions of how things should be. Since opinions do not hold up in court, I would no doubt be considered a hindrance to the legal system – again, something the judge would view unfavorably.

The only possible win-win solution was that I embrace the fable "Holding with an Open Hand" and release Jason to make this decision independently. Not an easy task. I truly want what is best for Jason. I can produce several strong reasons why I think living in Houston is better for him. But didn't I use Gilbran's writings to encourage parents to consider the child's path?

When I write these suggestions for long-distance loving, I write them for myself. When peace and joy are the result of my actions, I know I have tapped into wise action – action that needs to be shared with you. When I experience turmoil and frustration in my life, I know I must take a second look at myself – my thinking – and make changes. This is the same process I outline for you. Do not think for a minute that I am not in the same boat as you or that my boat is in some way better, stronger or more capable. In every moment I must look at what I am doing and why I am doing it. I accept as my own the words of Eleanor Roosevelt who said, "It is not fair to ask of others what you are not willing to do yourself."

When your child wants to discuss a change of residential location with you, consider the following:

- Why is your child making this request? (To dodge responsibilities, to please the other parent, to please you, to spend more time with the other parent, to get away from a difficult stepparent relationship.)

- Together evaluate the pros and cons of such a move by using a chart similar to this example.

*Building a Bridge*

| Situation | Pro | Con |
|---|---|---|
| Family | More time with Dad More time with siblings | Less time with Mom |
| Home | Less chores because more children to share in the jobs Familiar with area | No one at home after school |
| School | Knows the school (used to attend there) | Needs to be more consistent in schooling |
| Social | Has friends in Illinois | Will miss friends in Texas |

- Seek counsel for both yourself and your child. Consider meeting together and individually with a professional. This meeting would not be to persuade the child one way or the other, but to stimulate thoughts about the pros and cons. Encourage your child to make a decision only after it has been thought through carefully.

- Do some brainstorming on how you will handle the move.

    - When would it occur?

*Building a Bridge*

- How will this move affect the rest of your agreements with the other parent?
- When will you see the child – can you simply reverse the schedule you have now?
- Who would need to be notified? Family, friends, schools, medical professionals and others?

These moves are not easy on parents. When a child lives with us for any length of time, we grow as a family, generate routines and become comfortable. When the child wants to move, we feel a disruption in our lives. It hurts. We feel as if we are going through the whole painful cycle again.

We only have to experience pain if we choose to do so. The other option is to let go, live and love.

Sending a child to boarding school or a military academy is another decision that must be made with great care and caution. It would be wise to obtain a counselor's opinion prior to making such arrangements. Ask yourself, "Is this really what my child needs or is this simply a convenience?"

The fact is that if parents cannot handle a child, a judge can and may send a child to a boarding school. Do everything you – both parents together – can to make solid decisions for your child so the courts are not needed. If you need help, get it. Do not allow your pride to get in the way of making quality choices for your child.

Every possibility exists that the child's behavior is not only an opportunity for the individual healing process to occur, but for other members of the family to confront their problems as well. While it is human nature to want to shove the dirt under the rug, it eventually will need to be faced. It is better to do it sooner rather than later

*Building a Bridge*

## *Stepparents*

Who the other parent selects to be his new partner is none of your business or concern. The only right thing to do in dealing with a stepparent is to arrive at some common ground in communication. Actually, depending on how the other parent handles his affairs, you may have very few occasions for communication with the stepparent, but if/when you do, keeping it pleasant will be a real benefit. A note of caution: If you are dealing with an extremely difficult other parent, be sensitive to your comments. It is not unheard of that a little chitchat might get distorted and become a court issue.

My critical judgments of the stepparent do not mean that she is the person I describe, but it definitely means that when I judge this person, I am describing myself as a person who needs to judge. Evaluate the source of your judgments. Consider these questions:

- Am I still stuck in old thinking about the marriage?

- Am I jealous of the new relationship?

- Am I angry with myself about the status of my own life?

- Am I using this stepparent as a target for issues I need to work on within myself?

Sometimes when the children complain about situations or make comments involving the stepparent, the temptation to capitalize is almost overwhelming. I won't lie and say that I have never stooped to such comments. When I have, I don't like myself afterwards. What does work and generates a long-term positive effect is teaching the children how to deal with people and how to problem solve. Teaching them how to cooperate with others – whether the other person is you, your spouse or partner, another stepparent or any other individual – is a life tool that will forever benefit them. This course of action is healthy and productive.

While it is documented that many children have difficult stepparent relationships, there is every possibility that the children and this person are developing a loving relationship. When this happens, the children have, by choice, extended their family. It behooves us to show respect to this person, if for no other reason than as a courtesy to the children. If you exercise common courtesy, although you may not feel like it in your heart, it will come back to bless you and you will feel it. I am not saying it will come back directly from the other parent. Don't count on immediate courtesy from the other parent. Don't get upset regardless of their behavior. However, as a pure optimist, I don't want you to rule out the possibility of someday having real cooperation between you. Even the Hatfields and the McCoys have stopped feuding. It took over a hundred years, but the point is healing did happen. Remember the universal law that states whatever you give out, you get back? Why not put it to the test? Working together to raise happy, healthy children will bring peace to our own lives, peace to the children and will help heal our planet.

In addition, this person is with your children on a daily basis, and in all probability, is providing help and support in meeting their needs. If you are familiar with the efforts of full-time parenting, you can understand that the stepparent could be making a valuable contribution to your children. If you have not been involved in day-to-day parenting, you may not know the demands of such an endeavor, but I assure you that anyone engaged in such work deserves to be appreciated.

In working with relationships between the natural parents, stepparents and children, we must remember that we do not live in a perfect world with perfect people. We must learn to act respectfully and cooperatively. We must hope that each of us opens our hearts to learning through these relationships. We must never doubt the possibility of genuinely respecting one another.

Unfortunately, it is also known that many children have been abused – emotionally and physically – by a stepparent. To accuse another person of abusing your child is a deeply serious accusation, which could, if not proven, result in a lawsuit. If you suspect that your child is being abused, you need to contact the child protective services agency where your child lives. If you don't know how to reach that organization, a child services office in your area can assist you in locating the appropriate office. They will also have information on what signs indicate or suggest abuse, how to discuss the matter with your children and their other parent, and how to make a request for an investigation, if one is necessary.

*Building a Bridge*

While physical abuse reveals itself with cuts and bruises, a far deeper, but equally as painful, abuse, often goes unnoticed. Oliver Tuthill, founder and executive director of Autumn Tree Productions, a nonprofit agency created in 1995 to raise public awareness of emotional abuse, says, "It's sometimes called invisible abuse." Tuthill says emotional abuse is "a systematic disregard of a child's need for unconditional love. It can include bullying, negligence and isolating a child from others. It's the psychological consequences of the act that define it as abusive."

If emotional abuse is present in the relationship between your child and his stepparent and you are aware of this abuse, it will be difficult for you to address the issue. Because no visible evidence of the misconduct is present, only a trained professional will be able to diagnose and document the problem. Discussing the situation with the other parent will automatically put him in a defensive position. Even if the other parent knows that what you are saying is true, he will no doubt deny it.

In younger children there are a number of useful methods for getting an idea of how things are handled in the other household. I do not suggest these so you can snoop on the other parent or dredge up dirt to use against him. Here are some ideas for parents who feel their children are in abusive situations.

- Play house allowing the child to play both the mother and father. Observe the language and mannerisms of your child in each role.

- Play with puppets.

- Draw family pictures.

If you continue to suspect real trouble, consult a child counselor immediately and share what you have heard your child say or do. Then allow the counselor to work on your child's behalf without interfering with the process. The truth can only be determined when we are not manipulating to get it.

If your child is old enough to communicate the abuses, take her to a counselor and have the abuses documented. Ask the counselor to give you and your child ideas on how to proceed. After

*Building a Bridge*

the abusive behavior has been verified by a professional counselor, discuss the matter with the other parent in a very gentle, but direct, fashion. While this will be a very challenging conversation, you must protect the mental health of your child with the same assertiveness that you would use to protect the child's physical health. If, in the counselor's opinion, the abuse is significant, the child should be permitted to live in the other household, providing no additional opportunities for abuse exist in that home. If your child has brought these matters to your attention, your child probably has an opinion about where he wants to live. If this is the case, your child should tell the counselor so that can be documented as well.

Rather than approaching the situation with hostility, try to see this as an opportunity for healing. Because of the abuse demonstrated by this person, there is obviously inner work to do.

I want to say a word about movies and television programs that feature single parents, stepparents and blended families. Movies and television programs are in their glory when they depict intense drama. It seems that current scripts thrive on the most bizarre situations and most outrageous "solutions." Be careful using movie/TV dialogue in your life. Reel families are not real families. Using them as role models should be done with caution. For example, in the movie, "Stepmom," the characters portrayed by Julia Roberts and Susan Sarandon struggle to find balance in their involvement with the children. This is normal. The script unfolds to have Sarandon (the biological mother) diagnosed with terminal cancer. Suddenly the two women are working together beautifully and they magically blend into a fabulous family. I know that many stepparents fantasize about the biological parent leaving the planet, but rarely does that actually happen. In real life parents must learn to communicate and cooperate on a daily basis. Since these routine encounters aren't film worthy, we don't see them on the big screens. Watching these productions do offer us opportunities to observe, contemplate and evaluate, but they should absolutely not be considered training videos.

### *Stepsiblings*

The same thoughtful and gentle approaches that we use in dealing with any children should be applied to our dealings with stepsiblings. These children have become a part of a blended family because of the choices of the adults in their lives. We need to show them care and consideration when we have involvement with them.

My children have a stepsister and a half-sister, both of whom they consider sisters – period. When I send gift boxes or treats for holidays or special occasions, I include enough for everyone. If I am sending individual gifts, I include packages for each child.

Rising above parental "ownership" of children provides us countless opportunities to love children regardless of who they "belong to." You will find great joy in celebrating all children. It will be spiritually rewarding for you, a delightful experience for the children and an opportunity to create goodwill among the families.

Siblings – biological, step, blended or otherwise – will have their disputes. Sibling disputes have been around since The Garden of Eden – do you remember the drama I spoke about surrounding Cain and Abel? Sibling rivalry at its ugliest! Thankfully, day-to-day encounters among siblings are usually more manageable. Here are some suggestions for dealing with sibling rivalry:

- Don't compare your children. This creates a sense of competition for parental admiration, which can promote ill feelings.

- Appreciate and publicly praise each child individually.

- Establish sound family policies for behavior so everyone knows the boundaries.

- Teach your children problem-solving skills.

- Allow the children to work through their own quarrels. Only interfere when necessary, for example, before things get physically hostile.

- Parents should assist children in solution finding by offering suggestions, but only after the children have exhausted their own resources.

- Don't take sides. These arguments are never black-and-white. There is always gray area where compromise must be found.

*Building a Bridge*

- Establish a family policy outlawing words like hate and shut-up. Also discourage name-calling such as stupid or ignorant.

- If children do engage is physical fighting, separate them until they calm down. No one can think straight when his fists are clenched in rage.

- If the argument is intense, help them sort through the problems. You may want to insist on a written agreement. If this is what is called for, make each party sign it with parents as witnesses.

- When you see your children cooperating, tell them how much this means to you and the family. Our children want to please us, so praising good behavior generates more of the same.

- If things are hostile on a frequent basis, take some time to think about where the anger is coming from. Taking frustrations out on a brother or sister may be easier than dealing with a bigger problem.

There are several books available offering advice on how to blend families. Here is a list of a few, but consult your library or local bookstore for a more complete listing.

- *Strengthening Your Stepfamily* by Elizabeth Einstein and Linda Albert

- *Living in a Stepfamily without Getting Stepped on* by Dr. Kevin Leman

- *The Stepfamily: Living, Loving, and Learning* by Elizabeth Einstein

- *Stepfamily Living: Pitfalls and Possibilities* by Elizabeth Einstein

- *Stepfamilies: Myths and Realities* by Emily B. Visher and John S. Visher

- *Stepfamilies: A Cooperative Responsibility* by Fredrick Capalki and Barbara McRae

*Building a Bridge*

- For additional guidance, contact the Stepfamily Association of America at 28 Allegheny Avenue, Suite 1307, Baltimore, MD 21204 or at 800-735-0329 or at www.stepfam.org.

Another note on sibling rivalry may offer a positive spin on the subject. Sometimes the children will engage in games that pit the kids against the parents. There is an old war saying, "The enemy of my enemy is my friend." These games help the children to form a bond. How many episodes of "The Brady Bunch" offered the scenario of the children grouping as an allied front in an effort to out-maneuver the parents?

### *New Family*

Once my daughter asked if Fred and I planned to have other children. We answered, "No." Then she asked if we had thought of adopting. We said, "We had not." Then she said, "Well, are you going to get more kids somehow?" Jason piped in and said, "Sarah, no one is getting replaced!" Jason heard this from the movie, "Toy Story." Woody, the cowboy toy and leader of the toys, uses this line to calm the other toys when there is a panic over possibly being discarded. Their boy, Andy, is having a birthday and they fear a new toy will cause some among the toy family to go to the junk. To assure the toys, he proclaims, "No one is getting replaced!" (And by the way, no one does.) This is also an excellent example of how we learn by watching the characters in movies.

Children have a very real concern that they will be replaced when they do not live with you. They feel that since you don't have them, you'll get another child. Making children feel individually special is the job of every parent, but keeping long-distance children in touch with your family plans is especially important. Should you choose to add to your family, be sensitive to the emotional needs of your existing children. Communicate these events to them in a timely manner and do so with great love. Remember – extending your family – not replacing!

Before you plan to add to your family responsibilities, consider your present parenting responsibilities. Caring for new children at the expense of existing children does not serve to better the children of our world.

### *Building a Bridge*

## *Grandparents*

Not always, but quite often, when a parent becomes long distance or absent, the grandparents suffer. Hostilities toward the long-distance parent can spill into tensions toward the grandparents. Losing a parent is enough. Losing grandparents, who wish to maintain their own relationships, would be a true tragedy for the children. Do not unjustly punish the grandparents involved by trying to destroy or interfere with the development of their relationships with the children. If you, the long-distance parent, are not ready to be in communication with your children, allow the grandparents to exercise their rights.

Grandparents must also know their role in the children's lives and not become involved in the war between the parents. By remaining neutral and loving, they can offer the children a safe place to be loved and celebrated.

In blended family situations one of the most stressful times for the children is holidays. Everyone in the family wants to be with the children during these occasions, but the children simply cannot be in all places simultaneously.

To alleviate some of this stress, grandparents should create their own holidays – start some new traditions. They may want to celebrate half birthdays or choose a new date for major holidays or simply plan a periodic get together and celebrate many things at once. Learn to celebrate the occasions you have to be together rather than getting stuck in old, and often rigid, traditions. While honoring traditions can be fun, it can also create anxiety.

If grandparents live near the children, they can attend school open houses or school activities such as sporting events or theatrical performances. This gives them an opportunity to see the children while supporting their activities and interests. Grandparents can really help bridge the distance for a long-distance parent by videotaping programs or taking photographs.

*Building a Bridge*

In the agreement between the children's father and I, we stated that the children are to visit with my parents for one weekend a month or two days a month, depending on what can be worked out from the personal and school schedules. To date my parents have not had any real problems in making arrangements for the visits. I leave these arrangements up to my parents to work out with the children's father.

One incident happened that did take me by surprise. I became a long-distance parent at the end of October 1996. It had been planned that the children would spend first winter break with us. My parents had made plans to celebrate Christmas with Sarah and Jason a few weeks prior to December 25. I knew of these plans and prepared the gifts for mailing so they would arrive in time. About a week before the planned date, during a conversation with my mother, I learned that the children's father and his new family were joining my parents at my parent's home for the celebration. My mother told me of her plans for preparing hors d'oeuvres to serve while opening gifts and about reservations she made at a local family restaurant for dinner. She elaborated on what gifts she had bought the wife's daughter and their baby. Mom went on to tell me what gift she had purchased for the children's father and his wife!

To say that I was stunned is somewhat of an understatement. I felt that I was being betrayed. This episode was taking place about six weeks after my initial separation from the children. The last thing I was ready for was my parents inviting "the enemy" to their home for a cheery holiday get-together. To add to my aggravation, I had purchased gifts for his two children, but I had not considered buying him and his wife a gift. Fred and I discussed the matter and decided to put our (my) harsh feelings aside and act in the spirit of Christmas. We purchased a restaurant gift certificate for them. The wound seemed too open for all this "nice," but I reached deep within myself and went through the motions. I sent the box, and everyone enjoyed the holiday celebration and gifts.

*Building a Bridge*

This episode "worked" on me for quite a while. I discussed the "ordeal" with a couple of friends whose opinions I highly regard. They, too, were a little surprised with the arrangements. Then it hit me. First of all, my parents have the right to invite anyone they want to their home. Further, they have the right to take anyone they want to dinner. Secondly, it is a great gift to the children that we can all work together. While I did not initially appreciate the opportunity that the Christmas holiday afforded me, I was later happy that I extended the kindness. Now that I have my thinking straight, I am glad that I sent the gift. Third, my feeling of betrayal was clearly my lack of good thought processing. I was leaning toward victim territory – a place I hate to go! Since I do not want that frame of mind, I released the experience. I released the experience, but embraced the valuable lesson.

Through this experience I was able to learn a beautiful lesson that Dr. Wayne Dyer teaches: when you have the choice between being right or being kind…choose being kind.

### *Your Child's Friends and The Parents of those Friends*

The child's friends can provide a powerful resource of support for your child. Sometimes the friends have their own family issues to handle and can relate to your child's hurts and hopes. This allows both young people to express compassion and understanding. They can also share ideas and encouragement for working out their problems. Sometimes the friends have strong family networks, which become a support network for your child. You need to know your child's friends and the parents of those friends. These individuals offer your child a beautiful gift. Do not be jealous. The idea of a surrogate parent may not appeal to you, but children need the presence of thoughtful, caring adults in their lives. If you cannot be there for your children, endorse those adults who are. These people should not be considered a replacement of you, but a tremendous support for your child. Appreciate them for the contribution they make to your child's life. Tell them that you are grateful for them by writing a note or calling with a word of thanks.

*Building a Bridge*

Sometimes friends can bridge the distance between your home and their other home. Consider inviting your child's friends to visit on occasion. If there is great distance between you, consider having a friend join your child for spring break or for a week during the summer. If you live closer, perhaps a weekend stay can be arranged. Talk to your child about his/her close friends and discuss the future possibility of inviting a friend.

### School personnel/teachers

If you are preparing for your long-distance relationship or are at the early stages of one, I highly recommend that you meet with the school personnel and teachers before you separate from the children.

I had been very active at my children's school prior to my move. Before I relocated, I met with the teachers and shared with them my ideas for staying in touch. Because I had been a volunteer at the school and the faculty/staff were familiar with me, they were very open to my ideas. They knew they could trust me to contribute in constructive ways. Through my continued participation in the children's educational process, not only did the school staff see the children and I making the best of a tough situation, so did their classmates.

If you are not familiar with your child's school, you may want to write a letter of introduction. A sample letter might read as follows:

Dear (Principal),

This letter comes as an introduction of myself, Jane Doe. I am Susie Smith's mother. As you may know, I live in Another City, State and maintain a long-distance relationship with my daughter. Since she will be in your school this year, I want you and me to have an open line of communication, regardless of the miles between us. It is my hope that I stay current with her schooling and educational development, and therefore, look forward to receiving a copy of her report cards and status reports from you. When it is time for the parent-teacher conferences, I would like to make an appointment to discuss her progress and needs via telephone conferencing. If a situation or problem arises that requires more immediate attention, please notify me.

Susie's father and I share in the custody of Susie. While he does a fine job with her, I believe that my input in these matters is equally valuable.

I am enclosing some items that I hope will be helpful to us in our communication efforts:

- A letter for office records giving the principal, Susie's teachers and office personnel permission to call me collect at any time. I have listed all the telephone numbers where I can be reached and the times of day I am generally at those numbers. Please do not hesitate to exercise this right.

- A sheet of mailing labels with my home address.

- Five 9x12 mailing envelops and ten business-sized envelops. Each one is pre-addressed/pre-stamped.

As long distance parenting may be something you are unfamiliar with, I would like to share with you some of the ways we stay in touch:

(List what you do to stay in touch)

If I find that I will be in the school area, I will contact you, as I would very much like to meet you. I am looking forward to this school year for Susie. She is a delightful girl and I am confident you will enjoy her very much.

Sincerely,

NOTE: You may want to include a copy of the court-ordered decree. This can be optional. Check with the school on their policy regarding having this document on file, but be aware that they may ask for it. If you do choose to enclose it with your introductory letter, do so as an 'FYI' or 'For Your Records.' You do not want the school to have the impression you are sending this to proclaim your rights in a demanding legalistic manner.

*Building a Bridge*

In the event that serious medical or educational decisions need to be made, if you have a joint parenting agreement and the party(s) need to know this information, your letter should politely state your legal status.

I have drafted this letter as an example. If you need a letter for the school, you must write one to fit your specific situation and use words that are in line with your comfort level and integrity. For example, if you receive school information from the other parent, you will not need to ask the school to provide this.

Every school is different. Every principal has his own ideas regarding long-distance parents. Some principals have had less than pleasant experiences in these matters. I highly recommend that you give the school an opportunity to get to know you. While a letter of introduction is good, it is not a replacement for actually meeting you. Visiting the school and spending time with the principal and teachers will help you establish a reputation – which will open doors of opportunity for participating in your child's education.

- If you can arrange a visit, try to do so early in the school year. Most schools offer a parent information night at the beginning of the year and if possible, try to attend.

- If you cannot attend the parent/teacher introduction evening, ask the teacher to send you a copy of the curriculum packet. This will outline the teacher's lesson plan for the year as well as her policies on homework and standards for classroom conduct. You may also request a school calendar, which will specify the holiday/no school schedule. Also ask for dates of any special events that your child may be participating in, such as the class play, talent show, band/chorus concerts, or other events.

During a school open house, principals and teachers are very busy. If you want time to discuss long-distance parenting, make sure these parties have plenty of time to really focus on your situation. Make arrangements well in advance so they have time to think about how they might be able to communicate with you. If you request this meeting, you must be prepared for it. Consider the following:

*Building a Bridge*

- During a visit, outline your ideas for constructive contributions. These ideas should be developed PRIOR to the meeting. Review the ideas in Chapter 8 before your appointment. You might also benefit from talking to other long-distance parents to find out how they stay in touch. In addition, ask the principal of the school if she deals with any other long-distance parents. She may have some ideas of her own to bring to the table.

- Ask what ideas the teachers might have for your participation.

- Ask what the school policy is regarding mail and faxes to students.

- Ask what the school policy is on visitors in the classroom and lunchroom.

- Ask the teacher(s) if you may have a copy of the curriculum. This is where you will gather information about ways to participate. As you study the curriculum, you can create ideas for contributions to the lessons.

- Ask what time of day is a good time to contact the teacher or leave a message. Do the teachers have voice mail?

- Ask if the school or teacher has email available.

- Ask if the school has a web site or on-line newsletter.

- Ask if the school participates in any fundraising programs such as the Campbell's Labels for Education program or collecting soda can tabs. This is an easy way for you to support the school long distance!

- Meet the librarian and ask for a copy of her "wish list." Donating books to the library is another great way to participate. You could donate a book periodically or you could make the donation in honor of your child's birthday or simply make a financial contribution. (Every dollar makes a difference. Do not feel that you must make a large donation in order for it to be helpful.)

*Building a Bridge*

- Ask for the names and telephone numbers of the room moms. Connect with them for ideas on how you can contribute to holiday parties or other special occasions.

- Ask to meet with the school counselor. She can brainstorm with you on additional ideas. She can also provide your child with tremendous support on difficult days.

- Ask if the school has a parent volunteer weekend. This would be a great weekend to visit your child and participate with other parents in projects that will benefit your child's school. It will provide you an opportunity to be of help and also directly connect you with the parents of your child's friends.

- Ask if your school has an annual fundraiser such as a carnival. This would be another great weekend to visit as PTA is always in need of extra hands during these big events.

In my first experience with school, the school staff and faculty knew me quite well. My relationship with those professionals after my relocation was still positive and very cooperative. However, when the children were moved into a different school environment, my participation in their schooling deteriorated – in fact, the school made it very clear to me that they wanted nothing to do with me. I realized that they were prejudiced because of my label of long-distance parent and had no grounds on which to base their stereotypes since they did not know anything about me. They chose to be very cold when I made arrangements for a visit to the school. (I am pretty sure they had been given a description of me, but since they did not exercise the opportunity to get to know me for themselves, the children experienced a great loss.) I believe that the only reason they met with me then and subsequently kept me involved at the minimum they did was about concern of potential legal problems.

If you feel shut off from the school:

- Maintain contact when the opportunity presents itself

- Create a few opportunities of your own

*Building a Bridge*

- Let go of the situation and allow the universe to open the doors for you

- Pray, meditate and visualize

When the children were at the "less-than-receptive" school, I learned through my son that his classroom needed a pencil sharpener. He told me that the students were instructed to make sure that their pencils were sharpened at home and ready for school the next day. I immediately suspected this would turn out to be a train wreck of a plan, and saw an opportunity to help out. I went to the office supply store and purchased an electric pencil sharpener. It was not top-of-the-line, but it was good quality and one I could afford. I sent the sharpener to the school. On the return address space I wrote "School's Secret Pal" with my home address. The teacher, of course, knew the sharpener was from me, even though I had not enclosed a note. I loved it when Jason told me about the sharpener magically appearing. He said all his classmates were thrilled, and everyone lined up right away to sharpen their pencils!

I LOVE victory in kindness! Not only did the class get its much-needed pencil sharpener, they also received a message. I was able to very nicely say, "I am paying attention. I want to participate. I will find ways to help even if you don't tell me what they are." Touché!

Are you familiar with the poem, "Outwitted," by Edwin Markham?

> He drew a circle that shut me out –
> Heretic, rebel, a thing to flout.
> But Love and I had the wit to win:
> We drew a circle that took him in!

Educational professionals have been trained to handle the various life situations of children. They may have insight to assist you in handling long-distance parenting. Perhaps another student has a long-distance parent and the two students could find comfort in sharing what helps or bridges the distance. Or, if your child is having trouble dealing with your long-distance situation, perhaps the school

*Building a Bridge*

psychologist could meet with her and discuss the problems. Remember: These professionals are there to help your child.

DO NOT create any hindrances in their efforts to serve your children. DO NOT abuse the school personnel by sharing negative communication. Discuss with them issues that pertain directly to your child. Brainstorm with them on how to better your relationship with the children or new ways you might involve yourself in school programs or activities. If a time arises when sensitive subjects need to be addressed or handled, do so without incorporating blame toward any party. Simply handle the situation and contribute toward correcting the behavior or circumstances. I will warn you that if any uncomfortable situations arise from your long-distance situation, the school will probably not work with you. They have special issues for nearly every student in their care and cannot (will not and should not) deal with parent nonsense.

Each school district has its own policies regarding parental participation. Ask the principal of your child's school what the policies are. If they don't have any, suggest that they use your participation as a pilot test for creating policies.

Any and all efforts you make to connect with your child's school will benefit your child. Studies confirm that children do better in school and create healthier school relationships when the parents are involved in the educational process.

Make the effort!

### Medical/Dental Professionals

If you have joint legal custody, it is appropriate for you to send the medical/dental professionals a letter of introduction. For routine appointments or check-ups, you may not feel the need to be advised of treatment. However, should your child need any out-of-the-ordinary care, you may tell the medical/dental professionals that you want to be included in the decision-making processes which are afforded to you under the joint parenting agreement. In the letter of introduction you should indicate your address and telephone number(s) and extend the right to call collect.

*Building a Bridge*

My experience has been that medical and dental professionals are careful about talking to the long-distance parent. They generally expect the residential parent to handle the communication of information. I highly recommend that any dealings you may have with these parties be done with the greatest level of professionalism. Remain completely focused on the diagnosis and treatment options.

If there is a difficult medical decision to be made, you may need to provide a copy of the custody decree showing your legal right to be included in the process. Should you find yourself in this situation, keep only your child's best interest in mind. This is no place for a demanding attitude.

### *Attorneys*

It is a common practice of many long-distance parents to keep an attorney close at hand for ongoing discussions of matters that arise in the parenting of the children. If you use an attorney for consultation about parenting matters, don't be surprised if he at some point suggests legal action. My experience is that lawyers are looking for opportunities to exercise the law. Therefore, it is my opinion that keeping an attorney on retainer is much like keeping a loaded gun in the dresser. If you are not expecting any trouble, what's the point?

Maybe your response to that question is that by having an attorney at hand you feel safer. If that is your position, you need to take a careful look at your relationship with the other parent.

- Has the other parent given you a valid reason to keep an attorney at hand?

- Why does an attorney make you feel safer?

- Are you putting more trust in the attorney than yourself?

- Why?

Once the custody decision has been made, the attorney's job is done. Any other challenges, such as visitation problems, require a new retainer and contract. Before you solicit your attorney for matters, seriously consider if the services are really needed or if you can find

*Building a Bridge*

another way to handle the conflict. Should you require legal services, you must secure an attorney from the controlling jurisdiction.

If you feel the need to monitor the joint parenting situation, I recommend that you keep a written documentation of those situations that you feel present a problem for you or your children. The log should include the date and time of the situation for which you are writing as well as the important information about the matter.

I have on several occasions sent a letter to the children's father outlining my opinions of situations where I have held a different view from his. As a participating parent of the children, I am entitled to contribute my opinions and ideas to their lives. As a joint custody parent, by law, the other parent has a responsibility to hear my ideas. Whether he does or not is his choice, but by putting my thoughts in writing I have a documentation of my comments to him. It is appropriate and acceptable for a long-distance parent to address these issues with the residential parent when they neglect to address them with you. When writing a letter be sure to address only the issues at hand and not use the letter as an opportunity to belittle the parent or create additional problems.

As I mentioned previously, I had a situation regarding a school matter. While this was a real issue in my life, this is not the real letter I sent to the other parent. I have not included those real letters in this book as a matter of privacy, so this letter is an example.

A sample letter might read as follows:

Dear name,

> I am writing this letter regarding your decision to place the children in a private school. Our custody decree clearly states that we are to jointly make decisions regarding the children's educational and medical needs. By excluding me from this process, our agreement has been violated – an agreement we promised the judge we would honor. If this were a situation requiring emergency medical attention and you made a decision without me, I would understand. However, this is not an emergency matter as I am confident you had ample time to consider

*Building a Bridge*

moving the children to this school. Excluding me from the process is unacceptable.

Since you have officially enrolled the children in this school, and they have prepared themselves for this change, I will not disrupt the plan. However, I will not contribute to the tuition fees as you have requested. Since this decision was made independent of me, the financial responsibility will be yours. While I am sure you were counting on my financial assistance, this is not a decision I support, as the children had a very positive public school situation.

I will personally assure the children that I will continue to support their educational process in the same manner which I did at the public school.

While I am upset about this situation, it will not effect the child support payments and I do not intend to contact an attorney about this. But you can be sure that if you continue to make decisions outside of our custody agreement, I will not rule out the possibility of seeking legal counsel.

For the children's sake, I hope they are happy and do well at the new school.

Sincerely,

name


If you nood a format for writing a difficult letter, follow this example:

Dear _____,

Paragraph 1: establish the issue

Paragraph 2: explain your position

*Building a Bridge*

Paragraph 3: assure continued support

Paragraph 4: close focusing on the children

Sincerely,

Other suggestions for writing difficult letters include:

- Write the draft letter and do nothing with it for at least twenty-four hours. This will give you time to calm down, if necessary, and do rewrites. If calming down is not needed, you can still use the time to step away from the letter and rethink any possible changes.

- Seek counsel on the letter. Do not call every person you know, but asking a wise friend for a second opinion is a good idea. You might have this person read your letter and help weed out words that accuse or threaten. (When we are caught up in a situation, we cannot see these words for ourselves.)

- Type the letter, if possible. The act of typing makes a letter more professional and gives you an opportunity to create some emotional distance.

- Keep a copy of this letter in the event of future problems. Put the letter in a safe place, but don't leave it on top of your desk or dresser. By doing so, you will stay focused on the problem and block yourself from solutions.

I am not suggesting that you write letters about the day-to-day rearing of the children. I am suggesting that you write when you feel that important life decisions are being made without your input. While the point of this book is to create cooperation and communication, there are times and situations when we need to stand up for our parenting rights as well as protecting the children from a parent who may independently make decisions that are not necessarily in the child's best interest.

*Building a Bridge*

## Support Groups

Participation in a support group can be a valuable asset in dealing with long-distance parenting issues. Other parents who are in similar situations will understand your frustrations and concerns. Support groups can be found at churches, community centers or by contacting your local United Way office. A word of caution: every support group has its own personality. Get with a group of people who want to heal. Sometimes groups spend more time wallowing in the problems than time working for solutions. Try a group out. If it works for you, great! If not, look for another. Larger communities will generally have a variety of groups to choose from, however, smaller communities may not.

If you can't find a local group, create one. Tips for starting a support group are:

- Locate other long-distance parents in your area. If you don't know any, distribute flyers at work, libraries, community centers and churches. For a start-up program, you might try to locate a counselor or psychology professor and/or graduate student to assist you in the development of the group. Their expertise could be very helpful.

- Select a location for a first meeting. It could be your home, but a neutral location might be more appropriate. Possible locations are:

    - a church with an available room

    - a library conference room

    - a coffee shop or restaurant with a private room

At the meeting, pass around a sign-in sheet, which lists each person's name, telephone number and email address. Ask each person to introduce him or herself and make a short statement about their parenting status and relationship with their children. Encourage participants to think about what they want – or what their goals are – in long-distance parenting.

*Building a Bridge*

- Invite the group to study this book chapter by chapter together. Each person would study a chapter independently, then meet to review comments, thoughts, ideas, suggestions or simply share what the chapter meant to each person.

- Establish an outline for your meetings such as an introduction time, a sharing time, a book study segment, a closing thought or prayer, and a reminder of the next meeting and assignment. Keep the meetings focused. If individuals want to have additional sharing time after the "official" meeting, encourage them to continue privately. The meetings should be about one and one-half hours to two hours in length. Longer meetings will discourage participation. Shorter meetings offer people an opportunity to connect without feeling overwhelmed.

- The keys to successful meetings are:

  - exercise good listening skills

  - show respect for each person

  - resist the temptation to rescue anyone

- focus on healing and helping – don't allow each other to whine or wallow in difficultly

- take turns being the meeting facilitator

- establish a time-frame for the group, such as a six-week, eight-week or twelve-week commitment.

- If the group learns that it needs help in any particular area, for example, creativity, seek out a speaker for a presentation at the next meeting. Or perhaps you could all meet at a craft store and have a creative friend give you a tour while offering suggestions.

- Encourage each member of the group to claim the group as his own. Cultivate encouragement in one another. Really support one another. Remember that what you give out, you get back. Give out your best!

Another option for support group is through the Internet. Investigate some of these sites and see what they might have to offer you.

- http://www.total.net/~shenker

- http://www.innerself.com/Relationships/divorceandloss

- http://www.divorcecare.com

### Support Network

As I mentioned in the acknowledgements of this book, I had a strong and reliable support network to help me. During the legal proceedings I surrounded myself with friends who were rich in wisdom as well as some who had experience with custody matters. At the onset of my long-distance experience I embraced those friends who were prayerful and those who were creative. Each person in your circle of friends has something special and valuable to offer. Cherish your support network.

At the same time, respect yourself and your inner voice. Sometimes other people speak their ideas so loudly we cannot hear our own selves think. Take the input from your support network and season it with your own ideas and instincts. Also know that sometimes a close friend is greatly affected by our situation and becomes a negative influence in making sound decisions. In this case, do not give up the friendship, but make it clear that the topic of the custody matter is off-limits when you are together.

During my custody proceeding I had a dear friend who constantly made me feel like a bad mother because I was contemplating putting a stop to the legal dispute. She was outraged that I could call myself a good mother. She felt I should work to get full custody of the children no matter what the expense – financially or otherwise. This friend was much older than I and greatly influenced by traditional definitions of motherhood. She was a jewel of a person and I adored her. But she was also a fighter. I knew this about her and

*Building a Bridge*

respected her for being true to herself. However, I had to follow my heart in this matter. I soon learned that our relationship was healthier for not involving her in updates of the situation. After the decisions were made and I moved to Houston, she began to see how I was building a bridge for the children. She became my most enthusiastic supporter and applauded me privately and publicly for my efforts. She told me that during the legal proceedings she simply could not fathom how I could still be a mother to the children with 1,100 miles between us. She did not have my vision or faith. This was clearly a time when I needed to listen to my heart and follow my own inner advice. Do you have a friend you need to exclude from your matters with the children?

Custody proceedings are painful, ugly and draining. They pierce through our souls and rip us deep within. We are clearly not at our best. As a result, we feel needy. However, be careful to not wallow in whininess or self-pity. If you choose to drag your supporters through this muddy mess for a long period of time, they will grow weary of well-doing and soon you will find yourself without a support network.

Find ways to keep some balance in your life. If a friend invites you to a movie or golf game, go. If you are asked to help with a friend's children and are able, do it. By working to maintain some sense of normality in your life, you not only help yourself, you help your children and all around you as well. Your support network will see you putting forth effort to make the best of a difficult ordeal. This will recharge you and them – you will all have the energy and ambition to find solutions and resolutions.

When dealing the other parent or our current spouse/partner, we need to work for the finest relationships. When our primary relationships are in order, our relationships with the other involved parties in our children's lives will fall into place.

So often I felt that I had to bang my head against the wall in working with third parties. I would scream out, "Can't I just be Sarah and Jason's mom? Do I always have to meet with obstacles? Does every little thing have to be difficult?"

*Building a Bridge*

The answer to all three questions is "No." It took me a long time to understand that my heartaches and hardships were a by-product of my unresolved fears.

If you are having trouble with third parties, go back to Chapter 3. I did, and it made all the difference. For some things I had to go back several times. I still evaluate my fears. Every day offers me opportunities to look more carefully within myself.

*Building a Bridge*

# Chapter 7: Our Children at Home

There is a tendency in physically distanced families to think of the children as "visiting." While the children may not live in your home on a full-time basis, both your home and their other parent's home should be considered homes. This concept of "visiting" needs to be dismissed, as it holds no value for you as a family. It suggests that your child is only temporary in the family, and that is not an idea you want to promote.

There is an old saying, "There are two things we should give our children. One is roots – the other wings." Creating a solid home life for children gives them the roots – the foundation – they need if they are to grow and mature into healthy adults.

### Creating Schedules

Developing a schedule for the children to move from one home to the other depends on several factors: distance between homes, availability of parents (both emotionally and physically), ages of the children, schedules of the children, and financial abilities.

When the children live a great distance from the non-residential parent, getting together tends to be less frequent, but longer in duration. For parents and children that live many miles apart, the schedule will need to be made with consideration for school schedules, which generally means holidays. The best situation occurs when the parents can agree on a holiday rotation. When parents do not live too far from each other, children can enjoy shorter, more frequent time-sharing. Even regular or three-day weekends can be included in the schedule-making process.

Whatever plans you make for the children, be sure the children understand the schedule. The children should have their own calendars. (See Calendars, Chapter 8.) Note on the calendar for the next year when she will be going to her other home. This gives the children the security of knowing when they will be with the other parent and also protects those dates from other plans. Once you have created a schedule, make every effort to stick with it. For all parties involved it is frustrating, and sometimes expensive, to juggle last-minute changes and arrangements. It creates uncertainty in the children, which can produce insecurity.

All parties need to understand that as the children grow and develop their own interests and activities, the schedule will need to be altered. Accommodations for summer sports or music camps may need to be considered. Teenagers who want to have jobs or attend summer college sessions will have a limited availability for traveling. In these cases, the parent may want to make arrangements to come to the child's city for a get-together. As the children mature and create their own lives, parents will need to be flexible and put the consideration of the children's desires before their own desires. Make plans that are reasonable, sensible, and affordable.

When considering the length of the child's stay, consider your responsibilities at work. What does it benefit you or your child to have him to your home for six weeks in the summer, if you have to work every day? If you have to work, can he see other family? Does he have friends to be with? Is he going to be on his own more time than not?

If you know when your children will be home, you have a better opportunity for making yourself available during their stays. Perhaps you will need to make arrangements at work for altered

*Building a Bridge*

hours or take vacation days. Again, early planning will allow you to be creative.

For parents that have more than one child, some arrangements should be made during the children's stay that will allow the parent and each child some one-on-one time. This can be a short outing, a "date with dad," or errands with mom. But it is critical that you have some focused time with each child and that each child feels that he was given adequate opportunity to share his thoughts and/or feelings with you privately. A child is a unique human being who needs individual time with his parent for self-expression.

When you do have opportunities to be with your child, really be with them. Give them your attention. Turn off your cell phone. Leave a message stating a time when you will be returning calls and give an alternate number where people can secure assistance if they need immediate attention. An occasional work call during your time together might not be a problem, but if you find that you can't be away from the phone for even an hour, ask yourself if you are really focusing your attention on your child. Have you been in your boss's office attempting to discuss an important work issue, but find yourself getting only a tiny piece of his attention? Why? Because the phone is ringing, the secretary interrupts, and other co-workers pop in for a 'quick question.' How does this make you feel? Unimportant? Disrespected? Remember this when your child asks for time with you.

Be careful about "count downs." This is the function of counting down the number of days until you and your child will be together. Counting down is fine and fun and builds excitement. The caution comes because we do not want to teach our children to disregard today in anticipation of tomorrow. When we put too much stock into a future event, we have a tendency to ignore the precious moments that are offered us in the present.

### Home: From the Inside

Have you ever taken a moment to consider what your home is like? Sarah Ban Breathnach writes in her book, *Simple Abundance*, "Like it or not, the personalities of our homes are accurate barometers that reflect, through our surroundings, where we have been, what's

*Building a Bridge*

going on in our lives, and who we are – today, this moment – though not necessarily where we're heading."

- What is the overall energy of your home?

- Is your home welcoming?

- Is it closed up and cluttered or open and inviting?

- Does it have an odor or fragrance?

- Do people like to be in your home or do you rarely have others in?

- Is your home a place your child really considers home or is this just your house and she comes here to see you?

- Is your home child-friendly?

- Does your refrigerator feature your child's artwork and school papers?

- Do you have children's items available, such as books, movies or games?

     I am not suggesting that your home is in any way inadequate. I am asking you to take a look at your home and see how you might make it a more comfortable home for your children as well as yourself. Critics might say that since the children are only with us on a part-time basis, putting too much effort into how they feel would be a waste. I say that it is critical to make our home a home for our children as well, even if they are only with us one day a year.

**Additional reading suggestions:**

*Simple Abundance* by Sarah Ban Breathnach

*Living a Beautiful Life* by Alexandra Stoddard

*Building a Bridge*

### *Creating a Room for Your Children*

It is also critical that your child have a real place of his own in your home. The ideal situation occurs when your child is able to have his own room.

- If you have the good fortune of having an extra bedroom in your home, give your child permission to create his own space. Your child should be able to arrange the room as he likes and have his belongings remain in that room during those times when he is not home with you. Having a room gives the child a sense of stability and security.

- If you have a guest room, and that is where your child stays when he is with you, stop calling it the guest room. Allow that room to become your child's room and tell the guests they can stay is his room. This change in perspective will go a long way toward creating a healthy family environment.

- If you do not have a room in your home for a separate bedroom, it is very important that you establish a place for the children to sleep and keep their things. Consider these options:

    - Can a residential sibling share his/her room? Would bunk beds help? What about a trundle bed?

    - Do you have a space that could be converted into a room? (For example, an attic, basement, or walk-in closet.)

    - Do you have an area where you can put an extra bed or a cot? (A good cot .)

    - Do you have, or can you obtain, a separate dresser?

    - Do you have a separate closet that could be used solely for your child's belongings?

    - Could you shop garage sales or resale shops for an old seaman's trunk or hope chest to store her personal items?

*Building a Bridge*

- Could you purchase under-the-bed storage boxes (plastic or cardboard) for his things?

Regardless of what you use, make preparing this area a very special event. Make this personal by allowing your child to select a paint color for the dresser or inside of the closet, or select lining paper for the dresser. Whatever you do, make this a priority! It is critical that your child has a real place to call her own when at your home. She needs a safe place to keep her things when she is at her other home. Put your good energy and effort into this project and it will benefit both of you.

Now that I have encouraged you to create this space, I want to caution you on making this space a shrine. This happens when we create a shrine in honor of our long-distance child rather than creating a room our child can really enjoy and live in. Having your child participate in the creative process will help assure the room stays a "kid room." Also, when you are finished, step back and take a good look. Ask yourself, "Does this room reflect the life of a child or the existence of one?"

While you work to create a physical space for your children, do not forget they will need some emotional space as well. When making plans for your child to come home, consideration needs to be given to the emotional health of your relationship. If your relationship with your child is strained, it would be better to have two or three good days together rather than two or three weeks of misery.

- Does your child feel fully welcome in the home with you?

- Do your comments indicate that you have been looking forward to being with her or are you trying to figure out how to handle all the hassles (schedules, finances, and other adjustments) associated with her stay?

- Is your relationship such that you will be able to really share conversation with him or will this time together be several weeks of silently passing each other in the halls?

- Would you like to develop a stronger bond between you and your child? Try creating a scrapbook of times spent together. You and

*Building a Bridge*

your child can view it together and relive past good experiences, which will help in creating more fond memories.

### Pets and Plants

Consider pets and plants when thinking about your home. Children generally love animals and find great joy in caring for them. The unconditional love that pets offer make them attractive. I am not suggesting that you run out and buy a dog or cat, but I am encouraging you to give positive status to your family pet. An animal can bring people together in a gentle and friendly manner. Think not? Walk your dog through the park and see how many strangers stop to say hello.

As a note of humor, when we talk to our children on the phone many times the first thing they ask is, "How is Shadow?" We joke that when they are home we really need to lick their faces more!

Also, the next time your children are home, plant something together. If you don't have a yard, start a container garden or an herb garden. Consider planting a tree together. Watching it grow through the years will help you to remember that we are all growing. If you do not have your own yard, consider planting a tree at the community park or in your churchyard. (You will need permission for this, of course, but I bet planting a tree will be a welcomed offer.) Nurturing something together is a great way to strengthen your bond.

### Routines

The temptation to make a child's stay at home a grand festivity is a huge temptation indeed. I know first hand that when my children are home I want to entertain them with activities and outings. All this is fine, but making every day an event will soon wear you out.

There is also the risk of creating your own monsters. If you set the standard of living at the party level, it won't take the children long to adapt to that level and love it. Then on a day that you plan to stay home, they will feel deprived and cheated.

Establish family routines that make sense. Don't get into the convenient habit of going out to dinner every night. Prepare meals at home and let everyone take a turn at cooking. Outline the basic daily schedule. If the duration of the children's time at home is only a few days, create a plan of what you would like to do and who you would like to see. If the children are home for a longer stretch of time, the routines you set will make everyone more relaxed and comfortable.

When planning family outings, set a budget, then offer the children choices on what fun can be had in that price range. Many cities publish a magazine or weekly section of the newspaper, which features local activities for children. These articles give locations, telephone numbers, hours and prices. Often the magazines (which are generally available for free) offer coupons or additional information on the attraction such as what age group the events are prepared for, what type of clothing to wear, peak times, concessions, and other useful information.

There are lots of fun things to do together that don't require elaborate funds. Here is a short list to get your wheels turning:

- Prepare meals

- Eat meals together

- Exercise – walks, bike rides, jogging, aerobics to music

- Sing songs – songs you know or songs you make up

- Start a family gratitude journal

- Pray together

- Make up stories. Someone starts the story then the next person adds a sentence, and so on. Your stories can be crazy, silly, serious, helpful, whatever – just allow the story to take on a life of its own.

- Make a video of your child's favorite story or of family talent night.

- Do a household chore.

- Talk to each other.

- Check out videos from the library.

- Do a volunteer project.

- Read a book or magazine together.

- Draw or color.

- Write a letter to the grandparents.

- Look in the community section of the paper for ideas on open-to-the-public events such as community concerts or author appearances/book signings.

- Make a casserole and take it to someone in need or an elderly person who could use some company.

- Mow a neighbor's lawn when he is out of town on business or pick up his newspapers when he is on vacation.

If you have family and friends who want a chance to visit with the children, invite them over. The idea of having company while the children are home may not initially appeal to you, but dragging the children all over town and country to see others will be significantly less attractive. This does not mean that you have to feed and house everyone. Plan a pot-luck dinner or set the invitation for evening and serve coffee and dessert. (Note: the younger the children, the earlier you have guests, the better. Little ones are not always charming during evening entertaining.)

Often family and friends will extend invitations when the children are home. While attending a few get-togethers is great, don't get yourself or the children overbooked. The point of them being home is for you to share time together. Running from a friendly barbecue to another family function will only make everyone grouchy. If you receive an invitation that you are not sure about, discuss it with the children. Get their input on participation. Receiving an invitation is very nice, but you are not obligated to accept. Thoughtfully decide what is best for you and follow through on that decision.

*Building a Bridge*

Regardless of what you plan to do, make sure it really works for the adults. You are steering this ship – make certain your guidance is into manageable waters.

### Chores

Nothing says home like a little sweat equity. Household chores are great for children and create a sense of real contribution to the family. Have a little family meeting (at or after dinner?) and discuss what chores need to be done and solicit volunteers. If no one jumps up and down and shouts, "Pick Me! Pick Me!," start making some assignments. Don't go overboard, but each child having a chore or two is not out of line. They may grumble at first, but they will get into the flow and feel good about helping (although you should not plan on any verbal confirmations that they like it.) Not only do chores offer an opportunity for the children to contribute to the care of the home, everyone's participation prevents the adults from feeling overloaded when the children are home.

### Policies/Procedures

While we don't like to think about discipline when the children are with us, (who wants to dampen the excitement of being together?) it is necessary for children to understand family rules, policies and procedures.

Whether our children are with us one day a year or 364 days a year, it is the responsibility of parents to set boundaries that appropriately correspond with the child's level of maturity. Dr. Marianne Neifert, contributing editor of Parenting Magazine, says, "structure and rules not only make child rearing easier, they're also essential ... Far from squelching the spirit, rules are needed for kids to flourish." She offers parents the following pointers for establishing sound rules:

- Rules prepare children for the real world. Limits provide a framework so your child can understand what's expected of him and what will happen if he doesn't comply.

- Rules teach kids how to socialize. If you make it a policy to use polite words at home, your child will not only be more pleasant to be around, but she'll also learn appropriate ways to get what she wants.

- Rules provide a sense of order. Even little children tend to cooperate better when they know what's required of them, and that helps them gain a sense of belonging.

- Rules make kids feel competent. Clear limits tend to reduce power struggles because children don't need to constantly test you to discover where boundaries lie. This doesn't mean your kids won't ever test you; it just means that after the hundredth time they'll realize it won't get them anywhere.

- Rules reassure kids. No matter how often children act as if they want to be in control, having too much power is frightening. They intuitively know that they need an adult to be in charge, and they count on their parents to guide their behavior.

- Rules help keep kids safe. Children – and some grown-ups – often grumble as if rules were made by a bunch of spoilsports. The truth is that many household rules, like many laws, are designed to protect our kids: "No lighting matches" or "Wear a helmet when you ride your bike."

- Rules boost confidence. If you gradually expand the limits placed on your child, she'll become more confident about her emerging independence and her ability to handle responsibility.

When establishing rules, Dr. Neifert further offers these five tips parents to:

- Don't be too strict.
- Don't be too easy.
- Be consistent.
- Be expansive – allow room for growth.
- Give your child a voice.

*Building a Bridge*

First, the adult of the family needs to evaluate where the rules, policies and procedures are needed. If you are a single parent, you can obviously make your own list. However, if you have a partner, you will need to sit down together, privately, and review the various aspects of day-to-day living where limits and boundaries will be appropriate. While democracy in family life is important, you should not surrender your right of family leadership. Determine the issues, then decide what can be discussed as a family, and what matters you will leave to the children. This is important: Before you call a family meeting, the adults must agree to being unified. If the children suspect you are not, they will take advantage of this fact and there will be trouble. Do not skip the step of adult conferencing! Once you have had your adult meeting, call a family meeting. Make sure everyone understands the rules, policies and procedures that the adults have made. Then open the discussion to those issues where the democratic process can be exercised. During family discussion, the adults can take a moderator role by giving the children an opportunity to contribute their opinions, complaints, and ideas. Often children will surprise us by suggesting great ideas that really work! Actively listen to what they have to offer and be flexible enough to make modifications when it is reasonable. Children will support that which they have helped to create – so be sure to make them a part of the process.

Policies on what, you may ask? All those things we take for granted when the children are not home! These issues will present themselves immediately in day-to-day life, but here are a few thoughts to get your wheels turning.

- Where does dirty laundry go?

- Who puts clean laundry away?

- Who sets/clears the table after meals?

- What is the policy regarding how much time is permitted for television? What shows are OK and which are not? What time does the TV get turned off for the day?

- Do you have any procedures for telephone answering? (Many parents receive business calls at home and this is important to discuss.)

- Is it OK for your children to use the phone whenever they like? Where or who may they call? What's the policy for calling long-distance?

- Is your kitchen ever "closed" or may the children get what they want when they want it?

- Do you have a policy on candy and sodas? (One soda a day? No candy before noon?)

- Does your family pay allowance for chores?

- Do the children know the neighborhood boundaries?

- Are they familiar with the streets?

- Do they know their address and telephone number at this home when they are with you?

- Is the computer available to the entire family? Are there policies regarding the Internet? Do you need a schedule so everyone gets a turn?

- Do you have an open door for your child's friends or should they make arrangements for specific get-together times.

Once you have decided on the family policies, post them for all to see.

*Building a Bridge*

> ☺ The Stewart Family Policies ☺
>
> Updated on 6-1-99
>
> - Every family member is responsible for getting his/her own dirty clothes to the laundry room.
>
> - Every family member is responsible for picking up his/her clean laundry, which will be folded on top of the dryer. Check the hanging rack, too.
>
> - The television in the family room is for the whole family. The children are to work out a cooperative system for program selection. If that cannot be done, the parents will decide. The television gets turned off at 10 p.m. unless otherwise approved by the parents.
>
> - Allowances will be paid on Friday at dinner, provided the chores have been done in a quality fashion.
>
> - And so on …..

**"What the world needs are fewer rules and more good examples."**

**Anonoymous**

### Making Life Fun

So often as adults we get caught up in the project and forget the process. When this happens, we do not experience enjoyment in what we are doing. I want to encourage you to spend some effort in making tasks fun.

*Building a Bridge*

Many great magazines help parents create happy and healthy families. Before you subscribe to a dozen of them, visit your local library and review them. I am confident you will find one, or two, that provide information you can really use. By evaluating the magazine before you buy it, you will know if it will really offer you usable information.

While magazines can offer great ideas for creating family fun, do not discount the limitless source of creativity within you.

Here are two examples of how we have created fun in our family.

- Our son has learned to prepare a family favorite meal. This meal (my mother-in-law, Bea's, recipe) might be something he would not normally be interested in eating if called by its actual name: Ground Beef and Bean Casserole. When it is called "Beasie's Cheesy Beanie Burger Bake" it is suddenly fun and appetizing. Everyone wants seconds!

- One of Jason's chores is to clean his bathroom. YUCK! BOO! This takes chores to an all time low! When done creatively it can turn into total fun. Aunt Lisa showed Jason how to become "The Potty Patrol." Attired in his police officer's hat from his cops and robbers game, sun glasses (they tell me they are needed because the bowl will be clean, very bright and very shiny!), big yellow rubber gloves, cleaning solution and bowl brush. The entire process consists of Jason, dressed in his "uniform," scrubbing the bowl and singing "We're going to scrub that bowl as clean as can be" to the tune of "I'm gonna wash that man right out of my hair." It all sounds crazy? YES! It is! But it is fun, Jason does his chores, and we all take joy in the laughter.

Allow yourself to be silly, crazy and young again. It benefits our children, but it also benefits us. We need to lighten up and enjoy life. Let your children help you with this.

*Building a Bridge*

## Home: From the Outside

### *Friends*

When our children are home, we want to consume their every moment. We are so excited to be with them, we don't realize that we sometimes smother them with our attention. Resist the temptation to completely monopolize them.

A great way to share your children is to help them make friends. It is important that your child have friends at your home. Making friends at school is easy and natural for children, but when they do not attend school in your area, you will no doubt need to help them in meeting other children their age.

Before your children come home for their next stay, make some contacts. Start with the neighbors by asking the names of families in your area with children your children's ages. This will be easy if you live on a street with lots of children. If not, I doubt you will need to go too far to find great kids. It is not necessary for you to make introductions to these kids. Find out where they are so you can tap into them when your children are home.

Hanging out at the pool in the summer is a great way for kids to connect. Watch who your children are talking to and playing with. If your child indicates an interest in making friends with this person, give the child your telephone number or better yet, introduce yourself to the parents if they are at the pool, too.

Do you have a neighborhood newsletter? Check it out. Lots of neighborhoods sponsor holiday parties for children/teens.

Another great place for children to make friends is at church. If you belong to a church, you can connect your children with the children of other member families. One thing to consider in this case is that these children might not live in your neighborhood. Children need friends they can easily access, otherwise they will be asking you to drive them here and there. While an occasional ride may not be a problem, becoming a taxi service is one of a parent's least favorite functions.

### *Building a Bridge*

If these avenues don't pan out, enroll your child in a class or an activity he enjoys. Discuss with the instructor your child's availability and ask for ideas on what class might be best for your child to participate in.

It is critical that you help your child make some local friends. Whether your child is home for a week or an entire summer, he must feel that he is connected to more than just you during the stay.

NOTE: Make sure you know the children your child is hanging out with. Do not permit a careless attitude to develop in your child by thinking that while at your house he can do whatever he wants with peers – that is, enjoy a vacation fling without consequences. Introduce yourself to the new friend's parents. Make sure you exchange phone numbers. Let the other parents know of any firm family policies such as boundaries or curfews. When families are aware of each other's policies, kids are less likely to get into trouble. This will make for a much more pleasant family experience during your child's stay at home.

### *Church*

If your children are young and have not yet established their own preferences for spiritual development, take them to church with you. If they are older and agree to go with you, great! If your children are teenagers and have a different religious preference than you, consider alternating church attendance between your church and their church. You might consider attending their church services when they are with you so you can fully understand your child's religious preferences. Use this as an opportunity to discuss religion and spirituality, but do not engage in arguments about whose church is right.

Church attendance can be a powerful tool for strengthening the family. Not only can it create unity in your family, it can also serve as another opportunity for your children to connect with young people their own age. Children from your church are also more likely to have family values similar to your own, which may relieve some of your worries about who your children have chosen for friends.

*Building a Bridge*

You may be surprised to learn that children are interested in spiritual matters. There are a number of good books on the market supporting children in their quest for spiritual information.

- *Nurturing Spirituality in Children* by Peggy J. Jenkins, Ph.D.

- *The Complete Idiot's Guide to Spirituality for Teens* by Rev. William R. Grimbol

- *Raising Faith-filled Kids: Ordinary Opportunities to Nurture Spirituality at Home* by Tom McGrath

- *My Kids Grow and So Do I: A Parent's Tool for Practical Spirituality* by Johanna van Zwet

- *Getting There! Nine Ways to Help Your Kids Learn What Matters Most in Life* by Lisa Marie Nelson

- *What Stories Does My Son Need?: A Guide to Books and Movies that Build Character in Boys* by Michael Gurian and Terry Trueman

- *What Do You Stand For? A Kid's Guide to Building Character* by Barbara A. Lewis

If you are not personally interested in spiritual development, but find that your child is, do not discourage him. Each one of us must find our truth and pursue our journey of self-discovery. Perhaps your child can introduce you to new thoughts about the universe and how it works.

### **Family Business**

Whether you own a business or simply have the routine business of conducting a household, invite your children to help you. It is valuable experience for children to see the effort that goes into your work. It allows you to spend more time together and further allows your child to be of assistance to you – something kids love to be for their parents.

*Building a Bridge*

## *Community*

Allow your children to become familiar with your community.

- Introduce them to the neighbors.

- Take them on walks or bike rides so they are comfortable with the streets.

- Find a map of your area and teach them how to read it.

- Visit the library, community center and museums.

- Study local history and legends.

- Participate in community service projects or create your own opportunities to reach out by preparing a meal for someone in need, mowing an elderly neighbor's lawn, or picking up litter at the community park (wear plastic gloves!)

When your children become more closely associated with your town, they will have a heightened sense of home.

## *Good-byes*

When it is time for the children to return to their other home:

- Don't make them feel guilty about leaving

- Don't ask them to be messengers

- Don't ask them to keep secrets from the other parent

- It is easier for the children if they are delivering something to the other parent rather than leaving you. Encourage your child to take something with them for the other parent. Perhaps something you crafted together or a homemade treat or a souvenir from an outing.

*Building a Bridge*

Send them off with your love, blessings and support. Remind them when you will be talking to them and when you will be with them again.

Give hugs and kisses and all best wishes – then let go!

### Post Together Follow-ups

You might give some consideration to the practice of sharing a follow-up discussion with the other parent after your child returns to the residential home. I am not suggesting a blow-by-blow description of your time together, but I am suggesting that you share with the other parent information you think might be important. For example, if you have noticed that your son has not been completely honest in his comments, you may want to ask the other parent if he has noticed this also. Or if your child developed a cough or runny nose while at your house, the other parent should be told – especially if you gave the child any medications or took him to see a doctor. This does not mean you did not do a good job of parenting or caring for your child. It means the other parent should be aware. It is important the children know that both parents are paying attention and sharing information. When the children see you being honest with the other parent, you have established a quality standard. If you try to give the illusion of being the perfect family, your child will know that is a lie and act accordingly. Be honest with the other parent.

# Chapter 8: Step Five: Ideas for Staying in Touch

When we look directly at long-distance parenting, we might not see the wonderful and varied opportunities available to us for connecting with our children. But we do have at our disposal a wide variety of tools for staying in touch.

Since we live in an age of tremendous electronic capabilities, we have many options for communication. In addition to the obvious elements of telephone and computer, I want you to appreciate other resources as well.

### *Resources*

The availability of time and money will obviously play a role in the way we long-distance love. Lots of both make it very easy. Some of each is great. Little of both requires creativity and advanced planning. Stay open to all parenting ideas and learn to tailor them to fit your long-distance situation.

## Responsibility for Co-Communicating

Young children, under age eight, cannot be personally responsible for returning your long-distance gestures of love. For example, they cannot be expected to return your phone calls or send a reply to your letters. It is great when the adults they live with encourage them to do these things, but you should not count on that to happen.

Children ages nine through thirteen do have the ability to write a letter, color a picture, make a card, and put them into the mail. If they see you doing these things, it will spark a level of interest and excitement in them to do it as well. You may see more reciprocation in older children, particularly if the adults involved are sharing a cooperative spirit.

When children get to be in high school, ages fourteen through eighteen, they should share an equal responsibility in the communication process. If you send a letter or leave a message on their answering machine, it is not unreasonable to expect a reply. Extend to them the same courtesy you would any other person in regard to responsive time frames. Expecting them to sit down the very day they receive your mail to write an immediate reply is irrational. If you call to talk and say so on the message, give them a day to return your call. If you need to speak to them sooner, convey that on the answering machine. If you have a healthy relationship, they will want to reply to your correspondence and calls and will respond with respect.

If this is not happening, discuss it with them. An authentic relationship cannot be developed by one person. It takes two. If they are not participating, the relationship needs to be evaluated.

- Does this child need some time alone from me?

- Have there been outside influences at work trying to interfere with the relationship? (Don't start throwing accusations – they will lead to trouble!)

- Have the demands of school and/or a job been especially difficult or time-consuming?

*Building a Bridge*

As in any genuine relationship, these issues need to be addressed and handled, because continuous one-way communications will exhaust your energies and emotions. If the other party doesn't wish to communicate, focus on prayer, meditation, visualization and periodic correspondence until things are sorted out between you.

The remainder of this chapter outlines the ideas I have personally used and had success with. The following are some resources you should also investigate. The more ideas we gather the better the chance of finding those elements that work well for us.

- *101 Ways to be a Long-Distance Super Dad (or Mom, too!)* by George Newman

- *Dads at a Distance: An Activities Handbook for Strengthening Long-Distance Relationships and Moms Over Miles* developed by The National Institute for Building Long-Distance Relationships. These books can be obtained at http://daads.com or http://momsovermiles.com or by calling 865-946-4954 or by writing A&E Family Publishers, POB16659, Knoxville, TN 37996.

### Address Books

Keep an up-to-date address book handy at all times. Make sure you include the names, addresses, telephone numbers, pager numbers and email addresses of the people in your children's lives: other parent, extended family, friends, teachers, school, doctors, dentists, and others.

Give your child an address book. Help her fill it in with the names and numbers **she wants** – information from both families. Encourage her to write and call the people she cares about regardless which parent introduced her to that person.

Make pocket inserts out of envelopes so stamps and return address labels can be kept together. This makes sending off a card or letter efficient and easy. When tasks are easy, it is more likely they will actually be done.

*Building a Bridge*

You don't need to purchase an expensive address book. Watch the mail as many charities distribute them to generate donations. Insurance agents, real estate agents and doctors also pass them out to patients. Check your local dollar store as they often carry them as well.

### *Answering Machines*

What a fabulous invention the answering machine is and BRAVO! to the person who thought of this! We can leave a recording of our voice so when our loved ones come home they can hear us express our love. WOW! This is great! Don't miss out – use the answering machine.

If you call your loved one and the answering machine picks up, don't hang up and think you'll call again. Use this opportunity to leave a little surprise message:

- "The school papers you sent were great! Just thinking about you!""

- "I was driving to work, thought about you and I smiled! Thanks for the smile! I love you! Bye."

You may want to intentionally call when you know your love bug won't be available – an "on purpose" treat! You get the message!

If the other parent does not have an answering machine, give one as a gift. You need to be able to leave messages.

NOTE: The other parent may have deliberately chosen not to have an answering machine. If this is the case, discuss the matter with him/her. Are you the problem? Or is there another problem? Do not be quick to accuse. Express your concern and listen.

### *Books*

Books are valuable for many reasons: for resource information, for gifts, for entertainment, to establish a life-long love of reading, to share favorite stories, and to have a tangible reminder that you are thinking of your child.

*Building a Bridge*

- Read books. Reading parenting books helps us stay open to new studies on children, know what to expect from our child's age group, learn new ideas on parenting or be reminded of old ideas that still work. Every day there are new books available to help us with parenting and family issues. We are long-distance parents, but we are still parents. Read self help books on becoming a better person. When you read fiction, ask yourself, "What can I learn about life from the characters in this story?" Read the newspaper. The local paper in our area offers a weekly column on parenting, and Ann Landers' column regularly features letters and responses on effective parenting. Read children's books and publications. Stay current with children's literature and their favorite new characters.

- There are a huge variety of divorce-related books on the market. A listing of books for all age levels is available through www.divorceonline.com.

- Get an activity book for ideas on things to do together with your children. These books are available for kids of all ages and offer suggestions for a variety of fun times. Lots of cities have their own activity books. The book for our area is entitled "The Houston Area Guide to Great Places to Take Kids." It comes with coupons to many of the attractions. Check with your bookstore or Chamber of Commerce about a local edition.

- Buy two copies of a book that interests your child. Read the second copy yourself and discuss the story. You'll have a wonderful time sharing your thoughts on characters or speculating on what might happen in the next chapter. Want extra fun? After you read the book, rent the movie and share further discussion on how the book and movie differed. What was better? What was not? Did the casting director put the right actors in the roles?

- Record yourself reading a book. Then send the book along with the tape. Now you are reading together! A bonus benefit of reading to our children via cassette is that we make reading fun for them, which stimulates their interest in reading. If the long-distance child has a sibling or siblings that live with you, have that child read a character line or a portion of the book.

*Building a Bridge*

- Buy two subscriptions to a magazine – one for yourself and the other sent directly to your child. Now you not only have additional topics for discussion, you can also challenge one another on crosswords or other activities such as the crafts or recipes or experiments.

- Why not personalize a book? Take a book that is special to you – or both of you – and write messages in the margins.

### *Business Cards*

Have business cards printed with your name, address, telephone number(s), fax number, email address and any other information on how to contact you. Distribute these to: the other parent, the staff and faculty at your child's school, the doctor, the dentist, and any one else who has direct contact or responsibility for your child.

You can print these on your computer. By doing this you can make as many as you need and a few extras. You can also personalize some of the cards. For example, on the cards for the doctor and dentist you could include your insurance information.

### *Business Connections*

Get connected with businesses in your child's area that can help you with staying in touch. Examples of these businesses include: florist, cookie store, bakery, restaurant, bookstore, or entertainment place (Discovery Zone, Laser Quest, Bowling Center and others.)

Call, write or visit the business and introduce yourself to the manager or owner. Explain your long-distance situation and your need for their assistance.

- Ask if they have a brochure or menu available for you to keep.

- Can an order be placed over the phone or do they have a web site?

- Ask about payment options – do they accept credit cards? Which ones?

*Building a Bridge*

- Do they offer delivery? What is the charge from their store to your child's home or school?

- Ask if gift certificates are available.

- Search the Internet for businesses that your child enjoys such as clothing stores, book stores, toy stores, and so on. Can you purchase gift certificates via the web, which your child can use locally?

If you want to be creative with businesses, you will need to establish a personal relationship with the owner/manager of the store. When they know you are a trusted customer, you will become a valued one as well.

The newspaper in your child's community can be another valuable resource for a long-distance parent. If possible, subscribe to the paper. If it is a big city daily paper, take out a Sunday subscription. Before you subscribe, see if the paper is on-line. Not only will you be informed as to what is happening in the community and schools, but also you will keep up on new businesses and upcoming events. You might want to run an occasional "I love you!" ad to celebrate a birthday, a special accomplishment or simply to let your child know that you care. Placing an ad in this manner would also allow you to express your love to a child who has distanced himself from you. Get a keepsake copy of the paper and hold on to it. One day – when you are no longer distanced – you will have an opportunity to show it to your child.

### *Calendars*

You and your children each need to have calendars.

- Make sure you write in the dates that you will be together.

- Note birthdays

- Note special occasions (school concert, sports play-offs, and "kid" holidays. Did you know that March 18th is Absolutely Incredible Kid Day? It is. Really!)

*Building a Bridge*

- Take a page-a-day calendar and write notes on some or all of the pages. Use variety by writing silly notes on Saturday pages or sharing special memories on Sunday pages or randomly put in "I love you!" or "Thinking of You!" notes.

As children grow older, they should become more responsible for taking action to acknowledge special days. For example, a fifteen-year old should know to call or write for a dad's birthday without being reminded. By seeing the date noted on his calendar, he should be mature and responsible enough to take some appropriate action or solicit assistance from an adult. We should let our children know that gifting us is not important, but acknowledging us is deeply appreciated.

### *Cameras*

Photographs are a fabulous way to communicate. Remember the saying, "A picture is worth a thousand words."

- Make sure your child has a camera of his own even if it is a one-time use camera. Older children will enjoy a "real" camera as a gift. Encourage your children to take pictures of his friends, activities, school, and other things of interest. This is a terrific way for you to become familiar with life at their other home.

- Make sure you have a camera. Take photos of your home and your activities. And, of course, lots of pictures of them when you are together!

- Photos can now be emailed to you from the developer. You can forward them to your child, the grandparents and extended family members.

- Photos around your home and office can help to shorten the distance between you and your child. Keep lots of photographs out – old ones, new ones, silly ones, serious ones – all of them!

- While photos can help you, they can help your child as well. Make sure your child has some photos of you for his room, wallet, desk and locker. If your child is missing you, a little photo of you taped

*Building a Bridge*

at the top corner of his school desk might be a good way to bridge the distance.

### Cassettes

Audiocassettes are a wonderful way to send a verbal letter. Something special happens when hearing a loved one's voice. A great benefit of a cassette is that it can be played over and over. These can be especially wonderful for younger children, particularly at bedtime when it might be too late to place a call or when they want to hear your voice and you are unavailable.

- The cassette letter can be done all at once or a little bit each day throughout the week.

- Record yourself reading a book to your children.

- Between days or chapters, record a segment of music you both like or have enjoyed together.

- Record a song that means a great deal to you and then tell your child (on tape) why it is an important piece. Share your thoughts and feelings about this music. Whenever your child hears that song, he will think of you.

- Record yourself baking cookies. Send the dry ingredients (in airtight plastic bags or containers) along with the tape. Now you are baking together!

- Interview a family member on cassette. Reminisce about the day your child was born or a family event or a world event that your family participated in.

- Cassette tapes are also a great treat-bag gift. Send blank tapes so your child can make his own recordings. Send a pre-addressed, pre-stamped envelope along so they can send their tape to you. Select tapes from artists that you would like to introduce your child to.

*Building a Bridge*

- If you have older children, you can exchange cassettes of their favorite artists or record selections from the radio. This is great way to stay current with their music.

- You do not need newly purchased tapes. You can record over the previous tapes as a cost-saving method. Often you can find these old cassettes at garage sales and save a few dollars.

Cassettes are especially great for very little ones. When they hear your voice and see a photograph of you they have two ways of connecting. Then when you are physically together they have a heightened level of familiarity, which will make them more comfortable around you.

While making a recording and hearing your recorded voice for the first time might seem awkward, stay with it.

### *Computers*

Computers seem to be everywhere today, but I appreciate that many homes have not yet gotten "on-line." Use the tools you have available and do not think that you cannot love long-distance without a computer.

If you do have a computer or access to a computer that is connected to an on-line service (America On Line, Microsoft Network, or some other carrier) and your loved one also has on-line access, emailing each other can be a great deal of fun.

- Prepare an email in the morning that your loved one can receive after school. THIS SHOULD NOT COMPLETELY REPLACE YOUR TELEPHONE CALLS OR REGULAR LETTERS THROUGH THE MAIL!! This is an additional message. Children NEED to hear your voice and see your handwriting.

- Free cards are offered at www.bluemountain.com or www.funone.com or www.americangreetings.com.

- Get into a chat room and visit over the computer. The charges for a long visit on-line pale in comparison to a lengthy long-distance telephone call. Young children will not appreciate this aspect of

*Building a Bridge*

communicating. A child needs to be familiar with the keyboard, spelling, and basic writing skills before e-mail seems fun. Since children use computers in school, they become familiar at an earlier age, but be sensitive to your own child's abilities.

- If your child's friends have email access, and you know each other, you can stay in touch with them as well. This will also serve as an asset in strengthening your overall relationship with your children. Keep the emails simple and upbeat. Use the greatest level of discernment in determining appropriate information or humor.

- You can create cards and stationary with your computer and save on purchasing those items. Hewlett Packard offers idea kits such as "Make School More Cool" and "Make Your Business Stand Out." These kits are loaded with creative ideas for letterhead, business cards, bookmarkers, and suggestions for personalizing lunch sacks!

- Create a family web site. Some resources to assist you are:

- *The Complete Idiot's Guide to Creating an HMTL Web Page with Cdrom* by Paul McFedries

- *Creating a Web Site: How to Build a Web Site in a Weekend and Keep It in Good Shape* by Bruce Durie

- AOL HelpNet/Creative Basics at

    http://www.aol.nethelp/publish/aboutaolmyplace.htm

    http://pages.prodigy.net/create/navbar.html

- Search the Internet using the words web pages or free graphics.

- Search web sites for information on parenting. While there are MANY web sites for parents, here are a few you might want to check out:

    http://www.family.com     www.makinglemonade.com

*Building a Bridge*

http://parentsoup.com

http://parentsplace.com

http://parenttime.com

http://parenthoodweb.com

http://www.familyhood.com

http://custodywar.com

http://www.kidsource.com

http://familyinternet.com

If you don't own a computer, perhaps you have access to one through work, church, or your local library.

Remember: younger children might like to receive messages on the computer, but probably won't be able to really use the computer as a tool for communication until they are a little older.

### Cookie Kits

Prepare a "cookie kit" for the children. Decorating sugar cookies is fun and tasty! When I send these kits, I know that not only will they provide the children with a great activity, but they will also stir their memories of the fun times we had as a family decorating cookies and the follow-up frosting fights! Kit includes:

- Sugar cookies: homemade, purchased from a bakery or a package mix that requires only adding water or eggs - whichever is most convenient for you or fun for your children. Did you know that Mrs. Field's cookies are now available in packaged mixes? YUM!

- Box of frosting – usually white (Boxes of frosting are generally a little less expensive and are lighter in weight than canned frosting which makes the postage less expensive. The box mix also requires preparation, which gives the children another activity. I usually send white frosting because they can add food coloring and make the colors they want for decorating.)

- A container of sprinkles

  - A couple bags of candy for decorating (M&Ms are always a BIG hit!)

*Building a Bridge*

## *Suggestions for Shipping:*

Cookies are fragile and therefore need careful packaging. Cookies that arrive in a thousand pieces are no fun ☹ to decorate! Here are some tips for assuring their safe arrival:

Line the bottom of a box with a layer of folded newspaper pages. Place the decorating supplies on the outside perimeter of the box. Line the middle spot with a piece of bubble wrap (small bubble size). Then, place the cookies in the bubble wrap "well." The cookies should be in a plastic Baggie that is sealed tightly. Then blanket the cookie bags in the bubble wrap. Make sure the package is wiggle-proof by wadding up newspaper balls and stuffing them into the open crevices. Pad the top with layers of newspaper so the cookies and supplies are sandwiched between the bottom and top layers of newspapers. Close the box and shake it to make sure there is no internal movement. If there is movement, open the box and add more paper stuffing. If there is no movement, seal the box with mailing tape and address.

I like to write messages on the box:

- HANDLE WITH CARE – LOVE ENCLOSED!

- TREATS FOR MY SWEETS!

- SENDING SMILES ACROSS THE MILES!

Be creative with kits:

- A spaghetti kit with noodles, a can of sauce, and Parmesan cheese.

- A movie kit with a movie, popcorn and candies.

- A lemonade stand kit with a plastic pitcher, pre-sweetened lemonade mix, and a box of cups. You can include a handmade or computer designed sign. You might also add a little start-up change to get business rolling.

*Building a Bridge*

## Fan Clubs

Start a fan club with your child as the celebrity.

- Create official membership cards.

- Write a monthly newsletter highlighting your child's activities and involvements. Send it to the grandparents, extended family and close friends.

- Have a current "publicity" photo available at all times.

- Send periodic imprinted items to fan club members. (For example, t-shirts, bumper stickers, key chains, or other things.)

- Have a celebration when you see your child – flowers, cameras (paparazzi!), welcome home banners, or other decorations.

- Put flowers or balloons in your child's room so when he/she arrives home there is an atmosphere of excitement.

- Create a web site for your celebrity and keep it updated!

- When writing your child, above your return address, write:

    The Official Sarah Smith Fan Club, c/o your address

    The Jason Jones Fan Club Headquarters, c/o your address

## Fax Machines

A fax machine is a tool that might be overlooked when thinking of communicating, but you can use it when immediate attention is needed.

- Fax a "Thinking of you" note to school or home, particularly if your child is having a tough day – it will bring a smile and an instant "I LOVE YOU!"

*Building a Bridge*

- Fax your child an encouraging message before a big test at school. (In order to fax directly to school, you will need to obtain advanced permission from the school office. See School section, Chapter 6.

- Encourage the school to fax tests and important papers to you. This is a great way to celebrate a good grade with your child! (My children's teachers have used this as an incentive to do well on a test – "Hey, we'll fax Mom your spelling test later today – let's go for a 100!")

- Fax necessary information to teachers or doctors to assist in the care of your child when there is an urgent matter.

If you do not have a fax machine in your home, do not panic. This is an additional outlet for communication and in no way should be considered a necessary item. However, if you do want to send a fax and do not have a machine, many postal service stores and copy centers have fax machines available. Charges for using the machines generally range in price from $2-$3 for the first page and $1-2 for the following pages. Call around to the stores in your area for specific pricing information.

### *Gifts*

We are always looking for gifts that the children will enjoy (and are easy to mail!) Here are some ideas:

| | |
|---|---|
| Magazine subscriptions | Gift certificates |
| Fast food coupons | Cassettes/CDs |
| Books/bookmarks | |

- Use your imagination – but consider the postage charge when purchasing a gift. Sometimes a $3 gift can become a $10 gift!

- Get a copy of the book, *Free Stuff for Kids*. (Make sure the book is for the current year.) It is loaded with great gifts that are free or cost $1. Write to *Free Stuff for Kids Book*, The

*Building a Bridge*

Free Stuff Editors, Meadowbrook Press, 18318 Minnetonka Blvd., Deephaven, MI 55391 or call 1-800-338-2232.

NOTE: You know this, but I have to say it: The most valuable gifts we can give our children are our time, attention and creative energy.

### Letters

While letter writing may seem like an ancient form of communication, I still believe in the magic of receiving mail.

Most people think of writing letters as boring, but you can make it fun. The stationers currently have many great papers to select from – buy a small package or buy a sheet and envelope at a time for added variety. Or try some of these ideas on for size:

- Enhance your letter with cutouts from magazines or newspapers. If you are telling about your garden, add a picture of vegetables or plants or flowers or an actual snapshot of your prized plantings.

- Paste a letter together with words from the magazines and newspapers. (The way movies do with ransom notes.)

- Use colored pencils as your writing instruments. Use a different color for each sentence or paragraph.

- Stickers and stampers can add variety and excitement to your edges or can be used to illustrate your messages.

- If you use lined notebook paper, cut along the margin line to get a clean edge. Then you can hand stitch or machine stitch a binding. This is great fun – you have created a personalized book. If you don't sew, create the same clean edge, staple the pages together along that edge, then using construction paper or wallpaper cut a strip to fold over and glue on the edging. A method for making your own binding!

- Write letters in shapes or mazes for fun.

*Building a Bridge*

- Spray a touch of your cologne or perfume on the letter before putting it into the envelope. Did you know that our sense of smell has a memory? When your child smells your favorite fragrance, you will be remembered!

- If you have family pets, remember to include their names in the signature. Draw a paw or a little cat face or fish to add a little extra fun.

- Dwight Twilley, a long-distance dad, developed a fabulous idea of question letters. Instead of giving facts, he created questions in search of facts. Some of the questions were ridiculous, some silly, some serious, but all were great. His daughter loved the letters and so does mine. Since the book *Questions from Dad* is out-of-print, I have included as an example the first page of our letter. If you would like a copy of the book, as of this writing, the publisher has a hundred copies in stock. To order, contact Charles E. Tuttle Company, Inc. at 617-951-4080. The cost of the book is $16.95 plus shipping and handling.

*Building a Bridge*

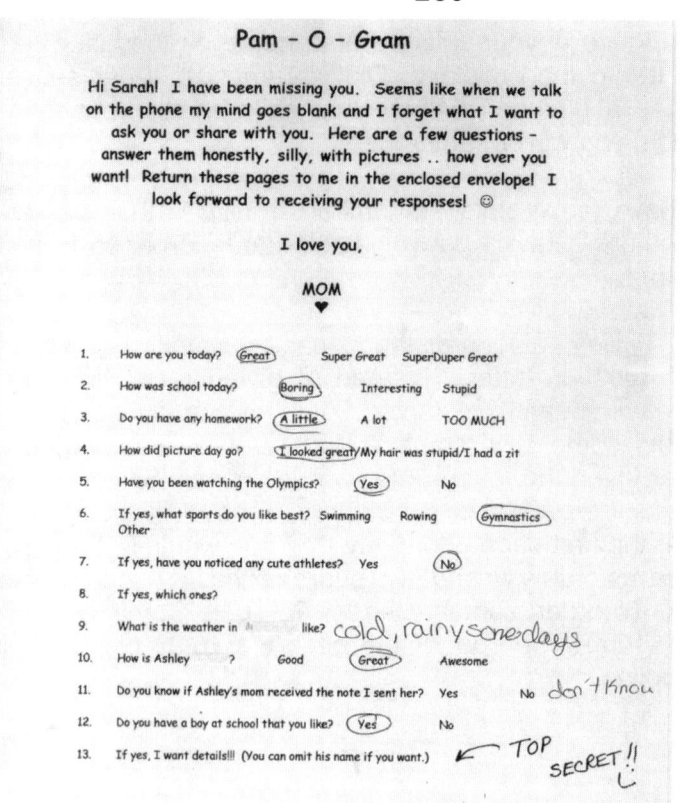

> **Pam – O – Gram**
>
> Hi Sarah! I have been missing you. Seems like when we talk on the phone my mind goes blank and I forget what I want to ask you or share with you. Here are a few questions – answer them honestly, silly, with pictures .. how ever you want! Return these pages to me in the enclosed envelope! I look forward to receiving your responses! ☺
>
> I love you,
>
> MOM ♥
>
> 1. How are you today? (Great) Super Great SuperDuper Great
> 2. How was school today? (Boring) Interesting Stupid
> 3. Do you have any homework? (A little) A lot TOO MUCH
> 4. How did picture day go? (I looked great)/My hair was stupid/I had a zit
> 5. Have you been watching the Olympics? (Yes) No
> 6. If yes, what sports do you like best? Swimming Rowing (Gymnastics) Other
> 7. If yes, have you noticed any cute athletes? Yes (No)
> 8. If yes, which ones?
> 9. What is the weather in ___ like? cold, rainy some days
> 10. How is Ashley ___? Good (Great) Awesome
> 11. Do you know if Ashley's mom received the note I sent her? Yes No don't know
> 12. Do you have a boy at school that you like? (Yes) No
> 13. If yes, I want details!!! (You can omit his name if you want.) ← TOP SECRET!!

- If you are pressed for ideas about letters The Written Connection may be able to help you. They offer a package of materials for a non-custodial parent. It contains twelve months of structured communication materials plus a guidebook. They can be contacted at 2633 E. Indian School Road, #400, Phoenix, AZ 85016, or by phone at 800-334-3143.

### Lunchtime Love Notes

Lunchtime love notes were one of the first ways I communicated with my children. When we lived together and I prepared their school lunches, I would put in a little love note as a luncheon surprise. When I became a long-distance parent, I adapted the idea for distance. The school was helpful because the teacher gave the note to the children just before lunch.

### Building a Bridge

Tools needed: Index cards (any size)

    Construction paper, wallpaper, or wrapping paper

    Glue stick                 Markers/colored pencils

    Candy or treat (flat)       Envelope addressed to school

Glue the construction paper to one side of the card. On the other side, write a simple note. Glue or staple the treat to the card.

I used the wallpaper from my daughter's room instead of construction paper. The wallpaper is a link to home as much as my note. It also adds a very personal touch to her card – it is her wallpaper. Wrapping paper or newspaper comics could also be used.

Keep the treat flat for easy mailing. Suggestions include: Hershesy's Miniture candy bars, fun size candy bars, Sunkist fruit drops or Twizzlers. FYI: Gum is not a good choice as most schools have a "no gum" rule. Also, with regard to mailing treats, keep in mind the temperature – it isn't much of a treat to get a melted, messy chocolate bar! (Ask my children – we learned this the hard way!)

- A purchased card can be used for these notes. The fun of sending a treat to school is that you are staying connected with your child at his school.

- Instead of a love note, write a joke on the card. There are a number of great joke books for kids on the market. Your children will be able to share the jokes with their classmates, which will make lunch more fun.

- If sending to an older child, they may not appreciate a "lunch time love note." Instead send a coupon for fast food. Forward a cartoon from the newspaper that will bring a laugh or send an article from the sports page or a magazine.

*Building a Bridge*

### Meet In The Middle

This is an excellent way to share time together and squeeze in a mini-vacation, especially as children mature and become more familiar with travel.

Here is how it works. If your child lives in Omaha and you live in Orlando, you could meet in Memphis for a weekend or spring break. Or if you have friends that you both would enjoy visiting for a weekend, plan a trip to visit them in their city. You don't need elaborate travel plans because the idea is to share a fun, spontaneous get together.

If you are in a city that you are not familiar with, here are some great places to visit:

- Visit a museum.
- Visit the zoo.
- Attend a sporting event.
- Attend a play or musical performance.
- Experience local culture.

It is very important that children spend healthy amounts of time in both their homes, but an occasional trip between regularly scheduled home times will be a memorable vacation for you both.

### Monthly Information

Each day of the year offers us opportunities to teach our children about history, people, holidays, faiths and their holy days as well as fun occasions for celebration.

The key to using the following information is to get ahead of the present. If you are reading information about the current month, look head to the next month. By doing this, you give yourself time to create ideas, work on projects, gather supplies or shop, without being pressured.

### Building a Bridge

While there are a wealth of ideas for each month, I am not suggesting that you follow-up on everything. Select one listing from each month and use that topic to connect with your child.

When looking at important dates, consider the following:

- What really happened on this date? Why was this important?
- Who were the people involved in this event?
- How can I teach my child more about this event?

  - Create a list of web addresses or a list of books for this topic that the teacher can distribute to your child's class.
  - Send a video of the important date's topic to your child's teacher.
  - Perhaps you have a family member who experienced this date in a special way. If so, record this person's account on cassette and send it to your child.
  - If you have a personal memory of this date, write it down or record it on cassette.
  - Share with your child how this historical event affects our lives today.

When celebrating the birth of a famous person, consider the following:

- Who is/was this person?
- What did/does he/she do?
- What characteristics of this person made him/her a positive role model? (Or a negative example can be powerful as well. We often learn what not to do by observing the conduct and consequences of someone else.)
- If you have a memory of this person from your childhood, share that memory. For example, did you see this person at a concert, in a movie, or in a sporting event? Do you have a favorite song, book or movie of this person? Did you read this person's work when you were a child? How

*Building a Bridge*

did it impress you? Did this person do something remarkable? What did this person do that demonstrated courage or commitment?
- Create a list of web addresses or books about this person.
- Write a letter to your child, or to your child's class, saying how this person has influenced your life.
- Create a list of quotes from this person. If you have a computer, make some business cards for your child. Put the quote on one side and an inspirational message, such as, "You Can Do It!" on the other. Teach your children values through voices of wisdom.
- Record on cassette something the person wrote or the music the person created. Or put together a collage of the person's life.
- Learn about the city or state where this person grew up.
- Donate a biography or autobiography of the person to your child's school library.
- If a documentary of this person's life is on TV, videotape it and send it to your child.

When preparing for holidays, consider these ideas:

- Does your child truly understand the meaning of this holiday? Does your child understand the traditions – how and why they are honored each year?
- Plan to do something at the same time although you are apart. For example, purchase two candles and send one to your child. Then plan to light the candles at a pre-planned time, such as 7 p.m. on Christmas Eve. This is just an idea. Use your own creativity and sound judgment when making a plan.
- Celebrate holidays by sharing with your child the meaning this day holds for you personally. Perhaps you have a special memory of this holiday. Be sure to tell your children these stories.
- For school participation, talk to the room parent of your child's class to find out what type of party or celebration is planned. Discuss ways you can contribute.

*Building a Bridge*

- When sharing gifts with your child, put some effort into your selection. Consider those items that hold meaning, such as personally inscribed books, charms for a bracelet, additions to a collection, photographs from special or shared occasions or gifts that encourage your child to become involved in something, such as sending a packet of flower seeds to celebrate spring (which would encourage your child to plant them).

Other faiths and their holy days:

- Study the traditions of other faiths and teach your child to honor and respect the religious choices of others by taking time to understand their beliefs and practices.
- Invite someone of another faith to tell you what their faith and its traditions mean to them personally. Conduct a recorded interview, if possible, and send the cassette to your child or your child's teacher. Take pictures of this person and send them along, too.
- Attend the service of other faiths for the pure experience of witnessing what they do. Feel the energy of the people. Are they peaceful? Excited? How were you welcomed? Share the story of this experience with your child. By allowing others to practice their faith, you allow yourself the freedom to fully embrace your own faith.

Resources:

For more information on the vast array of special days, birthdays and holidays, consult the following:

- *Day by Day Activity Book: 365 Days of Fun Ideas for Parents, Teachers and Kids* by Consumer Guide, Susan Ohanian
- *Kids Celebrate! Activities for Special Days Throughout the Year* by Maria Bonfanti Esche, Marie B. Esche and Claire Bonfanti Braham
- *Hands-on Celebrations: Art Activities for All Ages* by Yvonne Young Merrill, Mary Simpson and Sasha Sagan
- *Special Days Throughout the Year: Fifty Ready-to-Use Activities, Unit* 6 by Audrey J. Adair-Hauser

*Building a Bridge*

- *Top Notch 2, Teachers Tips, Seasons and Holidays* edited by Rosemary Alexander. This is a Scholastic Professional Book available through Scholastic, Inc., 2931 East McCarty Street, Jefferson City, MO 65102 or check your school's library.
- *Birthday Directory of Famous and Infamous People* by Dennis Crossland
- *Frank's Quotations: Creative Quotes from Famous People on Their Birthdays* by Franklin C. Baer
- *Foods to Grow and Learn On: Recipes, Literature and Learning Activities for Young Children* by Grace Bickett, Leslie Britt, editor.
- *Class Favorites: Take-to-School Treats for Every Holiday* by Leigh Ann Michael
- Http://funone.com  This site specializes in silly, unique and outrageous information!  Enjoy it!
- Search the Internet for the topic you select.
- Family and craft magazines offer ideas for upcoming holidays and seasons.  Check the periodical selections at your local library.

### *January*

Birthstones:  Garnet
Flowers:  Carnation

National Eye Care Month
National Hobby Month
National Oatmeal Month
National Soup Month
National Pizza Week (third week)
President's Day (third Monday)
Super Bowl Sunday (fourth Sunday)

NOTE:  Chinese New Year, the lunar new year beginning at sunset on the day of the second new moon following the winter solstice, can fall in January or February.  If you want to learn more about the Chinese New Year, check the calendar of the present year for an accurate date of celebration.

*Building a Bridge*

January birthdays and special days:

1 – New Year's Day*
2 – Isaac Asimov (children's author)
3 – Joan Walsh Anglund (children's author)
4 – Trivia Day
4 – Louise Braille (inventor of Braille method for blind)
6 – Carl Sandburg
8 – Elvis Presley
12 – Charles Perrault (author of fairy tales)
15 – Martin Luther King, Jr. Day
17 – Ben Franklin
19 – Robert E. Lee
20 – Inauguration Day (if there was an election last November)
21 – National Hugging Day
23 – John Hancock
23 – National Handwriting Day
27 – Wolfgang Amadeus Mozart
31 – Jackie Robinson

*Resolutions are very popular for New Year's Day. Why not make a resolution with your child? For example, resolve to write once a week or call twice a week. Decide on a resolution that you can honestly commit to based on the relationship you and your child share. Encourage your child to make a resolution and then support him in honoring that decision.

### Important January Days
### (Anniversaries, Birthdays, Family Days)

*Building a Bridge*

## *February*

Birthstones: Amethyst
Flowers: Violet, primrose

American Heart Month
Black History Month
National Children's Dental Health Month
Crime Prevention Week (second week)
President's Day (third Monday)
International Friendship Day (third week)
Mardi Gras (Fat Tuesday, day before Ash Wednesday)

*NOTE: Purim, the Jewish Festival to celebrate the delivery of Jews from Persia falls in February or March. Ash Wednesday is celebrated the seventh week before Easter. Consult the calendar for the present year for an accurate date of the celebrations.

February birthdays and special days:

   1 – Langston Hughes (poet)
   2 – Ground Hog Day
   3 – Norman Rockwell
   4 – Charles Lindberg
   5 – Hank Aaron
   6 – Babe Ruth
   7 – Laura Ingalls Wilder
   8 – Boy Scouts of America founded
   11 – Thomas Edison
   12 – Abraham Lincoln
   14 – Valentine's Day
   14 – G. W. Gale Ferris (inventor of Ferris Wheel)
   17 – Marian Anderson (singer)
   22 – George Washington
   26 – Levi Strauss
   27 – Henry Wadsworth Longfellow
       28 – Vaslav Nijinsky (ballet dancer)
       29 – Leap Year

*Building a Bridge*

## *Important February Days*

### *(Anniversaries, Birthdays, Family Days)*

### *March*

Birthstones: Bloodstone, aquamarine
Flowers: Jonquil, daffodil

National Nutrition Month
National Peanut Month
Poetry Month
National Women's History Month
Youth Art Month
Girl Scout Week (second week)
Spring Begins (on or about March 21, consult calendar for exact date)
Earth Day (first day of spring)
Good Friday (Friday before Easter)
Palm Sunday (Sunday before Easter)
Easter (from March 22 to April 25)
Art Week (last full week)

NOTE: Passover, the Jewish festival of freedom is celebrated in March or April. Consult the calendar of the present year for an accurate date of celebration.

*Building a Bridge*

March birthdays and special days:

1 – Yellowstone Park was created
2 – Dr. Suess
3 – "Star Spangled Banner" became National Anthem
4 – Jane Goodall (scientist who studied chimpanzees)
5 – Crispus Attucks Day
6 – Alamo was seized on this day
8 – International Women's Day
16 – Jerry Lewis
17 – St. Patrick's Day
18 – Rudolph Diesel (inventor of diesel engine)
20 – Fred Rogers (aka Mister Rogers)
21 – Cesar Chavez
22 – Marcel Marceau (pantomime)
23 – Roger Bannister (runner)
24 – John Wesley Powell (geologist)
25 – Aretha Franklin
26 – Sandra Day O'Connor
27 – Wihelm Konrad Roentgen (inventor of the x-ray)
30 – Vincent Van Gogh

### *Important March Days*

### *(Anniversaries, Birthdays, Family Days)*

*Building a Bridge*

## *April*

Birthstones: Diamond
Flowers: Sweet pea, daisy

Keep America Beautiful Month
National Humor Month
National Library Week (last week)

April birthdays and special days:

- 1 – April Fool's Day
- 2 – International Children's Book Day
- 4 – Maya Angelou
- 5 – General Colin L. Powell
- 7 – World Health Day
- 13 – Thomas Jefferson
- 15 – Income Tax Day
- 16 – Kareem Abdul-Jabbar
- 26 – John James Audubon (bird activist)
- 27 – National Youth Workout Day

**Important April Days**

**(Anniversaries, Birthdays, Family Days)**

*Building a Bridge*

## *May*

Birthstones: Emerald
Flowers: Lily of the valley

American Bike Month
Better Sleep Month
Mental Health Month
National Photo Month
National Physical Fitness Month
Be Kind to Animals Week (first week)
Asian-Pacific American Heritage Week (first week)
National Family Week (first Sunday and first week)
Mother's Day (second Sunday)
Indianapolis 500 (Sunday of Memorial Day weekend)
Memorial Day (last Monday)

May birthdays and special days:

    1 – May Day
    4 – National Weather Observer's Day
    5 – Cinco de Mayo
    8 – Jean H. Dunant (founder of International Red Cross)
    9 – James M. Barrie (author)
    12 – Limerick Day
    13 – Stevie Wonder
    20 – Dolly Madison
    25 – National Missing Children's Day
    26 – John Wayne
    27 – Rachael Carson (environmentalist)
    28 – Jim Thorpe

Graduations, which honor the completion of academic achievements, are celebrated mid-May through the end of June.

*293*

**Important May Days**

**(Anniversaries, Birthdays, Family Days)**

*June*

Birthstones: Pearl, moonstone, alexandrite
Flowers: Rose, honeysuckle

American Rivers Month
Dairy Month
National Adopt-a-Cat Month
National Tennis Month
Zoo and Aquarium Month
Family Day (first Sunday)
National Flag Week (week including June 14)
National Little League Baseball Week (week beginning second Monday)
Father's Day (third Sunday)
Summer Begins (around June 21)

June birthdays and special days:

  5 – World Environment Day
  7 – Gwendolyn Brooks (poet)
  10 – Maurice Sendak (author and illustrator)
  11 – Jacque Cousteau
  14 – Flag Day

*Building a Bridge*

17 – Barry Manilow
19 – Garfield (cartoon character)
21 – Daniel Carter Beard (founder of Boy Scouts)
22 – Ed Bradley (journalist)
23 – Irving S. Cobb (writer)
26 – St. Lawrence Seaway opened

**Important June Days**

**(Anniversaries, Birthdays, Family Days)**

*July*

Birthstones: Ruby
Flowers: Larkspur, water lily

July birthdays and special days:

2 – Thurgood Marshall (Justice, United States Supreme Court)
4 – Declaration of Independence signed
5 – P. T. Barnum (circus owner)
8 – John D. Rockefeller
9 – Elias Howe (inventor)
10 – J. A. M. Whistler (painter)
12 – Henry D. Thoreau
20 – Neil Armstrong
21 – Ernest Hemingway
26 – George Bernard Shaw
30 – Henry Ford

*Building a Bridge*

**Important July Days**

**(Anniversaries, Birthdays, Family Days)**

**August**

Birthstones: Sardonyx, peridot
Flowers: Poppy, gladiolus

August birthdays and special days:

    1 – William Clark (of Lewis & Clark expedition)
    1 – Francis Scott Key (author of "Star Spangled Banner")
    6 – Alfred, Lord Tennyson
    8 – Sara Teasdale (poet)
  10 – Smithsonian Institute founded
13 – Lucy Stone (women's rights leader)
13 – Annie Oakley
15 – Panama Canal opened
18 – Meriwether Lewis (of Lewis & Clark expedition)
25 – Leonard Bernstein (composer)

*Building a Bridge*

School begins mid-August through early September. Refer to the section on school in Chapter 7 for ideas on connecting with your child's school.

**Important August Days**

**(Anniversaries, Birthdays, Family Days)**

### September

Birthstones: Sapphire
Flowers: Aster, morning glory

All-American Breakfast Month
National Chicken Month
National Courtesy Month
Labor Day (first Monday)
Grandparent's Day (second Sunday)
National Hispanic Heritage Week (week after second Sunday)
United Nations International Day of Peace (third Tuesday)
Autumn begins (around September 21)
Good Neighbor Day (fourth Sunday)
Native American Day (fourth Friday)

NOTE: Rosh Hashanah, the Jewish New Year, and Yom Kippur, the Jewish Day of Atonement, occur in September or

*Building a Bridge*

October. Consult the calendar for the present year for accurate dates.

September birthdays and special days:

  4 – Newspaper Carrier Day
  6 – Jane Adams (women's rights and social welfare activist)
  8 – International Literacy Day
10 – Swap Ideas Day
11 – William Syndey Porter (aka O. Henry) (writer)
12 – James Cleveland (Jesse) Owens
15 – Agatha Christie
17 – Citizenship Day
21 – World Gratitude Day
24 – Jim Henson (creator of the Muppets)
26 – Johnny Appleseed
27 – Ancestor Appreciation Day
28 – Confucius

**Important September Days**

**(Anniversaries, Birthdays, Family Days)**

### October

Birthstones: Opal, tourmaline
Flowers: Calendula, cosmos

National Adopt-a-Dog Month

*Building a Bridge*

National Clock Month
National Pizza Month
National Popcorn Poppin' Month
National Roller Skating Month
Child Health Day (first Monday)
National Newspaper Week (first full week)
Fire Prevention Week (week containing October 8)

October birthdays and special days:

   2 – Charlie Brown/Peanuts (cartoon characters)
   4 – Gregorian calendar was adopted
   5 – Robert Goddard ("Father of Space Age")
   7 – James Whitcomb Riley (poet and writer)
   9 – Leif Ericson Day (Norse explorer)
10 – Martina Navratilova
11 – Eleanor Roosevelt
17 – Black Poetry Day
25 – Pablo Pisasso
27 – President Theodore Roosevelt
31 – Halloween

**Important October Days**

**(Anniversaries, Birthdays, Family Days)**

*Building a Bridge*

## *November*

Birthstones: Topaz
Flowers: Chrysanthemum

Aviation History Month
Child Safety and Protection Month
General Election Day (first Tuesday after first Monday)
Children's Book Week (second full week)
National Geography Awareness Week (second full week)
Thanksgiving (fourth Thursday)
National Family Week (week including Thanksgiving)
Latin American Week (last full week)

November birthdays and special days:

1 – National Author's Day
3 – Sandwich Day
4 – King Tut's tomb was discovered
6 – Adolphe Sax and John Philip Sousa (inventors of musical instruments)
7 – Marie Curie
11 – Veteran's Day
12 – Elizabeth Cady Stanton (women's suffrage activist)
13 – Robert Louis Stevenson
14 – Claude Monet
15 – Shichi-Go-San (Japanese children's festival)
16 – W. C. Handy (composer/bandleader referred to as "Father of the Blues")
17 – Homemade Bread Day
20 – Chester Gould (cartoonist)
21 – Hello World Day (you must say Hello to ten people)
25   Joe DiMaggio
26 – Sojourner Truth (first black person to speak out against slavery. Since her birthday was not recorded, she is honored on the anniversary of her death.)
30 – Samuel Clemens (aka Mark Twain)

NOTE: Hanukkah, the eight-day Jewish festival of lights is celebrated in November or December. Consult the calendar for the present year for an accurate date of celebration.

*Building a Bridge*

*300*

**Important November Days**

**(Anniversaries, Birthdays, Family Days)**

**December**

Birthstones: Turquoise
Flowers: Narcissus, holly

Winter begins (about December 21)

December birthdays and special days:

  1 – Rosa Parks
  5 – Jim Plunkett (football player)
  6 – St. Nicholas Day
  7 – Pearl Harbor Day
13 – St. Lucia Day
18 – Joseph Grimaldi (clown)
22 – Colo (first gorilla to be born in captivity)
    24 – Kit Carson
    25 – Christmas
    25 – Clara Barton (founder of American Red Cross)
    26 – Kwanzaa (holiday that observes African harvest festivals)
    27 – Louis Pasteur

*Building a Bridge*

29 – Charles Goodyear
30 – Rudyard Kipling
31 – New Year's Eve

**Important December Days**

**(Anniversaries, Birthdays, Family Days)**

**Pagers**

If you carry a pager, it could also be a great tool for staying connected to your child. Consider these possibilities:

Create a message code. For example, if your child wants you to call for a telephone visit, but nothing is urgent, he could simply leave his telephone number. But if he wants you to return the call quickly, he could leave his number with an added 911. Or if he has some exciting information to share with you, he could add 411. Perhaps you could design codes for each child. For example, if you have three children, assign them a number. The oldest child could be 1, the second, 2 and so on. Then a return call code could be the telephone number, 411, plus 1 or 2 or 3. This way you would know which child wants you to call.

Won't it be great when you get the 515-555-0000-411-123 code!

*Building a Bridge*

## Postal and Parcel Services

I am quite familiar with the negative attitudes that exists in the public's perception of the American postal system. But I want to encourage you to acknowledge the incredible job the post office has before them and appreciate the work they do under some often difficult circumstances. No other postal service in the world handles the volume of mail at the bargain low prices the USPS does with a very small percentage of mistakes. Next time you are at the Post Office, be sure to thank them for all they do in keeping you connected with your child.

While the weather is no doubt a factor in postal work and the volume of mail handled by the service is overwhelming, have you considered the role the consumer plays the efficiency of the system?

To avoid postal problems, the U.S. Postal Service recommends the following:

- Make sure the address you are sending to is correct – including the zip code.

- Make sure the addresses (return and shipment) are both clear on the envelope or package. If your handwriting is not easily read, type address labels or print carefully.

- Make sure any additional writing on the envelope or box does not interfere with the addresses.

- Make sure the addresses are separated enough so the delivery service is not confused by who is shipping and who is receiving. To reduce the possibility of question, use **FROM** and **TO**.

Sometimes shipments (other than general delivery through the US Postal Service) will require a telephone number. Be sure you have the delivery number and a day number (if different) available.

*Building a Bridge*

The United States Post office offers a wide variety of services and mailing options. For up-to-date information on these services, ask your postal agent for an information package or call the twenty-four hour answer line at 1-800-ASK-USPS (1-800-275-8777) or check the web site at www.usps.com.

Did you know that you can now purchase postage over the Internet? For information, log onto www.e-stamps.com or call 415-871-0139.

Are you aware that the Post Office also has shipping envelopes and boxes available to its customers? They come in a variety of sizes and are available in the customer service area. A bonus: They are free!

We also have available a variety of other shipping services:

- United Parcel Service at www.ups.com

- Federal Express at www.federalexpress.com

- Airborne at http://airborne.com

These shippers are located throughout the country. If you do not have Internet access, check the yellow pages for the local office.

I have also used the services of postal representatives, such as Mail Boxes Etc. The employees at these facilities are generally very knowledgeable and helpful. While they are convenient, they do charge for their expertise. If you send an occasional package, paying a little extra probably won't matter. But if you are going to send to your child regularly (which I hope you do!), you would be better off to purchase some mailing supplies at the office supply store and handle your own packaging.

*Building a Bridge*

## Same Time "Stuff"

Same time "stuff" means participating in the same activity at the same time even though there are miles between you.

- Watch the same program on television

- Read the same magazine or book

- Listen to the same music or exchange music with each other

    (Our parents may have hated our music, but wouldn't it have been a treat to have them at least give it a try?)

- Do the same puzzle

- Exercise by the same video or cassette or share the same sport

- Each of you keep a scrapbook

This is a fascinating way to be stay connected. During calls or times together you can share your thoughts and experiences. This makes for valuable conversation topics.

### Scrapbooks

Scrapbooks used to be popular and are once again. I can recall as a young girl sitting with my Grandmother and looking through the yellowed pages of her scrapbook. The pictorial of her life was magic to me. I could see her in her own youth and hear the stories of her life. Today's scrapbooks are fabulously creative. Scrapbook clubs are now popular which gives the members access to wonderful ideas and instruction. The materials used benefit from current technology as they protect photographs from the aging process. Check with your craft store for the newest products and information on local clubs.

In our hectic world there is so much we forget to tell our children, even when we have regular communication with them. If we are in a situation where we don't engage in regular

*Building a Bridge*

communication or times together, these scrapbooks can be a critical element in sharing our lives – even years later. By keeping a scrapbook we document ourselves.

Children do not always understand long-distance separation. Divorces, job changes or transfers are very confusing for them to comprehend. Even if the nature of the long-distance circumstance is understood, there are always things we don't share with them. These scrapbooks can be a treasure when children have matured and are more open to hearing about the reality of life's situations.

You do not need to write volumes in a scrapbook – a few occasional notes can highlight photos. Add movie ticket stubs, snapshots, playbills, take-home menus, greeting cards, or other things of interest. Magazine or newspaper articles on subjects you are both interested in could be included. Perhaps a photocopied page or two of a book you've enjoyed or an ad or label from your favorite food would bring your scrapbook to life.

Consider creating a scrapbook of your times together. You and your child will have great fun taking photographs of each other and collecting materials for your scrapbook when on outings. You can view the pages together and relive past good times.

For young children, there is a darling picture book entitled *Carl Makes a Scrapbook* by Alexandra Day, which features some great scrapbook pages.

Additional scrapbooking resources are:

- America Online keyword scrapbooking, which features a chat room, message boards, ideas, articles, web links and a free home page.

- *The Complete Idiot's Guide to Scrapbooking* by Alpha Development Group

- *Scrapbook Storytelling: Save Family Stories and Memories With Photos, Journaling and Your Own Creativity* by Joanna Campbell Slan

*Building a Bridge*

- *10-minute Scrapbook Pages: Hundreds of Easy Innovative Designs* by Rachael Boehme

- *My Mother and Me: A Memory Scrapbook for Kids* by Jane Drake, Scott Ritchie (illustrator) and Ann Love

- *My Father and Me: A Memory Scrapbook for Kids* by Jane Drake, Scott Ritchie (illustrator) and Ann Love

**Special Notes of Love and Support**

When we are aware of special occasions in our child's life, it is great to show our support of these events. Here are some ideas for offering encouragement:

- Send a note of encouragement or support for an upcoming soccer game, spelling test, finals, speech class presentation, or other occasions. On the outside of the envelope, make sure to write: OPEN JUST BEFORE _____.

- Send a note of congratulations for a project or an assignment well done. Also celebrate your children when they make good decisions or behave in honorable ways.

- A fax sent to school before a test or event can be an excellent way to say that you are sending your best thoughts.

- Support the tradition of going out for a treat after the game by enclosing a coupon or cash for ice cream, pizza, or some other favorite food.

- For your child's school open house, you might send a plant or floral arrangement to brighten the office or library. An arrangement of helium balloons would be a hit with the students.

Showing that you care and are interested in every area of your loved one's life will bring huge rewards. Any funds spent in these efforts will be returned in priceless ways.

*Building a Bridge*

## *Summer*

While you may look forward to the summer with your children, planning for these stays can cause terror about how to handle schedules. Anticipating your needs is the critical element here – DO NOT WAIT UNTIL THE LAST MINUTE!

Summer is meant to be a time for young people to have fun – it is their vacation break from school – their work. If you have an agreement that says the children are to be with you for six weeks during the summer, you need to make arrangements for them to enjoy those six weeks or lessen your agreement so they can be free to make other enjoyable plans. When I say, "enjoy," I do not mean that they should be constantly entertained. It is not right, however, for us to bind the children to our agreement, then put them in daycare environments simply so we can exercise our "right" as outlined in the decree.

Here are some thoughts for making summer arrangements:

### *Evaluate your needs*

Look at your calendar and determine:

- How many workdays are involved?

- What meetings, events, engagements are already scheduled that cannot be changed?

- Is there any work holidays scheduled during the time frame (For example, July Fourth or Labor Day)?

- Can your work schedule be altered at all? (For example, with floxtimo.)

- Could you take vacation days one at a time to accommodate a three-day weekend every week?

- If you have a spouse/partner, could his schedule be adjusted to help out – by alternating flextime with your

*Building a Bridge*

work schedule or by planning a few alternate vacation days?

If your spouse/partner does not work outside of the home, be considerate enough to ask if he/she is prepared to give your children the amount of time and attention they deserve. If so, that is wonderful. If not, be respectful of your partner's choice.

### *Evaluate your child's needs*

- How many workdays did you calculate?

- How many work hours are in each of those days?

- List places and people you want to talk to for gathering ideas on how they are handling summer. That list should include neighbors, friends, coworkers or anyone with a same-age child.

- Find out what family members would like the first option on these days. If the children can spend time with other family, great.

- If not, you need to seriously consider the best interest of your children. Do you really want them to stay with you and spend their time in a daycare? If for whatever reason (your decision or a mutual decision between you and their other parent) the children are with you and you need daycare, check into the following:

- For younger children: Consider private residence, professional, church-sponsored or YMCA day care programs.

- For older children: Consider the following: camp, church youth groups, park districts or college sponsored "Kids on Campus" programs.

- For working age children: Investigate work co-ops at your office or inquire about internships available at other companies, or help them secure their own job (fast food restaurants, gas stations, swimming pools, or other opportunities.) Here is an idea worth investigating: If your teenager worked at a nationally established business in your community, could she transfer to a location near her other home at the end of the summer?

When determining arrangements for older children, discuss the matter with them and get their input. Kids can surprise us with great ideas, and sometimes they are easier to please than we might think. Plus, as children mature, they develop their own interests and activities, so the decreed schedule may need to be altered. Older children may prefer to attend summer school, work, or participate in some other activity. Do some brainstorming together, come up with two or three ideas and determine which one looks like the best bet. Make it clear that you will make every effort to work things out for the benefit of all, but the bottom line is you have to work, and they have to be in a positive situation. With older teens, keep in mind you will have to make the best mutual decisions with respect, because the older kids get, the more they know the direction they want to go.

- Make a plan. Make good use of your time together. Enjoy some summer! Have fun! Sit down together and make a list of things both you and the children would like to do.

- Camping, fishing, hiking, swimming, biking, reading, beach party, library club, movie camp, visiting children's museum or zoo, rollerblading, ice skating, bowling, attending vacation Bible school, or other activities.

- Check out your area "kid" magazine. Most big cities sponsor a publication that outlines current events designed for families.

Have you seen the movie, "Jungle to Jungle?" This movie is a great example of the mischief kids can get into when out of their element and unsupervised. This movie also gets a powerful message across – your child WANTS to be with you.

- Have you seen the movie, Jungle to Jungle? This movie is a great example of the mischief kids can get into when out of their element and unsupervised. This movie also gets a powerful message across – your child WANTS to be with you.

*Building a Bridge*

## Consider Your Finances

Arrangements for summer always generate additional expenses. You might need to save throughout the year to accommodate the day care needs or activity expenses you will experience in the summer. DO IT! If you aren't financially prepared for this summer, ask about reduced rate programs or scholarships for those activities your child is interested in. Perhaps you could do some bartering to cover daycare expenses or arrange a payment plan with a daycare center.

## Consider the Other Parent's Needs

If the residential parent also works and has no spousal or partner or family support for summer, he/she too will incur additional expenses for childcare. If you cannot help out by having the children with you, then you should consider sending extra money to help cover these expenses.

I cannot impress upon you enough the importance of getting your summer plans in order well in advance of summer. If you cannot personally be with your children, make arrangements that they will be enthusiastic about. If you don't, next summer will not only be hot, it will be hell — that is, if they will consent to coming to your home the next summer.

Summer with your children will be what you make of it. Putting effort and creative energy into the planning phase will go a long way toward making summer the pleasant and memorable experience it is designed to be.

## Talents and Hobbies

Every person has a talent or hobby that he can use to enhance a long-distance relationship. BE CREATIVE!

I like to write and therefore, have come up with a story line called Pam-O-Grams. This is a catchy title for a written report about the area where I live. The subjects of the stories have been about local flowers, insects, animals, and trees. The goal of the stories is to familiarize the children with their home in Texas. I write one report a month and send it to the teacher with a visual aid to complement the report. I have sent ant farms, stuffed animals, dried Spanish moss, whole pecans and pecan cookies, for example. By writing these stories I have been able to communicate with the children, but also contribute to the class. As the children grow older, my story lines will obviously change. Perhaps I will stop using the writing as a means for connection and use, or develop, another talent or hobby.

I appreciate that many people would find writing a story a burden. The intent here is that writing is something I enjoy and I am sharing that enjoyment. If you sew, woodwork, bake, craft, or travel, share your interest with your long-distance love. Using your hobby as a way to communicate with your child may bring new meaning to your leisure time activity.

Classroom curriculum plans are an extremely valuable asset to have on hand. I am confident that most teachers would be glad to share their outline for studies with you. These lesson plans can help you in preparing something that can perhaps enhance a study. You should discuss your plan with the teacher and see what suggestions he might have on how your contribution can help.

Here are some hobbies and ideas for using them:

- Woodworking: make a special chair for the students to sit in when reading to the class or a bookcase where the teacher can keep treasured stories.

- Baking: Offer to supply special treats for holiday parties or events.

- Gardening: Prepare a video or written instructions for planting seeds. Send along a kit so the students can plant their own seeds while you give the directions.

- Painting or Sculpting: Do a profile on your favorite artist and send along a piece of your work using that artist's method. You could also donate a piece of your work to be auctioned in a school fundraiser or placed in the library.

*Building a Bridge*

## *Telephone*

While parents know and appreciate the value of this marvelous invention, talking to young children on the telephone can be a frustrating and fruitless event. Young children sometimes do not have the concept of how the telephone works. They are often easily sidetracked and can get the sillies to the point that they cannot be understood. Fear not, as they grow older all this will change!

While children are young, more tangible means of communication will be better received, such as, cards or small toys with a love note. These are things they can hold and enjoy long after the receiver is put down.

Older children will have no problem using the telephone, but may still experience some reluctance to really open up emotionally during a telephone conversation. This can happen for a variety of reasons which might include: a lack of privacy on their end of the line, a low comfort level with the phone, a preference to share difficult information in person, or simply inconvenient timing as they may be engaged in another activity or obligation.

Long-distance children will learn to use the telephone earlier than others. They need to – it is a necessary tool in their lifeline to you. Here are ways you can assist your child with using the telephone:

- Establish some time frames for when it is appropriate to make calls. (Not before eight a.m.? Not after nine p.m.?)

- Teach children about the different time zones. What may be eight a.m. at their home may be six a.m. at your home.

- Prepare an address book for your child using printing so they are able to read your writing without confusion. Include all data that can assist them in keeping them in touch with you, family and friends. Include pager numbers, fax machine numbers and email addresses. Although they may not use these numbers immediately, the book will be useful as they grow older.

*Building a Bridge*

- Teach your child some procedures for telephone etiquette. If you are looking for some solid ideas for telephone manners, ETI-KIDS has a great video. They can be reached at 1-888-497-9888 or on the Internet at http://www.nlci.com/etikids. (For information on manners in general, try these two videos: Manners, Who Needs Them, ASIN 1882751000 or Table Manners for Kids – Tots to Teens, ASIN 6302918928.)

For calls you make to your child, it is best to select a time that is good for your child to receive calls. Discuss the matter with the other parent and figure out a time that will allow your child to really share a good conversation with you. BE CONSISTENT with this time. If you arrange to call every Sunday evening, then do it. If you are not going to be available on Sunday evening, call BEFORE your scheduled time. If your child is not home, leave a message. Make sure you honor your word for calling consistently. As your relationship matures and the children advance in age you can be more flexible.

To enhance your child's opportunity for communication with third parties, purchase a phone card for him. They are very popular now and widely available in various denominations. When the value of the card has been exhausted, the cards can be recharged over the phone with a credit card. This allows the child to make long-distance calls without the charges being billed to the other parent. The third parties receiving the calls will be thrilled to hear from the child and the child can stay connected. You can also obtain a printout listing the calls your child makes. This listing, like the one you receive for your at-home phone bill, will include the number called, length of the call, and the time of the call.

There seem to be a zillion long-distance carriers in business and all of them call at dinner to hawk their services. Since long-distance parents rely on the telephone so greatly, we might feel like a target audience. Shopping around is the smart thing to do. In Timothy Barmann's article, "Long-distance Plans Not As Simple or Cheap As They Seem" (Houston Chronicle, Nov. 29, 1999), he shares these ideas for finding the best long-distance service:

*Building a Bridge*

- Decide.com offers a variety of ways to compare different long-distance plans. It tracks and constantly updates plans from the largest seven carriers. You can also get information about prepaid calling cards and wireless telephone service plans.

- Trac, at www.trac.org, provides a similar service for long-distance calling plans, called WebPricer. It's not as sophisticated as Decide.com, but offers a detailed charge of plans as well as a comparison of the 10-10 services. Note: The chart costs $5.00.

- A Bell Tolls, http://abelltolls.com, offers tables to compare long-distance calling plans, calling cards, international plans and toll-free numbers. The site also evaluates the extra fees company charge, which can make a difference in what you pay.

- For discounts on long-distance service, check out http://www.longdistancediscounts.net.

- Another tool for long-distance calling is the Internet. Research these websites:

  - Buddy phone (PC to PC only, but offers a very decent quality voice transmission.) http://www.buddyphone.com

  - Yahoo (PC to telephone although the voice quality can suffer a bit due to Internet congestion and system slow downs.) http://www.messenger.yahoo.com

Shop around, ask friends about the pros and cons of the plan they use and above all, remember those wise words of "caveat emptor" which mean "let the buyer beware."

### *Travel*

Long-distance families are always involved in some form of travel. Whether you live five, five hundred or two thousand miles from your child, arrangements need to be pre-planned. Regardless of the form of transportation you use, here are some general tips to consider:

*Building a Bridge*

- If your child needs to alter her school schedule to accommodate travel arrangements, the residential parent should notify the school office and teachers as early as possible so the child's class work will not suffer. It is not a good practice to allow children to miss too much school for traveling, but leaving school early once in a while or missing a day before a holiday break should not cause harm. However, be considerate of the children's involvement in pre-holiday festivities at their school. It wouldn't be fun for your child to miss every party or "free day" because of travel to your home.

- It will be well worth the investment to purchase a good piece of luggage. The carry-on with wheels is the answer! It is large enough to accommodate clothing and extras, but small enough to be a carry-on. The wheel feature allows young children to be responsible for maneuvering their own belongings. This piece, plus a school-type backpack, should be the limit. The backpack should be a carry-on and contain items for snacking and entertainment. (Children like to stay close to their belongings as it gives them a sense of security, so they will fill every piece of luggage you give them.)

- Register your children with the Ident-A-Child program. In the event of an emergency, information will already be on file. You will receive an ID card, which will be a great asset until your child obtains a driver's license. Ident-A-Child can be reached at www.ident-a-child.com or PO Box 310213, New Braunfels, TX 78131-0213, 830-620-0744. Ident-A-Kid is another program you might investigate as well. They are located at PO Box 543, Mt. Enterprise, TX 75681, 903-822-3125.

- Put the child's name, address and telephone number on all his luggage and carry-on bags. It is smart to put the information from both homes on these tags.

- Review the appropriate actions for children to take when approached by strangers. These are:

- Never go with any person unless you have permission from your parent.

*Building a Bridge*

- Never take anything from anyone you don't know – even if it is an item that belongs to you. (Strangers often use this tactic to lure children.)

- Get help from an adult you can trust, such as a police officer or security guard. If necessary, scream so people will notice you.

- Establish a password that only the child, you and the other parent know. If your child uses this word, you will automatically know that he child is in danger or trouble.

- Teach your child how to use a pay phone and make sure she has change in her pocket. Also, teach your child how calling collect works.

- Introduce them to security personnel. Assure them that this person is employed solely to maintain a safe environment for travelers. They should be comfortable in approaching these people when they feel uncertain of their surroundings. Show your children the airport courtesy phones and instruct them on how the phones work. In an emergency any number they dial will get them a person and that is what they will need.

- Encourage your child to use the washroom **prior** to departure. While this may sound standard, last minute hugs and kisses can cause everyone to forget. It is better for the children not to be up and down during travel.

### The Backpack

Regardless of the method of travel, a backpack can be a valuable travel asset. Pack some snacks that the children really like. When traveling by plane, not many adults like airline food, so asking a child to partake is inviting a disaster. The length of the trip will determine the volume of a snack bag – candy and a fruit may be fine for a two-hour trip, but a five-hour journey will require a brown bag meal and probably a couple of treats. If your child wants a beverage from home, make sure it is in a container that they can handle easily and which will not spill everywhere if they drop it.

*Building a Bridge*

If your child takes medication and the timing of a dose falls within the travel period, consult your physician about the matter. You may want to obtain a letter from the doctor that your child can keep in his backpack in the event of an emergency. If your child has a serious illness (for example, diabetes), if would be wise for him to wear a medical alert identification bracelet. Pack a book, game, toy, walkman or whatever will keep your child entertained for the length of the trip. Sending along a favorite doll or bear as a friendly comfort is a great idea as well as providing a playmate. Send along a sweater or light jacket as sometimes air conditioning can feel chilly when just sitting.

### Traveling by Airplane

Many people are now using the Internet when making travel plans. Often great savings can be obtained which are very attractive for those long-distance parents who might be making a lot of arrangements during the course of a year. However, if you are not familiar with using on-line travel services, make sure you fully understand the agreement before you click OK. Often times the arrangements cannot be changed in any way and if you need to change a date or time, you will be charged a penalty. There ARE great deals to be purchased through the Internet; I am only encouraging you to make sure you are fully aware of what you are buying.

If you are not comfortable using the Internet or do not have Internet access, a good travel agent is worth his weight in gold. Since on-line booking of reservations has become so popular, many travel agents charge for their services so be sure to ask your agent if their agency has a service charge policy prior to using them.

Another option for obtaining tickets is to call airlines directly for schedules and fares. Airline reservation personnel can be very helpful and do not charge for their services. Contact information is listed in this chapter.

The airlines do, however, often charge a surplus fee for children traveling alone. It can range from $20 to $40. Check with your travel agent or airline for the exact details as each airline seems to have a little different contract for unaccompanied minors. If you do not get the details up front, you are certain to have a surprise when you check-in! Pay the fee, especially if your child has a flight requiring connections. When the fee is paid, the airlines must care for your child. They have personnel assigned to take your child to his next flight. You may think this is unnecessary, but what will your child do if the connecting flight is delayed or cancelled? What if weather keeps the flight delayed for a long period of time? Will your child be safe alone in the airport? Will he have enough money for lunch or dinner? In a worse case scenario, where would she sleep? If you have paid the fee, the airline is responsible for handling these matters and informing you about the care they have arranged. Have you seen the movie, "Planes, Trains and Automobiles?" Travel madness is only funny when it happens in the movies.

It is best to make travel arrangements for early in the day. In all likelihood, in the event of a delay, the children would still have plenty of time to secure the next daytime flight. Daytime arrangements are critical if there is a connection to be made. Do not reserve a flight with a late connection, as there are too many possibilities for problems. Having children fly direct eliminates many of these headaches. Even if a direct flight is a few more dollars, it may be well worth it.

Airlines also offer special meals for children, if you make arrangements in advance. Again, discuss the available options with your travel agent when making the reservations.

Get to the airport in plenty of time. Don't put yourself or the children in the position of running through the airport in fear of missing the flight.

Check the luggage. While this may take an extra minute at the arrival area, it is the best way to handle baggage. This should be standard practice until the child is old enough to get the luggage in and out of the overhead compartment **on his own**. Airplanes are a madhouse at arrival and the sooner the children get off the plane the better. The delay of trying to get their belongings from overheads will be more trouble than time saving. While the flight attendant is available to help the children, I prefer

*Building a Bridge*

he stay focused on the care of the children rather than concern for the luggage.

Make certain you know which airline you are using for this particular trip. When making travel arrangements, you might use the airline that is offering the least expensive ticket rather than the same airline every time.

Keep your thinking and comments straight! Do not discuss travel horror stories or a recent airplane crash or your personal anxieties about flying. Children follow the lead of adults. Filling their minds with your fears will have a direct impact on their traveling experiences.

Teach your children to be pleasant and courteous travelers. Above all, instruct your children to be respectful and appreciative. Airline personnel are fully responsible for your child's well being while in flight. We must show these individuals our gratitude.

If your children use a Walkman, game boy, or other electronic device, make sure they understand there will be a time when they cannot play with it. You might mention to the flight attendant to remind them of this policy because chances are they will not be listening when the announcement is made.

Stay at the gate until the plane is in the air. If there is a last minute delay or cancellation, your presence will keep your child from being stranded.

When picking your child up from the airport, be sure you are early. There is no worse feeling for a child than not to have her parent at the gate when she arrives. While it is scary to be in a busy airport without an adult, your not being there suggests a message that maybe you aren't excited to see her.

The telephone numbers and website addresses of airlines are:

- American, 800-433-7300, http://www.aa.com

*Building a Bridge*

- Continental, 800-523-3273, http://www.flycontinental.com

- Delta, 800-221-1212, www.delta.com

- Northwest, 800-225-2525, http://www.nwa.com

- Southwest, check local listing, http://www.iflyswa.com

- TWA, 800-221-2000, http://www.twa.com

- United, 800-241-6522, http://ual.com

### Traveling by Bus

Greyhound Bus Company's policies and procedures for handling unaccompanied minors (children eight through eleven) are as follows:

- The origin agency must be open at the departure time, and the destination agency must be open at arrival time. (No pick-up or drop-off at flag stops or highway stops.)

- The trip must not exceed five hours and must be during daylight hours.

- Transfers are not permitted.

- A parent or legal guardian must sign an "Unaccompanied Child Form," which releases Greyhound from any responsibility.

- An adult must meet the child upon arrival.

- The child must pay the adult fare.

If you have questions or want additional or specific information regarding your child using bus service as a travel means, contact your local bus company or Greyhound at 800-231-2222 or http://www.greyhound.com.

*Building a Bridge*

## Traveling by Car

A positive car vacation – does such a beast exist? Well, I believe so! Here are some tips and ideas that are sure to endorse success….

- Plan ahead the time and place you will pick up or meet your child. Be courteous and call if there are going to be any last minute changes. For a lengthy drive, meeting at a fast food restaurant at the mid-point (or predetermined location) is a great idea – if the residential parent will agree and participate. Get the telephone number of the establishment where you plan to meet in case of an emergency or lengthy delay. Creating a situation in which the other party could worry is only fueling an opportunity for a hostile confrontation. Should the other party be running a few minutes late, or if you arrive early, you have access to washrooms, beverages and foods. There might also be a play place where your child can work off any restlessness.

Dr. T. Berry Brazelton emphasizes the importance of prompt arrival in his work, *Touch Points*:

> "Visitation should be clear, dependable, and on time. Even a fifteen-minute wait is an eternity for a small child. A visit from an absent parent becomes a symbol to make up for what he fears most – desertion. If you are a non-resident parent and must be late, call the child. When you arrive, say how sorry you are to be late. Speak to the child before you speak to your ex-spouse."

- Consider weather conditions. In seasons that present the most difficulty for driving, plan to drive in the daylight as much as possible. If you are traveling where weather can be spontaneously nasty, make sure your vehicle is emergency prepared with a flashlight, flare, pillow, blanket, crackers, water, jumper cables or other items you may feel helpful. A cell phone is obviously another valuable asset. If you don't have one, consider borrowing one – especially if weather is a factor.

*Building a Bridge*

Traveling a long distance in the car? Here is a great way to keep the children from driving you crazy with "Are we there yet?"

### *Make a Treat Bag*

Take a gift bag and fill it with small toys and a variety of candies. Every hour on the hour, those who have been good in the car can reach into the treat bag (NO PEEKING) and pull out a treat! Instead of focusing on a long episode in the car, the children (and adults!) focus on the next opportunity to reach into the treat bag. Stay with the rules – you must be good to have your next treat bag turn and the most important rule: No one is allowed to ask, "Are we there yet?" Saying this automatically disqualifies you from your next treat! ☹ The no-peeking aspect creates an excitement about making a selection. You just never know what special item will be selected next.

Toy ideas for the treat bag: Bead games (the type with the little metal ball in an enclosed plastic case), small tablets, pencils, bubble necklaces, kazoos (if you are up to it!), little books, and plastic animal noses. Check your local party store or dollar store for these items. Look where party treat bag goods are sold. You could also save the toys from cereal boxes or fast food restaurants to include in the treat bag.

Candy ideas: Discourage chocolate as it melts and creates a mess. (Except Tootsie rolls, they are OK.) Lollipops, gum (if children are old enough to be responsible with gum, otherwise it can be a nightmare) and individually wrapped candies all work well. It is a good practice to keep wet wipes in the car at all times. A container of diaper wipes works great!

### *Trading Places*

- Is a procedure that will help to alleviate car craziness. Each time you stop the car (lunch, potty breaks, or gasoline) rotate seat positions. Whoever is in the front gets to be the co-pilot by helping the driver with the map, watching for road signs, and radio control. The passengers in the back seat can play games, read, or nap. This makes the trip more interesting for

*Building a Bridge*

everyone and there is less opportunity for travelers to get bored with each other.

- Play car games: "I Spy," "License Plate Bingo," write in notebooks or color (colored pencils are better in the car than crayons because crayons can melt in the heat. Have a small sharpener available if you use pencils.)

- Kid tapes: Bring along a cassette or two with music just for the children. While these songs may drive you crazy, they are better than listening to whining.

### Hotel Accommodations

If you are in need of hotel accommodations, consider the following when making arrangements:

- Is the hotel you are selecting in a safe neighborhood?

- Is it close to restaurants and/or other locations that you will be frequenting?

- Is it affordable?

- Does it offer any extra services? (For example, kids stay free, complimentary breakfast, or other freebies.)

- Is there a pool? (Swimming is a great way for the children to work out car-itis without leaving the hotel.)

Make reservations as early as you can so that your room is secured. Do not wait until the children are tired and cranky to find a place to stay.

### Traveling by Train

Train travel may be an option that you will want to consider. Amtrak Customer Service has provided the following information regarding children and train travel:

*Building a Bridge*

Children from eight to eleven years of age may travel unaccompanied under the following conditions:

- Travel must be done during daylight hours only

- Travel must be on train only and not on any Amtrak thruway bus carriers

- Travel must be to and from stations staffed by Amtrak personnel (that is, no travel permitted to or from non-staffed stations or stations staffed by other carriers.)

- Travel is not permitted which involves a transfer of trains or train to bus transfers.

- The child in question must be interviewed by the station masters at the points of origin and destination (destination is waived if travel is only one way.)

- The person accompanying the child to the station for the interview must sign a release form.

- The unaccompanied child must pay a full adult fare and no discounts would be applicable other than those offered on the train route in question. (That is, no coupon or other promotions would be applicable.)

- Children under eight years of age are not permitted to travel unaccompanied regardless of the circumstances.

- Children over eleven years of age may travel without the above noted restrictions.

If you would like more information, contact Amtrak at 1-800-USA-RAIL or at http://www.amtrak.com.

**Additional reading suggestions:**

*The Penny Whistle Traveling With Kids Book* by Meredith Brokaw and Annie Gilbar

*Building a Bridge*

*Traveling With Children in the U.S.A.: A Guide to Pleasure, Adventure, and Discovery* by Leila Hadley

### Treat Bags

Tools needed:  Baggies ®, brown paper lunch sacks or seasonal treat bags

Treats

Ribbon, curling ribbon or yarn

Fill 'em up! Candy is a great addition to these bags -- other goodies you might want to include are: pencils, erasers, book marks, fast food gift certificates, small toys, photos of yourself or family pets, magnets, postage stamps, small writing tablets, stickers, a new toothbrush, you name it!

Occasionally treat bags turn into treat boxes! Then I include: a box of favorite cereal, a package of favorite store bought or homemade cookies, a canister of chip-type product, books, snap shots, T-shirt or sweatshirt, puzzle, whatever your cherub loves! Pass-along letters are great to send also. If you receive a letter from a friend or relative and your child would also enjoy reading the letter – pass it on!

### Video Recorders

Video cameras are an excellent way to be together. Share thoughts, do a project, tour your home highlighting any changes you have made, have friends send a hello, or show the family pet. The ideas here are endless!

- Share thoughts (another verbal and visual letter).

- Read a book.

- Do a project: Bake cookies, do a craft project.

- Do a project for school: send the video along with the needed materials. On the video go through the project step-by-step.

### Building a Bridge

- Video events or parties.

- Videotape a show or program to share that might not be available where your loved one is located.

- If you have family or friends in your child's area that have a video recorder (or you can supply them with one) ask them to record school plays, concerts, or sporting events when your child participates.

- Make a movie together. Be silly, sing or dance to your favorite songs, share jokes, do a craft, act out a favorite story or talk to each other. When you are apart and want to be together you can share your movie.

While video cameras are a wonderful tool, when video taping your child, please be considerate of his wishes. If he asks you to stop recording his activities, stop. It is a violation of his privacy to continue after he has requested otherwise.

*Building a Bridge*

*Building a Bridge*

# Chapter 9: Available Support

Pioneers in long-distance parenting were brave souls basically on their own. Past support for parents trying to create or maintain a relationship with their children was slim-to-none – in fact, most of those parents met with tremendous resistance.

Today our society recognizes how critical it is for parents to have a relationship with their children. Children need, and want, to know who their birth parents are. They have questions and concerns and curiosities. In the past decade, as psychologists, psychiatrists, and clergy have worked with clients and communities, they have seen how critical it is that this painful family element be handled – and with a sense of urgency.

If you are looking for support and guidance in your efforts to create and maintain a relationship with your children, here are a few places to contact. (This is certainly not a complete list, but will get you headed in the right direction.)

- Mark Bryan, author of *The Prodigal Father*, outlines a plan for absent fathers – a "how-to" on working through the grief and reconnecting with estranged children. He can be reached at The Father Project, PO Box 38-26-66, Cambridge, MA 02238-2666.

*Building a Bridge*

- The National Center for Fathering can be reached at 10200 W. 75th Street, Suite 267, Shawnee Mission, KS 66204 or 913-384-4661, 1-800-593-DADS or log onto their web site at http://www.father.com. Their mission statement is "to inspire and equip men to be better fathers."

- MOMs Living Apart from their Children can be reached at 2 Old Littleworth Road, Dover, NH 03820 or at http://www.nh.ultranet.com/~lavietes/.

- Dr. T. Berry Brazelton, M.D. is considered an expert in child rearing and parenting. In his syndicated column, Families Today, he answers questions that have been submitted by confused and concerned parents. If you would like his opinion or advice on a parenting matter, you can write him at Dr. T. Berry Brazelton, c/o New York Times Syndicated Sales Corp., 122 E. 42nd Street, New York, N.Y. 10168.

- Pale Horse Publishing offers information on a web site http://www.custodywar.com where a variety of products are featured. The subjects range from how to handle a custody proceeding to how to heal the hurts and how to help our children. Most are updated annually.

Other great web sites for parents to reference are:

> http://www.us.net/indc/101ways.htm
>
> http://www.us.net/indc/journal.htm#Top
>
> http://www.dadsanddivorce.com/links12.htm
>
> http://www.fathermag.com/807/LongDistDad.shtml
>
> http://www.fathermag.com/

Internet resources for children are:

> http://www.kidsturn.org

*Building a Bridge*

http://www.rainbows.org

http://www.sandcastlesprogram.com

These individuals and organizations are working to heal the painful wound of parents separated from their children. I, too, want to be part of the solution. You may contact me at the following places:

- On the Internet at www.buildingabridge.com

- By mail at P.O. Box 591037, Houston, TX 77259.

These avenues of support are available to you so you can access help when you feel you need it, but I also want to hear your success stories. The objective is to create healthy relationships with our children, and I want to share in your celebration!

*Building a Bridge*

## Chapter 10: Final Thoughts

Throughout this book I've encouraged you to build a bridge between yourself and the other parent. While it is critical that we establish this solid foundation of communication and cooperation, it is also important that we keep in mind the bigger picture.

I hope you have been able to build a bridge from your home to the home of the other parent. The bridge you have built is a foundation. Now look beyond. This foundation is also the foundation of your child's future.

Our ultimate parenting goal should be to work ourselves out of a job. As we work on our own bridges, we establish a powerful positive example for our children to follow – an example that creates a solid foundation for their adult life. Every stone that strengthens your bridge will be a characteristic your child will be more apt to personally embrace as well.

*Building a Bridge*

By working to build a healthy relationship with your children, the other parent and involved third parties, you give a precious and priceless gift to your child – a solid childhood which will promote a better opportunity for a solid adulthood.

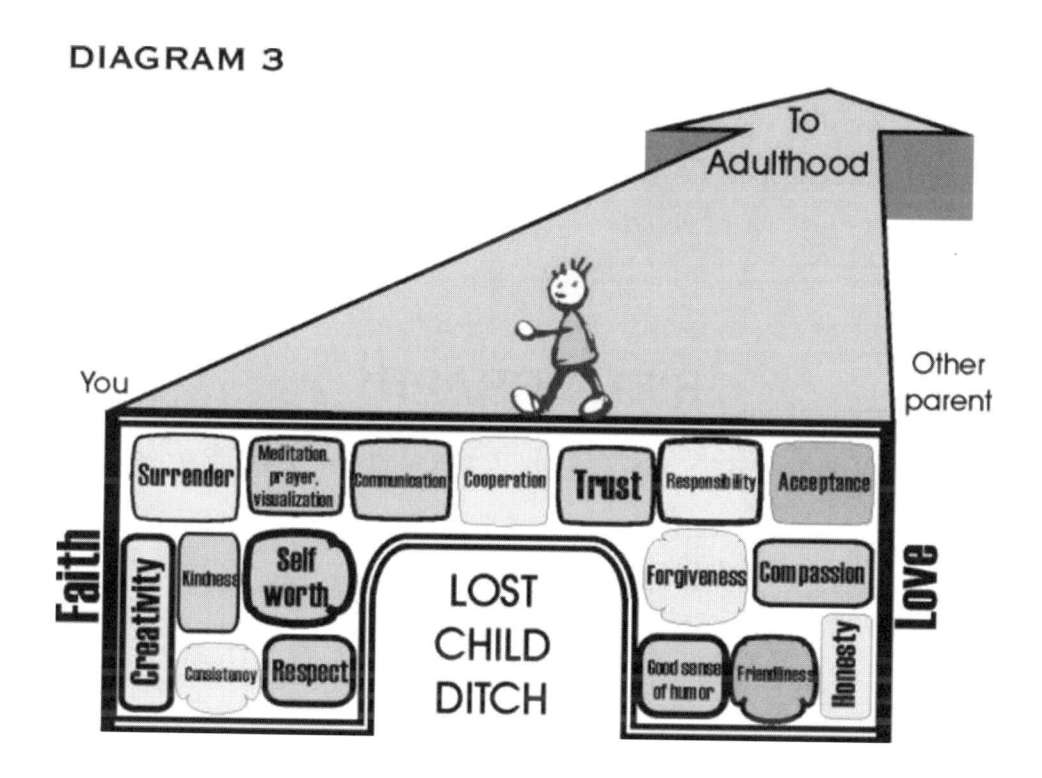

**DIAGRAM 3**

*Building a Bridge*

# BIBLIOGRAPHY

Allen, James. *As A Man Thinketh*. New York: Barnes & Noble, Inc., 1992.

Ballard, Carroll, director. "Fly Away Home." Jeff Daniels, Anna Pacquin and Dana Delany. Columbia Pictures, 1996.

Ban Breathnach, Sarah. *Simple Abundance*. New York: Warner Books, 1995.

Barmann, Timothy C. "Long-distance Plans Not As Simple or Cheap as They Seem." Houston Chronicle, November 29, 1999.

Bottorff, J. Douglas. *The Practical Guide to Prayer & Meditation*. Unity Village, Missouri: Unity Books, 1995.

Brazelton, Dr. T. Berry. "Adults Should Value Children's Differences." Houston Chronicle, August 16, 1998.

_____. *Touch Points*. Reading, Massachusetts: Perseus Books, 1992.

Bittle, Jerry. "Shirley & Son." United Feature Syndicate, Inc., 2000.

Bryan, Mark. *The Prodigal Father.* New York: Three Rivers Press, 1997.

Carlson, Dr. Richard. *Don't Sweat The Small Stuff for Teens.* New York: Hyperion, 2000.

Columbus, Chris, director. "Stepmom." Julia Roberts, Susan Sarandon and Ed Harris. Columbia Pictures, 1998.

Dyer, Dr. Wayne. *What Do You Really Want For Your Children?* New York: Avon Books, 1985.

_____. *Real Magic.* (Cassette program.) Niles, Illinois: Nightengale-Conant, 1992.

Edelman, Marian Wright. "What Every Child Needs." Family Circle, April 4, 1996.

Faber, Adele and Mazlish, Elaine. *How To Talk So Kids Will Listen & How To Listen So Kids Will Talk.* New York: Avon Books, 1980.

Friedman, Dr. Sonya. "Isn't It Time to Please Yourself?" [excerpt from On A Clear Day You Can See Yourself] Redbook, February, 1991.

Gibran, Kahlil. *The Prophet.* New York: Alfred A. Knopf, 1993.

Grief, Geoffrey L., *Out of Touch.* New York: Oxford University Press, 1997.

Hardwick, Charlotte. *Win Your Child Custody War.* POB 1447, Livingston, TX: Pale Horse Publishing, 2001.

*Help & Where to Find It*, POB 1447, Livingston, TX: Pale Horse Publishing, 1999.

Hay, Louise. *You Can Heal Your Life.* Carson, California: Hay House, Inc., 1984.

Heller, David. *My Mother Is The Best Gift I Ever Got.* New York: Villard Books, 1993.

Helmstetter, Shad. *What To Say When You Talk To Yourself.* New York: Pocket Books, Simon & Schuster, 1982.

Hickey, Elizabeth and Dalton, Elizabeth. *Healing Hearts, Helping Children and Adults Recover from Divorce.* Seattle, Washington: Gold Leaf Press, 1997.

Hughes, John, director. "Plains, Trains and Automobiles." John Candy and Steve Martin. Paramount Pictures, 1987.

"I Dream of Jeanie." With Larry Hagman and Barbara Eden. Columbia TriStar Televesion, NBC, Culver City, CA, 1965-1970.

Jeffers, Dr. Susan. *Feel The Fear And Do It Anyway.* New York: Ballantine Books, 1987.

Lansky, Bruce, Hooper, Heather, Mallon, Melanie, Gagne, Joe, White, Danielle, editors. *Free Stuff for Kids.* Minnetonka, Minnesota: Meadowbrook Press, 2000.

Lasseter, John, director. "Toy Story." Voices of Tom Hanks and Tim Allen. Pixar Animation Studios, Disney Enterprises, 1995.

"Marcus Welby, MD." With Robert Young. Owner, Culver City, CA, ABC, 1969-1976.

Markham, Edwin. "Outwitted." *The Best Loved Poems of The American People.* New York: Doubleday, 1936.

Maxwell, John. *Failing Forward: Turning Mistakes Into Stepping Stones for Success.* Nashville, Tennessee, Thomas Nelson, Inc., 2000.

Mellody, Pia. *Facing CoDependence.* New York: HarperSanFrancisco, Harper Collins Publisher, 1989.

Miller, Sy and Jackson, Jill. "Let There Be Peace on Earth." *Wings of Song.* Unity Village, Missouri: Unity Books/Unity School of Christianity, 1984.

*Building a Bridge*

Moshier, Carmen. "We Make Our Own World." *Wings of Song*. Unity Village, Missouri: Unity Books/Unity School of Christianity, 1984.

Neifert, M. D., Marianne. "Why Kids Need Rules." Parenting, March, 2001.

Oddenino, Michael. *Putting Kids First*. Salt Lake City, Utah: Family Connections Publishing, 1995.

Orr, James, director. "Man of the House." Chase Chevy, Jonathan Taylor Thomas. Walt Disney, 1995.

Pasquin, John, director. "Jungle to Jungle." Tim Allen and Martin Short. Disney Enterprises, Inc./TFI International, 1997.

Petty, Jo, editor. *Apples of Gold*. Norwalk, Connecticut: The C. R. Gibson Company, 1962.

Ramirez, Marc. "For Many Children, Emotional Abuse is an Often Ignored, Invisible Enemy." Houston Chronicle, March, 16, 1999.

Reynolds, Eleanor. *Guiding Young Children: A Child Centered Approach*. Mountainview, California: Mayfield Publishing Co., 1995.

Rice, David L. *Because Brian Hugged His Mother*. Nevada City, California: Dawn Publications, 1999.

Rodrigues, Janette. "Shining the Light on Suicide." Houston Chronicle, July 29, 1999.

Salt, J.S., editor. "How To Raise the Perfect Parent." McCall's, October, 1997.

Santrey, Laurence. *Young Albert Einstein*. Mahwah, New Jersey: Troll Associates, 1990.

Sark. *Succulent Wild Woman*. New York: Fireside, 1997.

Scofield, Rev. C. I. *The Holy Bible.* The Scofield Reference Edition. 1906. New York, New York: Oxford University Press, Inc., 1945.

"The Brady Bunch." With Robert Reed and Florence Henderson. Paramount Pictures Corporation, a Viacom Company, ABC, Burbank, CA, 1969-1974.

Tipping, Colin. *Radical Forgiveness.* Marietta, Georgia: Global 13 Publications Co., 1997.

Twilley, Dwight. *Questions from Dad.* Boston, Massachusetts: Charles E. Tuttle Company, Inc., 1994.

United Technologies Corporation. "Don't Be Afraid To Fail." Wall Street Journal, 1941.

Vanzant, Iyanla. "Let Us Pray." Acts of Faith (newsletter.) 1999.

Veerman, David R., senior editor. *Student's Life Application* Bible. Wheaton, Illinois: Tyndale House Publishers, Inc., 1997.

Walsch, Neale Donald. *Conversations with God, Book I.* New York: G. P. Putman's Sons, 1996.

Wilcox, Ella Wheeler. "Whatever Is – Is Best." *The Best Loved Poems of the American People.* New York: Doubleday, 1936.

Williamson, Marianne. *A Return to Love.* New York: Harper Collins Publishers, 1992.

_____. *A Woman's Worth.* New York: Ballantine Books, 1993.

Zukav, Gary. *The Seat of the Soul.* New York: Fireside, Simon & Schuster, 1989.

## *Index*

Abandonment, 49
Acceptance, 12, 22, 107, 117, 120, 121, 185, 187, 219
Acting responsibly, 22, 87, 88, 89, 185
Address Books, 273
Alienation, 15, 21, 26, 42, 50, 100, 186
Anger, 20 - 21, 26, 37, 45, 54, 67 - 78, 115, 117, 121, 125, 127, 170, 186, 229
Answering machines, 274
Apologies, 71
*Apples of Gold*, 37
April, 299
Arrogance, 22, 26, 79, 186
Attorneys, 241
August, 303

Balance, 212
Being alone, 143
Blame, 22, 26, 73, 87, 88, 106, 113, 158, 159, 168, 186, 215, 240
Books, 274
Boundaries, 66, 72, 85, 88, 89, 173, 175, 220, 228, 260 - 263, 267
Brainwash, 80
*Bridge Builder, The*, 39
Business cards, 276
Business connections, 276

Calendars, 17, 252, 277
*Call to Action*, 132
Cameras, 278

Cassettes, 279
Change of residence, 100, 220
Child support, 170
Child's Bill of Rights, 115
Childhood experiences, 182
*Children Learn What They Live*, 187
Children's friends, 137
Chores, 260
Church, 267
Co-communicating, 272
Communicate, 59, 141, 230
Community, 269
Compassion, 22, 32, 69, 70, 130, 131, 144, 181, 182, 185, 206, 214 - 216, 233
Computers, 280
Connectedness, 144
Cookie kits, 282
Cooperation, 124
Counsel, 104, 105, 166, 167, 222, 243, 244
Courtesy, 22, 37, 116, 185, 218, 225, 272, 324
Creating a room for your children, 255
Creating schedules, 251
Creative ability, 118
Creativity, 22, 83, 87, 119, 121, 173, 185, 246, 265, 271, 292

December, 308
Despair, 22, 26, 90, 186
Difficult questions, 108
Do not compete, 97
*Don't Be Afraid to Fail*, 36

*Building a Bridge*

Emotional abuse, 226
Envy, 97
Example for our children, 22, 193, 199, 340

Failure, 207
Family business, 268
Family, new 230
Fan clubs, 284
Fax machines, 284
Fear, 21, 26, 108, 190, 191, 320, 344
February, 296
Focus on contributing, 91
Forgiveness, 22, 52, 123, 157 - 162, 185, 214 - 216
Friendliness, 22, 185
Friends, 266

Gifts, 285
God, 12, 33 - 35, 41, 50 - 53, 56, 65, 67, 70, 71, 76, 77, 78, 85, 91, 117, 120, 125, 156, 164, 165, 169, 185, 195, 196, 206, 208, 209, 216, 346
Good-byes, 269
Grandparents, 61, 105, 115, 118, 119, 231, 232, 259, 278, 284
Greed, 103
Grief, 22, 26, 117 - 118, 120, 186, 336
Guilt, 22, 26, 117, 122, 123, 153, 186

Hatefulness, 22, 26, 127, 186
Hero complex, 83, 132
Hobbies, 318
*Holding With An Open Hand*, 165

Holidays, 113, 142, 152 - 155, 176, 228, 231, 252, 277, 290, 292 - 294, 315
Home
  from the inside, 253
Honesty, 13, 21, 22, 54, 70, 176, 185, 218

Imperfection, 211
inferiority, 21, 26, 131, 132, 186, 211
Integrity, 181

January, 294
Journaling, 16, 29, 40, 65, 78, 92, 210, 211, 314
July, 302
June, 301
Justice, 68

Kindness, 22, 37, 41, 42, 54, 178, 185, 233, 239

Laziness, 22, 26, 140 - 142, 186
Legal system, 87, 89, 166 - 169, 172, 221
*Let There Be Peace On Earth*, 196
Letters, 288
Letting go, 164
Listening, 22, 27, 51, 126, 146, 147, 156, 246, 327, 331
Loneliness, 22, 26, 144, 152, 186
Love, 5 - 341
Lunchtime love notes, 288

March, 297
May, 300
Medical/dental professionals, 241

Meditation, 50, 57 - 60, 64 - 66, 85, 208, 273
Message board, 29
Mini-vacation, 290
Miracles, 33, 155
Money, 28, 80 - 82, 99, 102, 130, 138, 143, 169, 170, 172 - 175, 271, 318, 326
Monthly information, 290

Negative thinking, 27
November, 307

October, 305
*Outwitted*, 239

Pagers, 309
Parent's Bill of Rights, 116
Patience, 207
Perseverance, 207
Pets, 257
Physical abuse, 226
Plants, 257
Policies/procedures, 260
Post together follow-ups, 270
Postal and parcel Services, 310
Prayer, 50, 51, 54, 56, 60, 64 - 66, 216, 246, 273
Problem solving techniques, 150
*Prophet, The*, 61

Regret, 22, 26, 156, 160, 186, 217
Release the past, 123
Resentment, 22, 26, 121, 153, 163, 170, 186
Residential parent, 213
Respect, 13, 22, 43, 44, 49, 54, 62, 66, 73, 76, 80, 83 - 85, 89, 98, 102, 103, 110, 116, 134, 152, 185, 196, 197, 202, 217 - 219, 225, 246, 247, 272, 293, 317
Response chart, 128
Routines, 257

School personnel, 234
Scrapbooks, 312
Self-abusive behaviors, 138
Self-pity, 22, 26, 31, 176, 186, 248
Self-worth, 22, 185
Sense of humor, 73
Separation, 38, 42, 50, 60, 64, 102, 107, 143, 184, 232, 313
September, 304
*Serenity Prayer, The*, 169
Society, 23, 104 - 107, 109 - 111, 113, 117, 336
Spiritual development, 22, 185, 267, 268
Spite, 22, 26, 54, 178, 186
Spouse or partner, 217
Stepparents, 224
Steps to personal fulfillment, 197
Stepsiblings, 228
Summer, 315
Superiority, 22, 26, 79, 106, 180, 186
Support group, 31, 114, 245, 247
Support network, 29 - 31, 40, 176, 177, 233, 247, 248
Surrender, 22, 52, 98, 164, 168, 185, 262
Symbolic exercises, 29, 40

Talents, 318
Teachers, 206
Telephone, 320
Things kids love to hear, 136
Things kids want from their parents, 134

*Building a Bridge*

Travel, 323
  Airplane, 325
  Bus, 328
  Car, 329
  Train, 332
Treat Bag, 330, 333

Video recorders, 334

Visualization, 33, 50, 58 -, 60, 64 - 66, 118, 273
Volunteer work, 138, 205

*We Make Our Own World*, 205
*Whatever Is – Is Best*, 120
Wisdom, 22, 38, 41, 54, 137, 165, 166, 169, 192, 247, 292

## About Pamela ...

Pamela writes a regularly featured column in Small Change News entitled For Fabulous Families. The column is designed to assist all families with an emphasis on guiding non-traditional families. Small Change News is a Clear Lake (Houston) area paper with the mission of providing positive information and inspiration to its readers. Archived articles are available for reading on the website – www.buildingabridge.com. Pamela also writes for children and is presently creating books using kid-friendly characters to help children deal with divorce issues.

Pamela is a trained Stephens Minister and caseworker with the Family Outreach of America program. In addition, for the past four years, she and her husband have been a couples match for a boy through the Big Brothers/Big Sisters program. On the grass roots level, she is a volunteer for Children Without Borders, a program that gathers donated school supplies for poverty stricken schools throughout the world. She also joins the staff and readers of Small Change News on a monthly "Hug the Homeless" pilgrimage to reach out to the Houston area homeless.

## About Joy Goodgame and Frank Mitchell ...

Joy Goodgame and Frank Mitchell are co-creators of the cover for *Building A Bridge*. They are both students at Southwest Texas State University. Joy's major is Communication Design. She plans to use her lifelong love of art for both professional enrichment and personal enjoyment. Ms. Goodgame can be reached at www.joygoodgame@hotmail.com. Following graduation in 2002, Mr. Mitchell's goal is to pursue a career with a graphics firm. He can be contacted at frankmitchell12@hotmail.com.

*Building a Bridge*